John Smailes is chair of the Australian Motorsport Hall of Fame, flagship of the Australian Motorsport Council, which is the peak body of Motorsport Australia, Motorcycling Australia, Karting Australia, Speedway Australia and the Australian National Drag Racing Association.

Just 93 heroes belong to the Hall of Fame—a recognition rate of far less than one per year since motorsport began in Australia 124 years ago. It's an exclusive gathering and each inductee's achievements are celebrated at www.australianmotorsporthall offame.com.au.

John's career spans journalism, commentary and communications. He was managing editor of the 60th-anniversary history of the Confederation of Australian Motor Sport, now Motorsport Australia. For Allen & Unwin he has written *Climbing the Mountain*, the autobiography of Allan Moffat OBE; *Race Across the World*, the incredible story of the 1969 London–Sydney Marathon; *Speed Kings*, the story of Australians and New Zealanders at the Indianapolis 500; and *Formula One*, the first book exclusively on Australians and New Zealanders in F1. He has also recently written *The First to 1000*, the autobiography of Dick Johnson AM.

In response to demand, Allen & Unwin recently re-released John's book *Mount Panorama*, the full history of one of the two most historically revered racetracks in Australia. *Phillip Island* completes the double.

www.johnsmailes.com.au

I0895717

PHILLIP ISLAND

THE INSIDE STORY OF AUSTRALIA'S FASTEST RACETRACK, OUR HOME OF MOTORSPORT

JOHN SMAILES

ALLEN&UNWIN
SYDNEY • MELBOURNE • AUCKLAND • LONDON

First published in 2024

Copyright © John Smailes 2024

All rights reserved. No part of this book may be reproduced or transmitted in any form or by any means, electronic or mechanical, including photocopying, recording or by any information storage and retrieval system, without prior permission in writing from the publisher. The Australian *Copyright Act 1968* (the Act) allows a maximum of one chapter or 10 per cent of this book, whichever is the greater, to be photocopied by any educational institution for its educational purposes provided that the educational institution (or body that administers it) has given a remuneration notice to the Copyright Agency (Australia) under the Act.

Every effort has been made to trace the holders of copyright material. If you have any information concerning copyright material in this book please contact the publishers at the address below.

Allen & Unwin
Cammeraygal Country
83 Alexander Street
Crows Nest NSW 2065
Australia
Phone: (61 2) 8425 0100
Email: info@allenandunwin.com
Web: www.allenandunwin.com

Allen & Unwin acknowledges the Traditional Owners of the Country on which we live and work. We pay our respects to all Aboriginal and Torres Strait Islander Elders, past and present.

NATIONAL LIBRARY OF AUSTRALIA

A catalogue record for this book is available from the National Library of Australia

ISBN 978 1 76147 121 6

Index by Puddingburn
Set in 12.5/17.5 pt Minion Pro by Midland Typesetters, Australia
Printed and bound in Australia by the Opus Group

10 9 8 7 6 5 4 3 2 1

FSC www.fsc.org MIX Paper | Supporting responsible forestry FSC® C001695

The paper in this book is FSC® certified. FSC® promotes environmentally responsible, socially beneficial and economically viable management of the world's forests.

To the memory of my esteemed cousin
Ian John Heads OAM
(15 February 1943–25 March 2024).
Awarded the Medal of the Order of Australia for services
to the media as a sports journalist, author and mentor.
Member of the National Rugby League Hall of Fame.
Kennedy Foundation Awardee for Lifetime Achievement
(excellence in sports journalism).
And, as always, to
GT Jenny.

Contents

List of Maps

Prologue

Wayne Gardner, 1987 world motorcycle champion and Australia's first in the Senior category, was spent, tired beyond words.

It was Sunday, 9 April 1989, and there were just minutes to go before the start of Australia's inaugural World Motorcycle Grand Prix, the grand prix for which he was largely responsible. He knew he couldn't go on.

'I'm too tired, Don,' he said. It was just the two of them—Gardner, 29, already a veteran, and Donna Forbes, 27, his girlfriend of eleven years and soon to be his wife—just two kids from the 'Gong alone in their flimsy caravan at the rear of the pits at Phillip Island racetrack, newly built, near as close as you can get to Tasmania from Australia's mainland.

For two years, even while he was winning his world championship, Gardner had lobbied hard for this moment; he had put his time, determination and, surprisingly to him, considerable influence with politicians and business leaders into securing an Australian Motorcycle Grand Prix and a spectacular place to run it. 'No one knew the effort we put in,' he later recounted.

And now, on the cusp, it had all caught up with him—all the radio and TV, all the gladhanding and 'important' meetings, all the demands on his attention when he should have been concentrating solely on staying alive at 300 km/h.

'I can't do it, Don.'

Donna, blonde, feisty, more than his girlfriend—she was his 'muse', as she put it—didn't hesitate. 'We're here because of you. *They're* here because of you,' she told Gardner, referring to the 90,000 fans (who knew there were that many in Australia?), plus a massive TV audience, the biggest ever for a motorcycle race. 'Go and kick arse.'

Still he didn't move.

Donna went again: 'Unless you want to give it to Doohan.'

That lit the spark.

Gardner left the caravan, marched across no-man's land to the new Phillip Island pits, head down, stony-faced, ignoring the well-wishers, and slammed the door shut. Donna followed closely, carrying his helmet and placing it on a bench. Gardner scooped it up and put it on as soon as he could: 'It's like a mask.'

The mighty Honda NSR500—not as mighty as it once was—was fired up. Gardner prepared to race. 'If you don't win, don't come back,' was Donna's final advice.

He won.

'I was a tough bastard, a real hard man,' Gardner said many years later. But he needed Donna.

PROLOGUE

Wayne Gardner holds a unique place in Australian motor sport. Along with circuit designer, constructor and visionary Bob Barnard, he created a circuit of such magnitude that it is revered throughout the world. The history of Phillip Island as a motor-racing venue spans a century. It has been through five distinct phases. Heroes have been made in each. This is its story.

Part One

The Road Course
1928–1940

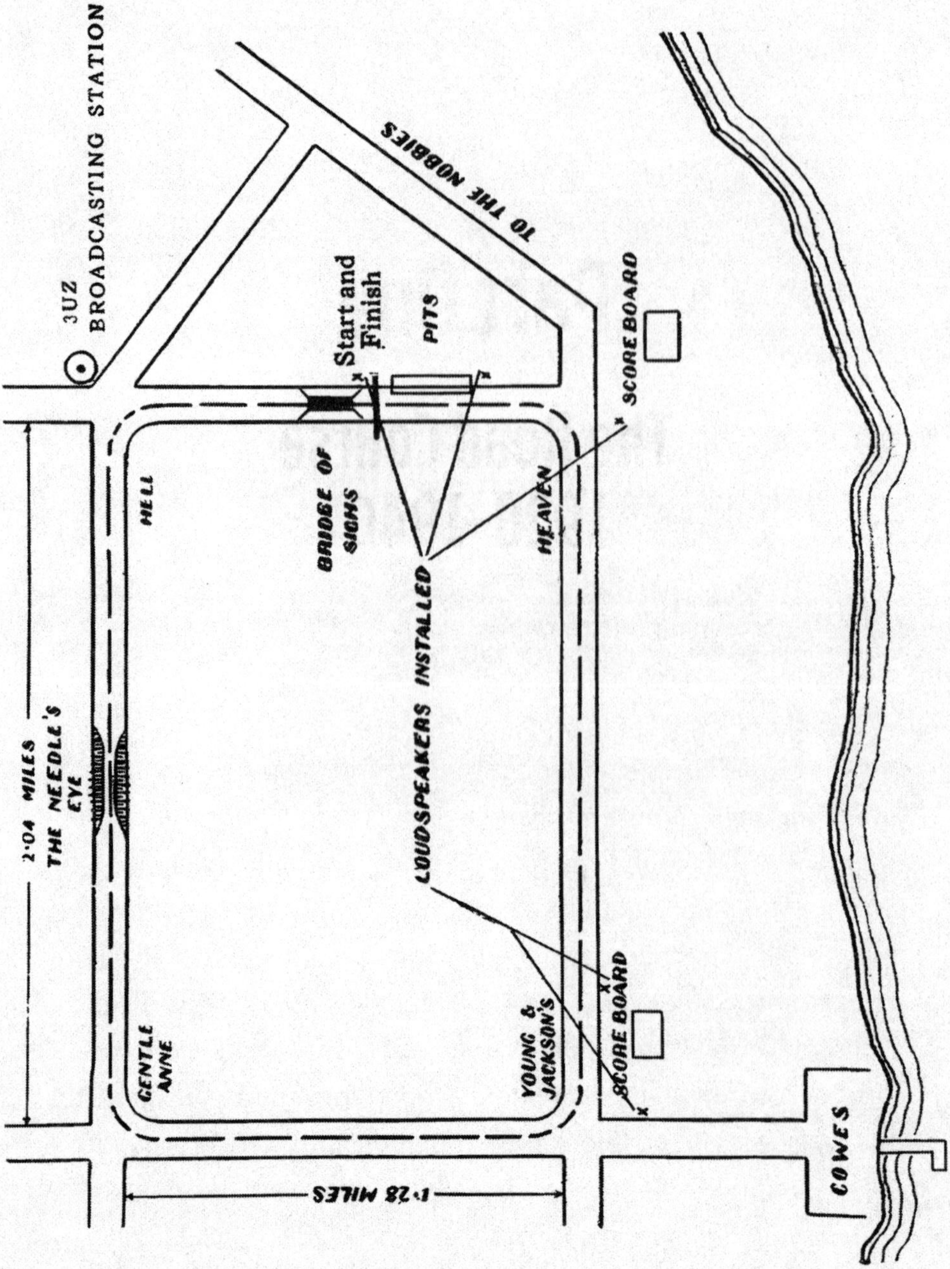

Phillip Island Pre–World War II Road Circuits, 1928–1940
Rectangular Grand Prix course, distance: 10.4 kilometres (6.5 miles)
Triangular 'short' circuit, distance: 5.28 kilometres (3.3 miles)

1

The Making of Phillip Island

AKT Sambell couldn't believe his good fortune.

As the most ambitious (and possibly only) property developer on Phillip Island, he needed to attract Melbourne people with money to get them to invest in his subdivision.

Sambell was a century ahead of his time. It was the Roaring Twenties (the 1920s, that is) and he had grand plans. He'd build a championship links golf course, only nine holes—a miniature St Andrews—then create a whole community around it: quality homes on big blocks, an upmarket commercial area with designer shops and top-end restaurants, even a hotel he'd call a 'guesthouse' to give it that exclusive, personal touch.

To top it off, it would be within waddling distance of a recently discovered penguin colony, one of the most compelling this side of the Antarctic. One day, Sambell reasoned (quite correctly, as it turned out), the nightly Penguin Parade would be world renowned.

Sambell had already given his dreamworld a name: Summerland. So much better than 'The Nobbies', which is what the locals called it. His grand golfing estate would be perched on top of one of the most magnificent coastlines not just in Australia but the world.

All he needed was to get people to come.

That didn't prove easy. It wasn't called an island for nothing. The drive down from Melbourne on goat tracks was arduous enough, but when you got to within cooee of your destination there were five kilometres of Western Port Bay to be crossed from the Mornington Peninsula, or a swift-flowing tidal channel of several hundred metres on the eastern side if you chose to drive all the way around.

Sambell became the ferryman, buying barges and punts, even a redundant Sydney Harbour ferry (he bought two, but one sank). Still he was well short of his projections. For all his ambition, Phillip Island continued to be tightly held by the few cashed-up Melburnians who already held substantial land there and perhaps weren't keen to share.

And then a group of blokes arrived, looking for a place to run a motor race.

They were committee members of the recently formed Victorian Light Car Club (VLCC) and they coveted the island for all the reasons Sambell was trying to overcome. Its isolation would enable them to run a road race without the draconian restrictions placed on them by authorities on the mainland.

But they were hardly proposing it happen in a bubble. This was an event craved by competition-starved racers and the burgeoning Australian motor industry. Both represented the growth sector of the economy. Cars weren't cheap and racing them required massive cash injections.

The motor industry was booming. By the end of the 1920s, more than 100,000 vehicles would be registered on Victoria's roads, and they were stacking them on at a rate of almost 30,000 a year. Motoring in the 1920s was a money-making machine.

The 100 Miles Road Race would bring as many high-net-worth individuals to the Island as AKT Sambell's ferries could carry. The name was a bit wimpy, though. The big thinkers were already saying it should be called the Australian Grand Prix, the country's first.

On 30 December 1924, the Victorian parliament banned motor racing on public roads.

Its *Highways and Vehicles Act*, tabled that day, was largely seen as a positive document, outlining the state's obligation to build highways to carry the state's fast-growing vehicle population. Just shy of 200,000 people, all of them voters, held driver's licences and the number was growing exponentially. But section 18 was a killer: 'If any motor car is used on a highway for purposes of racing or of trial of speed the driver or the person in charge thereof shall be liable to a penalty of not more than Fifty pounds.'

It was the death knell for free-range motorsport.

To be fair, motoring enthusiasts had enjoyed a sensational run for more than twenty years. The first Australian motoring event is generally agreed to have been a gathering of single-cylinder

De Dion-Boutons on the Sydney Cricket Ground on 1 January 1901, the day of Federation. Soon interstate speed records captured public imagination.

In 1905, Dunlop tyre executive Harry James, the great-uncle of Peter Brock, organised a five-day, 565-mile (909-kilometre) trial from Sydney to Melbourne. Of 33 starters (23 cars and 10 motorcycles), 21 made it home. Harley Tarrant on his Argyll was declared outright winner after an additional 140-mile (225-kilometre) tie breaker. Tarrant took nearly 24 hours to make it to Melbourne. Twenty years later the record stood at 9 hours 16 minutes on roads not substantially better. Wizard Smith (twenty interstate records) and AV Turner (four Sydney–Melbourne records) became local legends.

Speed wasn't necessarily injurious. AV Turner raced for 40 years and retired without a serious accident.

But you couldn't blame authorities for being concerned.

Self-regulation was the key. In 1903, both the Royal Automobile Club of Victoria (RACV) and the much more grandiosely titled Royal Automobile Club of Australia (the NSW version) were formed. Harry James started the Melbourne club with 57 members—roughly equal to the number of cars in the state at the time.

The clubs took on advocacy roles, pressing for road upgrades, influencing driving regulations before some bureaucrat did it for them, and even becoming the licensing authorities. They also governed motorsport.

Motorsport energised sales.

It was an era for entrepreneurs. Cessnock-born Rupert Jeffkins was riding mechanic for the great Ralph DePalma when they almost won the 1912 Indianapolis 500 (their Mercedes ground to a halt while leading with less than two laps to go). Back in Australia, the big-talking Jeffkins persuaded mega-wealthy Melbourne sports promoter John Wren and Sydney lord mayor James Joynton Smith to back him in closed-road speed events in both cities with the strapline: 'If Excitement Hurts You, Stay Away'. The ventures made motorsport an entertainment spectacle.

Jeffkins was the promoter of the Motordrome, an impossibly banked, 45-degree, one-third-of-a-mile (535-metre) concrete oval perched on the banks of the Yarra. The Motordrome was killing people. Enthusiastic crowds started calling it the Murderdrome. It was giving legitimate motor racing a bad reputation.

Arthur Terdich saw the storm coming.

The Terdich family were furniture manufacturers, specialising in fly-proof gauze doors. Arthur turned their company into motor-body builders. Most new cars arrived on the Melbourne docks as rolling chassis needing bodies, seats and touring luxuries. Specialist local body builders, like Terdich, finished the job. Pretty soon Arthur was making real money. Naturally, he spent it on fast cars. He raced, rallied, hill-climbed, time-trialled. Whatever weekend pursuit took the fancy of the cashed-up car set, he was in it.

But the RACV offered no future in racing. It had become a business serving the broader motoring public, consumed by the need to keep fragile motor vehicles on the road with road service and to maintain some economic stability in the event of collisions with insurance. Motorsport was an irritating side issue and a potential embarrassment.

There were 700 road fatalities in Australia in 1925, the first year that casualties were counted. For the automobile clubs it was hard to argue the case for road safety in parliament when the perception, and maybe even the reality, was that their own members were tearing up the countryside.

On 5 November 1924, an RACV breakaway group formed the Victorian Light Car Club to go motor racing in an organised way. The two clubs were joined at the hip. The RACV would retain a sporting committee guided by the VLCC, and one member would belong to both organisations, providing a clear channel of communication. Arthur Terdich was the man.

Just one month later, when the state legislature pulled the handbrake on street racing, the VLCC saved the day where, most likely, the RACV would have buckled under.

Arthur and his VLCC committee challenged the resolve of the rule makers. They were ambitious. It was one thing to run hill climbs and gymkhanas on private land (which they did), but what about something serious: a grand road race, like those in Europe?

A purpose-built road-racing track was beyond their comprehension. No one had built a permanent motor-racing circuit in Australia. It would be 1955 before the 1.5-mile (2.4-kilometre) Port Wakefield track in South Australia opened the floodgates for many more. The VLCC's vision was set on the established principle of closing a piece of public road.

So, they tested the waters.

Although opposed by the Country Roads Board in Victoria, they staged a straight-line sprint—a flying mile—on the Laverton Road west of Melbourne. They formed a partnership with police to set up roadblocks to make it safe. The police overachieved. Their roadblock—1.6 kilometres from the event—delayed and disrupted traffic so much that even Terdich and Harry James, trapped on the wrong side of the barricades, missed their starts.

The event still ran, though, and a precedent had been set. With the right permits and the right assistance, and with a bit of PR liberally applied to local authorities, it was possible to use public roads to go racing.

But where?

How, ultimately, did Phillip Island become the unlikely location of choice? The answer, perhaps, lies with the great Australian historian, the waggish Manning Clark.

In his boyhood, Clark lived on Phillip Island for two years between 1922 and 1924, courtesy of his father's itinerant Church of England ministry. 'The people he was courting were all Anglicans,' Clark said of his father in his memoir *The Puzzles of Childhood*, 'all members of Yarraside in Melbourne who had holiday homes down Lovers' Walk or between Ventnor and the Nobbies.'

'Yarraside' was Clark's tongue-in-cheek description of cashed-up, bourgeois Melburnians. He described exactly the people in the same social set as Arthur Terdich and his committee, and the same people AKT Sambell was pursuing.

Clark knew Sambell, the businessman with a home in 'Yarraside' and ambition on Phillip Island: 'He was interested in all those developments which would attract the holidaymakers and weekenders to the Island. He thought big: he had ideas for a new ferry from Stony Point to Cowes, for a car punt and later a bridge from San Remo to Newhaven, and for better roads on the Island.'

In 1927, Arthur Terdich led the exploratory expedition to the island Manning Clark called his Swanee River, his special place.

Phillip Island, 101 square kilometres of towering basalt columns standing proud against the mighty seas of Bass Strait, an amalgam of woodlands and wetlands, has always been a holiday destination. Even its First Nations inhabitants, the Bunurong people, came and went, moving between mainland Australia and the island according to the season. They called it Millowl.

On 5 January 1798, surgeon and explorer George Bass arrived with a crew of six after an epic journey in an open whaleboat from Sydney Cove. He named his discovery Phillip Island after his boss, Arthur Phillip, the governor of New South Wales. Phillip returned the compliment by naming the body of water beneath the island Bass Strait.

Bass did the island no favours. For centuries, the Bunurong had trodden lightly on the land. By 1801, gangs of sealers had arrived to harvest the bounty. Within twenty years the seal population was decimated, the ecosystem had vastly declined and the Bunurong didn't visit anymore.

In 1844, Scottish settler John D McHaffie and his brother William, late of Wigtownshire and more recently station owners from Moonee Ponds, secured the lease of the entire island for an annual fee of £10. They cleared the dense scrub by setting it alight, a fire 'seen for days on the adjacent continent', ran sheep, and introduced deer, hare, pheasants, partridges, quail and grouse. Their run lasted for twenty years.

In 1868, the Victorian Government declared the island was on the market. The great Victorian gold rush, which started in the 1850s, had swollen the state's population and there was a pressing requirement to provide pioneer settlers with land they could farm. Phillip Island presented one opportunity. The land ballot carved the island into 157 allotments of up to 160 acres (65 hectares) each. The McHaffies retained more than 600 acres (243 hectares) of the best land.

Commander Henry Cox, commissioned to create the first accurate chart of Western Port Bay, decided that the shape of Phillip Island resembled that of England's Isle of Wight, so he named its landing place Cowes, after its English counterpart. Ventnor, another town on the island, was also an Isle of Wight knock-off.

Farming was tough going. By the turn of the century, only 50 settlers remained. The ones that stuck it out did well. Mini dynasties were built, the backbone of an island culture that prevails to this day.

Tourism became a parallel industry. An advertisement in *The Phillip Island Standard* said it all. 'Come down to this Finest Pearl of the Southern Seas with its setting of crystal waters and azure skies,' it proclaimed. 'Leave the heat, dust and flies of summer or the cruel frosts of winter, say goodbye to the monotonous routine, or nerve racking trouble, and realise the joy of life in an island holiday where all breezes are sea breezes.'

Manning Clark's Yarrasiders built holiday homes. They were gentle times; Clark, aged nine when he arrived on the island, celebrated them in his biography: 'We travelled in a jinker, a single-seater carriage drawn by a horse [called Ginger] . . . on a moonlight night when the moon seemed to be travelling at the same pace as we were . . . Ginger raised his tail gracefully and farted with every step in the stately trot he turned on when the world was shrouded in the beauty of the night.'

His words are lyrical but also offer insight—when it came to cross-island transport, there were few alternatives to horses. In 1922, 'locals travelled on horseback while visitors drove cars. In the main street of Cowes, in the holiday season between Christmas and Easter, the locals gawked at them, as though they were invaders from outer space.'

Arthur Terdich, Bill Scott and Jack Day mapped out a near perfect 6.5-mile (10.4-kilometre) rectangular racecourse. Perfect—except that the roads were rough-hewn, more suited to Clark's jinker than to any sort of race car.

Sitting in the bar of the Isle of Wight Hotel in Cowes in 1927, the committee members determined not only the direction of travel—clockwise—but also named the corners.

Starting and finishing on what is now Ventnor Road, race cars would head down to Heaven Corner, a distortion of the name of the Evans family who lived there (now the corner of Ventnor Road and Berrys Beach Road), then east to Young and Jacksons Corner, named for their favourite Melbourne hotel (corner of Ventnor Road and Thompson Avenue). Next they headed south to Gentle Annie Corner, named after a popular if somewhat risqué folk ballad (Gap Road and Ventnor Beach Road), then west through Needle's Eye cutting (Ventnor Beach Road) to Hell Corner (Ventnor Beach Road and Berrys Beach Road) and then north, uphill, to the finish. A narrow bridge just before the finish was named the Bridge of Sighs—a cue to take a deep breath before the next lap.

The roads, though, needed major work. And the local council was unwilling to pay.

There was a problem with the council.

Municipal government was first declared on Phillip Island in 1871, shortly after the land ballot. But as the grand ballot experiment fell away, a diminishing number of ratepayers made it difficult for the council to remain solvent. Amalgamation with nearby Woolamai Council on the mainland was the only solution. There was growing concern that island matters were being given short shrift.

After World War I, and with the island's economy recovering thanks in part to tourism, a group of dissidents (or were they visionaries?) formed the Phillip Island Severance Party. Pretty soon, half of the island's residents, it seemed, were prepared to secede from the mainland.

On 21 March 1924, the island called a referendum. The breakaway movement failed by just 70 votes. Debate continued. On 26 March 1927, a new poll came down in favour of secession, this time by more than double the number—150 votes. The Severance Party was quick to take that result to the state parliament.

The VLCC committee had landed in a hotbed of local politics. Even as they were planning their ambitious race meeting, the matter of island governance was a red-hot issue that was still in limbo.

In the circumstances, it was remarkable that the existing council paid any attention to the motor-racing proposition at all. But they did—they allocated £25 to road reclamation. It was an inconsequential amount, but the council's pledge meant far more than the cash injection.

By granting the funds, the council had green-lighted the project. The VLCC had found a place to stage its road race. Official permission was granted on 17 January 1928. A lot of work needed to be done in a truly short time.

The locals pitched in. Working bees were part of the island's culture. Road crews comprising islanders and VLCC members knocked the steep crown off the roads and widened them where possible. AKT Sambell, a civil engineer, was building a road to Summerland and to the Penguin Parade beyond (it, too, would open in 1928). He loaned his expertise and his equipment.

Except for some blue metal near the start/finish line, the Phillip Island circuit was entirely unsealed. Bill Scott worked for the Commonwealth Oil Refinery, a fuel and lubricant giant. He hit them up for drums of waste oil. The oil would help settle the dust.

The VLCC's 100 Miles Road Race was held on Saturday, 31 March 1928, and it was a runaway success (see chapter 3).

Half a year later, on the afternoon of Tuesday, 18 September, AKT Sambell celebrated the passing of the *Phillip Island Shire Act* (no. 3585). In a landmark decision, the Victorian state parliament rubber-stamped the proposal to create the independent shire of Phillip Island, separating it from the mainland.

It was the second-smallest municipality in the state.

On 31 October 1928, the first meeting of the Phillip Island Council was held in the Mechanics' Institute in Cowes. Albert Keaston Trenavin (AKT) Sambell was elected unopposed as shire president. His development was assured—as was motorsport on the island.

The first item on his agenda? Better roads.

2

The Incredible Story of a War Hero

It was dawn on 25 April 1915 when Adelaide brothers Arthur and William Waite, both attached to the 3rd Australian Field Artillery Brigade, entered hell.

Sixteen thousand Australians fought their way ashore on Gallipoli that day. Two thousand of them were killed or wounded.

There was no place to set up artillery. Field artillery was useless in the face of the Turkish fusillade. William, a captain, and his younger brother Arthur, a corporal, could only dig in. It was not a fair fight. Turkish commander Mustafa Kemal Atatürk, first president of the republic of Turkey, told his troops: 'I don't order you to attack; I order you to die.'

By evening, Australian commander Major General William Bridges, and Lieutenant General Sir William Birdwood, who was in charge of the combined Australian and New Zealand forces, had proposed an immediate withdrawal. General Sir Ian Hamilton, commander-in-chief of the Mediterranean Expeditionary Force, refused. A month later Bridges was dead, shot by a Turkish sniper.

More than 8000 Anzac soldiers died in the Gallipoli campaign. Eighteen thousand were wounded. The most successful part of the campaign was the December 1915 withdrawal. The brothers Waite survived.

Arthur Waite hero-worshipped his big brother. William (Bill) Charles Nightingale Waite, born 1880, was the eldest of seven children of second-generation licensed victualler William Nicholas Waite, proprietor of the Stag Hotel on Rundle Street, Adelaide (it's still there), and his wife Anna, nee Weston. Arthur Cyril Roy came along fourteen years later.

Arthur was just five when Bill took off to fight in the Boer War as a corporal in the 1st South Australian Contingent, then signed up for a second tour of duty as a lieutenant with the 6th Imperial Bushmen in the Transvaal. He was mentioned by Lord Kitchener in despatches and returned to sleepy Adelaide a hero.

When their dad died in 1909, Bill became head of the family. Arthur was apprenticed with engineering firm J.H. Southcott. On 4 August 1914, England declared war on Germany. Recruitment offices opened across Australia on 10 August. Just nine days later young Arthur, not yet twenty, walked into the army's office in Morphettville, South Australia, and signed up.

Contemplate the dinner-table conversation that night. Bill had survived one war—twice. Now his baby brother sought to risk death. Their widowed mother could not have been pleased.

Next day, Bill, aged 34, enlisted too. Bill's mission—to care for Arthur—was clear.

Because of his previous service, he entered as a lieutenant and before they sailed he was promoted to captain. On 1 November 1914, the first convoy of 38 transport vessels and four warship escorts set out with great determination from Bunbury in Western Australia bound for England. On board were 21,500 Australians, 8500 New Zealanders and 12,000 horses.

Mid-voyage, the convoy changed course for Egypt—there was simply no room to accommodate or train the Anzacs in England. They passed by Port Said for Alexandria and disembarked on 3 December.

Then hell opened its gates.

Arthur Waite was evacuated from Gallipoli on 18 July 1915. He'd not been wounded. Instead, he'd developed an inguinal hernia. The top of his right leg had become swollen and his testicles felt as if they were the size of melons. The pain was excruciating. For several days before, his division had engaged in a gunnery duel with the Turkish. It had taken almost two months under relentless enemy fire for the South Australian contingent to heave their artillery—trench mortars and even a 1500-kilogram howitzer—into a position where they could inflict mortal injury.

Arthur bugged out on the hospital ship HS *Ansonia*, bound for the UK via Malta. On 27 July he was admitted to the military hospital in Hampstead. There he met nurse Irene Austin.

The Austin family had already given their only son to the war.

Vernon James Austin, Irene's younger brother by two years, had fallen victim to a lone sniper on 26 January 1915 as he walked with his commanding officer on a recce near La Bassée, in the region of northern France and southern Belgium known as Flanders.

'I need hardly tell you what a gloom it has cast over officers and men of my battery, as everyone was so fond of him. He was such a cheery little chap,' his commander, Lieutenant Colonel Henry Sandilands, wrote to the bereaved parents. They brought his body back to England for burial.

Vernon was born in 1893 to an English father and an Australian mother. His father had mapped his career path in the family business. But Vernon, who studied at the King's School, Canterbury, was headstrong. He enlisted in the Officers' Training Corps and was commissioned in the Special Reserve of the Royal Artillery as second lieutenant. The family business could always come later.

It was some business. Vernon's dad was Herbert Austin—later Sir Herbert and then Lord Austin—and he owned the Austin Motor Company.

As a means of interesting the lad in the family firm, Herbert had allowed Vernon to play with the products. He raced and rallied them with moderate success, and when war was declared he'd been due to sail for Russia to participate in a race organised by SPAK—the St Petersburg Automobile Club, with headquarters on Nevsky Prospect.

Five months later he was gone, and with him Herbert's succession plan. Herbert's daughters, Irene and her sister Zeta, were not considered suitable for high office.

But there was a spark between Arthur Waite and Irene, and Herbert and his wife Helen couldn't help but be pleased.

Herbert had an affinity with Australia. Born in Buckinghamshire in 1866, he was just eighteen when he set out for Australia to seek his fortune. Three years later he'd married Melbourne girl Helen Dron and secured an interest in the world's first sheep-shearing machine company, owned by fellow expat Frederick York Wolseley.

It was a revolutionary device, powered by a petrol-fuelled stationary engine. But poor quality control in its manufacturing let it down. In 1893, Wolseley and the Austins, including Irene (born 1891), retreated to the UK where they could rely on the excellence of the skilled labour force in Britain.

Sheep shearing is seasonal. In the downtime, the Wolseley factory began making bicycles, then Austin built two prototype three-wheeler cars. Neither Wolseley nor his board could see a future in the motor industry. In 1905 Herbert struck out on his own.

By the time of the war, he was producing more than 1500 Austins annually in a multitude of engine sizes and body style and was the fourth-largest motor manufacturer in the UK. He employed 2300 people and even built Austin Village to house them.

When he gave the factory over to the war effort, it earned him his knighthood, and the Belgian government awarded him the Order of the Crown of Leopold II for employing Belgian refugees and giving them shelter.

Arthur Waite and Irene Austin enjoyed a classic wartime romance. They wed on 16 October 1918, one month before the armistice ended the Great War. Brother Bill, now a lieutenant colonel, attended the wedding, then a week later sailed on the steamer *City of Karachi* back to Adelaide, invalided home. Bill had remained in Gallipoli when Arthur was repatriated and was one of the last to be evacuated. He'd been wounded twice and won the Military Cross for his bravery at Lone Pine.

His service was exemplary. He fought in France and received the Distinguished Service Order for his action at Fromelles, Ypres and the Somme.

Arthur served largely in staff appointments, first in Egypt then in France. His hernia continued to give him grief, evidenced by the walking cane at his side at his wedding. But he nonetheless received the Military Cross and was promoted to captain in January 1918.

Bill forged a career as an Adelaide livestock auctioneer and when World War II broke out, he re-enlisted. He was made camp commandant at the Wayville Barracks, then deputy director of recruiting at Keswick Barracks. For 29 years he led Adelaide's Anzac Day parade mounted on a white charger. He died on Christmas Day 1973, aged 93.

For the Austin family Captain Arthur Waite was the hope of the side. He wasn't Vernon, but he was close.

The Austin Motor Company was in trouble. Servicing the war effort had seriously depleted its cash reserves. Patriotically, Austin had slashed profit margins to build armaments.

The postwar marketplace had not bounced back, and volume was not enough to sustain the factory, at least not with the expensive mid-sized cars they were making. To make matters more complex, in 1914, Herbert Austin had floated the company, capitalised at £650,000. Understandably, his new investors were more demanding of immediate results than his family was—and they were harder to handle, too.

To top it off, Herbert, now in his fifties (considered old at the time), had taken his eye off the ball. In December 1918 he'd bowed to the will of the people and agreed to represent them as the Conservative MP for Kings Norton, Birmingham. You can't do both.

A big idea was needed, and in 1921, Sir Herbert and his son-in-law had one. They'd make a car for the common man—fifteen years before Volkswagen had the same idea—and they'd build it on a production line to rival that of Ford's Model T. It would be so cheap that it would cost no more than a motorcycle-and-sidecar outfit.

For the concept to work, profit margins would have to be infinitesimal. For that reason alone, the shareholders wouldn't buy it. The risk-to-reward ratio wasn't in their favour. Rebuffed, Austin started a skunkworks. The plans for his baby car were drawn by eighteen-year-old draftsman Stanley Edge in the billiard room of Austin's home. Three prototypes were built in a corner of the factory.

It set the Austin family on a collision course with their new shareholders, who revolted. Austin Motor Company was briefly put into liquidation, then bailed out almost immediately by the issue of £1.5 million in debentures repayable over five years. The purpose had been to loosen Austin's grip on his company. It was a ploy. As part of the 'rescue', the banks insisted three senior external directors were appointed, and Austin was removed as managing director. As the man with his name on the hubcaps, he was allowed to remain chairman.

And then, miraculously, the Austin 7—696cc and 7.2 horsepower (5.3 kilowatts) of mini-magic—got up. Austin extracted his revenge by charging a family royalty of two guineas for every car sold. They made 290,000 of them and wiped out the cyclecar industry.

Arthur Waite—handsome, six feet tall, straight of back, not yet 30, and a war hero (everyone who survived Gallipoli was)—became the super-salesman. He spearheaded a racing-based promotional blitz. He set class speed records on the steeply banked Brooklands circuit in Surrey. Then in 1923, with his trusted riding mechanic Alf Depper, he took a race-prepared Austin 7 to Monza in northern Italy and won the International Grand Prix for Light Cars.

This was the biggest of big deals. Bentley was carrying the British flag on the Continent and would win the Le Mans 24 Hour race in 1924. But a year earlier, Waite's baby Austin had blown away the opposition on their home soil. Buyers couldn't help but be impressed.

Seven-mania spread the world. Austin 7s were manufactured under licence in the USA, Germany and France. Datsun in Japan survived a court action for knocking off the design and instead assembled under licence. Baby Austins arrived as rolling chassis in Australia, available to seven local coach builders. The completed 7s were sold under local names such as Comet and Meteor.

Sydney Albert 'S.A.' Cheney, a true Australian retail pioneer, saw the potential for a more lineal approach. In 1926, he secured the Victorian, NSW and South Australian agency for Austin, promising Sir Herbert he'd attack Ford, which had established manufacturing plants in each state to build its market-leading Model T.

Arthur and Irene Waite came with the deal. Sir Herbert and Lady Helen thought a change of climate would be good for the kids. Their marriage had not yet been blessed with offspring. Perhaps a summer or two in Australia would do the trick. They were packed off with instructions to double Austin's market share Down Under.

Arthur made immediate contact with the VLCC and when he learned of their plans at Phillip Island, he telegraphed his father-in-law: 'Send my race car.'

On 31 March 1928, Waite and riding mechanic Guy Barranger, a fellow AIF veteran, won what retrospectively became the first Australian Grand Prix—not in class, but outright, which was a surprise to all (see Chapter 3).

Five weeks later, on 4 May, the winning Austin 7 was the smallest car on display at the biggest motor show then held in Melbourne, at the Royal Exhibition Building in Carlton. The trajectory could only be upward.

But the Great Depression stopped that. Total Australian car sales had smashed through the 100,000 ceiling in 1929, peaking at 104,000. A year later, as shock waves from the New York Stock Exchange's 1929 Black Thursday crash created a global financial catastrophe, total deliveries plummeted to 40,130. By 1932, just 13,921 new vehicles were sold. Cheney, listed on the stock exchange, went into liquidation. Arthur and Irene had already retreated to the United Kingdom, but their anticipated clear succession was no longer an option. In their absence, the board's control had tightened.

In the 1930 Ards Tourist Trophy (TT), a 660-kilometre enduro in Northern Ireland won by Tazio Nuvolari on Alfa Romeo, Arthur crashed his works Austin 7 on lap seven. He never raced again.

Arthur became a director of the Austin Motor Company, in charge of sales, service and promotions, but he did not ascend to managing director or chair.

Sir Herbert Austin was created Baron (Lord) Austin in 1936 and died from a heart attack in 1941, after once more seeing his factory given over to another war effort. His peerage did not pass on.

In 1952, the Austin Motor Company merged with Morris Motors to become the British Motor Corporation. The Austin badge was phased out in 1988.

Arthur Waite passed away on 25 January 1991, aged 96. He and Irene never had children.

3

First Shots—The Prewar Grands Prix

Arthur Terdich hadn't expected to win, but halfway through the 100 Miles Road Race in 1928, that's the way it was working out.

Terdich was Victoria's Bugatti distributor, and his Bugatti Type 40 was a standard four-seater with a fabric body built at his family's bodyworks. They called the pointy-tailed shape a Torpedo, which was a bit of a misnomer—it was still a tourer. He'd stripped the guards from the car and fitted a fat exhaust. But as good as the three valves per cylinder 1500cc in line four was, it was no match for the purpose-built, straight-eight grand prix Type 39, or its four-cylinder clone the Type 37.

Luck, though, was going his way. SC Cox's straight-eight Type 39 failed to start. Iron filings were found in the sump—not sabotage, but simply the crankshaft scoring an own goal after an over-rev. Jack Day's Type 37 had gone off into the bushes early after a spot of overdriving. Day was still in the race, pushing to make up time, but a fair way back. Things were looking good.

An unexpected challenge had come from a pesky Austin 7, that of the 'British' driver Arthur Waite—sensational on the corners and brisk on the long straights. But Waite had taken a pit stop at half distance and he was now nine minutes behind. Terdich was fuelled to the end, no pit stop needed.

And then . . .

The Type 40 coasted to a halt at the back of the circuit—no spark, caused by no fuel. Terdich thought fast. He flagged down Stan King's Austin 7 and caught a lift back to the pits to get a churn of petrol. King dutifully waited and then drove Terdich the other half-lap back to where they'd left the Bug. Except it wasn't there.

Terdich's riding mechanic had found a faulty fuel feed, fixed it, and driven the Bugatti back to the pits to look for the boss. By the time the confusion was sorted, Captain Arthur Waite had assumed the lead, which he held to the finish.

Terdich was left to fight Day for the honour of being the first Bugatti home—in fourth place.

The race had been a bold experiment on several fronts. Support had been so overwhelming that the VLCC had to reject entries.

Captain Arthur Waite's bundle from Britain had arrived, but when he opened the box it was the wrong car. The factory had received an offer they couldn't refuse for their lightweight Austin 7 racer, so they sent him a 'sports prototype', supercharged, the only one in the event with a revolutionary four-speed gearbox. To save weight, the extra forward gear replaced reverse in the tiny casing. There was precious little time to prepare. Waite and riding mechanic Guy Barranger drove it only once, in a back lane of Melbourne, where they confirmed a top speed of 144 km/h.

The prototype 7 turned out to be a blessing. The lighter GP Austin would surely have broken up on Phillip Island's rough surface. Waite's international experience simply allowed him to outshine the locals, setting a new standard for grands prix to come. He drove his car like a metronome: similar time every lap; light-fuelled at the start, with a planned and superbly executed five-minute pit stop at half distance for fuel, oil and a spanner check. No fuss, no panic, no emotion. Let the others crash around him.

There was a salacious suggestion that Irene Waite had arrived at Phillip Island in a Model T Ford. Her dad had failed to ship her favourite 7, a pretty one-off special with a body by coach builder Gordon England. Irene had stamped her foot in protest and got aboard a Ford. Later, Arthur had a local replica of his race-winning car built for her.

The big winner was Phillip Island. AKT Sambell's ferries were at capacity—and so was accommodation. Teams arrived a week before, preparing for the race, which was to occur on the Eight Hour Day holiday Monday. Road closures were perfunctory at best. Three competitors rolled in practice; another two crashed heavily.

And then it rained—bucketed down.

On Sunday, the day before the race, Arthur Terdich tested the track and pronounced it unsuitable for competition. The options were as bleak as the weather—cancel or postpone until the following Saturday. The committee took the second choice. But there was no way to tell the spectators, many of them already en route.

Sambell's ferries disgorged thousands of passengers at the Cowes wharf that Monday morning. It was, the local paper claimed, the largest single gathering ever on the island. They could, quickly, have turned into a mob.

The VLCC hastily convened a half-mile (800-metre) sprint on the only piece of circuit that was not a quagmire. The track between Heaven Corner and Young and Jacksons Corner squeezed in just enough room.

The Bugattis blitzed it. Jack Day's Type 37 was quickest at 83.8 mph (134.8 km/h) in 21.48 seconds; then 21-year-old Sid Cox's straight-eight Type 39, which averaged 80.5 mph (129.5 km/h) in 22.36 seconds; and Terdich's Type 40 at 77 mph (124 km/h) in 23.36 seconds. The fastest non-Bugatti was Arthur Waite's 750cc Austin 7, at 73.5 mph (118.3 km/h) in 24.48 seconds—a fair way off, but still best of the rest.

Most of the crowd went home satisfied. Quite a few stayed for the week, taking shelter where they could. It was a more relaxed time then.

Miraculously, most who went home came back. AKT Sambell mustered more ferries. There were no official crowd figures. Melbourne's *Age* newspaper (2 April) estimated 'several thousand'.

Organisers started the race in four classes, sorted by cubic capacity: two waves in the morning, two in the afternoon, each class separated by five minutes. That meant there were two races, each of 100 miles (161 kilometres), with a leisurely lunch in between. The winner would be decided on fastest elapsed time. The plan was perfect—the execution less so.

They put the two equally matched middle classes together in the morning, and the baby cars with the outright contenders in the afternoon, guaranteeing the Bugattis a clear track. But the morning race cut up the fragile road, handicapping the afternoon starters.

Also, no one had factored in the pace of Waite's Austin. He was in the first afternoon wave, so quick that when the Bugattis took the starter's flag he was already through Turn 4 and in Terdich's mirrors, almost one lap up in a sixteen-lap race.

Terdich responded. According to *The Age*:

> Mr. A.J. Terdich, driving a Bugatti, narrowly escaped being hurled to death when rounding Hell's Corner. His car skidded alarmingly but was saved from crashing into the deep ditch by some straw bales. He had been driving at about 95 mph [153 km/h] on the straight. There were several close shaves when cars just grazed each other while travelling at top speed, but the day passed off without anyone being injured.

There was a hint of disappointment in that report.

The Melbourne motor industry celebrated. It was a victory for the mass market: an Austin 7 first, in 1 hour 46 minutes 40 seconds (90.56 km/h), Johnny McCutcheon's Morris Cowley, overall-second in 1 hour 50 minutes 10 seconds (87.1 km/h), 3 minutes 52 seconds ahead of third-placed Cyril Dickason's Austin 12. None of them standard, of course, but each a brand name with broad appeal on Melbourne's Elizabeth Street mile of motors.

One week later, 7 April, the motorcycles were on. The Victorian Motorcycle Union, a grouping of half a dozen marque-centric clubs, had been overlooked by the VLCC. The bikers went ahead anyway, using an extension of the grand prix circuit on a long, winding and tortuous track known as the Rhyll Course. It was Easter Saturday and Alec Finlay, one of the owners of Melbourne's BSA franchise, won the Victorian Solo TT over a punishing 200 miles (322 kilometres) in 4 hours 13 minutes 30.4 seconds, an average speed of 47.34 mph (76.18 km/h).

He was a massive 23 minutes clear of the second placegetter, Tasmanian Reg Hay. Every one of the estimated 1000 spectators applauded their heroism.

The Rhyll Course was a horror. Its extension, out to Rhyll, had been designed with naive ambition—more motocross than road race. The car-race portion had massively degraded after the grand prix the week before. The elongated motorcycle course added ten kilometres of what was essentially bush bashing. It was astonishing that ten of the twenty starters even finished.

The common link between cars and bikes had been one man, Phil Irving. Thirty-five years later he'd be the engineer who'd design and build the Repco Brabham engine that powered

Sir Jack Brabham to the only F1 world championship ever won by a driver-constructor.

In 1928, 25-year-old Irving was co-proprietor of a motorcycle shop in Ballarat, and a committee member of both the VLCC and the Victorian Motorcycle Union. Superhuman feats were his stock-in-trade. He was lying second in the TT when his clutch began to slip. He pulled into the pits, hacked some rubber from a car mat, relined the clutch and rejoined. It was one of the few times his ingenuity failed. The bike stopped.

Phil used the same motorcycle in the sidecar race. 'I set off in a blur without even my goggles,' he wrote in his autobiography, 'and consequently approached Gentle Annie much too fast, ran off the road and stopped in a clump of scrub. The thick stems bent over and exerted a sort of crab-pot effect which defied our efforts to free the outfit so it stayed where it was until the race was over.'

The Rhyll Course would never be used again; hurt by the experience, motorcycle racers would not return to the island for three years. There'd been some justification to going back-to-back with the cars. Infrastructure could be shared, and the pits, constructed for the cars, were free for the bikes. On the flip side, the cars had drawn a huge crowd and covered themselves with glory—the bikes, not so much. Perhaps it had been a mistake to go in the first place.

But motorcycle competition was on the cusp of positive change. In 1928, the Victorian Motorcycle Union morphed into the Auto Cycle Council of Australia (ACCA) and affiliated for the first time with the Auto-Cycle Union of Great Britain. The ACCA opened the door to international competition and to Australians becoming world champions. When the bikes did return to Phillip Island in 1931, it would be with a much-changed management structure and an entirely different outlook.

4

The Bugs' Clean Sweep

There was no room for doubt. The name 'Australian Grand Prix' appeared as an addendum, almost an afterthought, on the Phillip Island race program in 1929. But surely, that's what it was. For good measure, the first race in 1928 had been retrospectively coronated. It would not be until 1931 that the Grand Prix took prominence in promotion.

The 1929 race distance had been doubled to 200 miles (322 kilometres), conducive to a grand prix. Phillip Island had joined an elite group. Grand prix racing was still new to the world. The French had started it in 1906. Monaco had entered in 1929. In 1930, only three others existed: in Italy, Belgium and Germany.

Phillip Island was firing. AKT Sambell's own Summerland development was powering ahead. Street plans were laid out and approved. Golfer Alex Russell, winner of the 1924

Australian Open, was contracted to design the links, and he became Australia's first professional golf-course designer on the strength of the commission.

Whatever the VLCC wanted, it got.

A small parcel of land was reclaimed from property owners so that Gentle Annie, Hell and Heaven corners could be properly rounded, promoting higher mid-corner speeds and greater opportunity for overtaking. A bridge builder was brought in to make the Bridge of Sighs two metres wider on each side. The only non-passing zone would be at the Needle's Eye. The signalling and mechanical pits were moved for easier access. The landowner, possibly Sambell, willingly acquiesced.

The Phillip Island Council, with Sambell as its president, imposed a tax on local businesses to pay for it all. Sambell's own ferries would contribute a shilling for every fare onto the island. Hotels and B&Bs would pay two shillings and sixpence per person for everyone staying over the race weekend. The money went straight into the road-building program.

All competitors and their cars, and all officials, travelled free on the ferries. Spectators could leave their cars in free secure parking at Stony Point on the mainland but needed to pay to get to the island.

Most importantly, practice was allowed on course for the full week before the race, never mind the disruption to local traffic. Competitors were warned not to abuse the privilege.

In the circumstances, it was desirable a marque with cachet should win. Bugatti obliged. The French car with the Italian name won four Australian Grands Prix in succession between 1929 and 1932—three with its supercharged Type 37A and one with its naturally aspirated straight-eight Type 39. The feat of four-in-a-row for a manufacturer at Phillip Island has been matched but never surpassed. It was another 85 years before Casey Stoner achieved it, in MotoGP for Ducati (2007 to 2010).

The spindly, raucous Bugattis, with an exhaust note that sounds like sheet metal being shredded, were simply supreme. And they hammered the race record down. Arthur Terdich, the Victorian Bugatti distributor, won in 1929 in a time of 3 hours 14 minutes 22 seconds, an average speed of 61.7 mph (99.3 km/h). Next year young Bill Thompson, the NSW Bugatti distributor, cracked the metric tonne winning in 3 hours 6 minutes, an average of 65.5 mph (105.4 km/h).

Carl Junker, a nervous novice, used his unsupercharged Type 39 to undercut the three-hour barrier in 1931—2 hours 54 minutes 50 seconds, averaging 69.87 mph (112.44 km/h). In 1932, Thompson took no prisoners with the greatest reduction in race time over the four years—2 hours 40 minutes 11 seconds, averaging 76.27 mph (122.74 km/h). To reinforce his dominance, he set a new lap record of 4 minutes 49.4 seconds, at an average of 82.6 mph (132.2 km/h).

In the beginning, it was possible to communicate with Ettore Bugatti directly. Most owners, including an elite group of Australians, did. The eccentric Milanese, born into a family of Art Nouveau designers, had established Automobiles E. Bugatti in Molsheim in the Alsace region of either Germany or France, depending on which country was claiming sovereignty at the time.

Bugatti was brilliant. His Type 35 Grand Prix series, encompassing the 37 and the 39 and built between 1924 and 1930, was a runaway success. In the hands of private owners, the Type 35 claimed more than 1000 race victories, at its peak averaging fourteen victories a week. Orders rolled in and Ettore appointed a UK agent, Lieutenant Colonel WL Sorel, on the Brixton Road in London. For English-speaking countries especially, Sorel became the new go-to man.

In Australia in 1929, there were nine Type 37 Bugattis and two straight-eight Type 39 GP cars. Seven were entered in the Australian Grand Prix. Arthur Terdich imported his, a Type 37A, in late 1928. He wanted no repeat of the previous grand prix's stuff-up. A supercharged car had won; it was the way of the future, so he specified the 'blower' too.

You don't throw money away. Terdich got around the government surcharge on the importation of fully built-up vehicles by bringing the Bug in without its rear bodywork. He used his own furniture-making skills to craft a rear end just like the real thing.

Twenty-two-year-old Bill Thompson (Chapter 5), an emerging ace from Sydney, entered a naturally aspirated Type 37 for its owner (and his benefactor) Dr Arthur Burkitt, a lecturer in medicine at the University of Sydney. Burkitt would be Thompson's riding mechanic.

Another red-hot 22-year-old, Reg Brearley from Prahran, persuaded T.E. Barnett, a shareholder in Bugatti's Victorian distributorship, that he was the driver to bring results. Barnett had imported two Type 37s, one for his son Dudley, who never raced. That car went to Brearley, who found the funds to buy it.

It was hot and dusty in private practice. Stones and rocks were flung up. Arthur Burkitt copped a stone straight into his goggles and Thompson retired to the pits while the professor recovered his cool.

To settle the surface, the Commonwealth Oil Refinery covered the track in used oil. Then it rained. The amorphous mess required a day and night of clean-up. Parts of the grand prix track would be hard-baked by midday. Other parts required sand—plenty of that on the island—to soak up standing water.

They started in four waves, all on the track together. The first to 200 miles (322 kilometres) would win.

Thompson was out after five laps. Engine failure was the official reason; an over-rev was the most likely cause.

Young Brearley drove like it was a sprint. He thrilled the crowd with lurid slides. It was testament to his skill and daring that he brought the Bug home second to the measured drive of Terdich (he'd learned the value of restraint from Arthur Waite), the two Bugattistes separated by more than fifteen minutes. Fast-charging Bill Lowe, much later Australia's first Ferrari agent, was third in a French-built Lombard just two minutes behind.

The best news came at the prize-giving dinner, held at the Royal Automobile Club of Victoria three months later. The grand experiment that had been road racing on Phillip Island had been successful. The Victorian Government, lobbied hard by the Phillip Island Council, agreed to pass a bill allowing motor racing to be held on public roads for a maximum of twelve days each year. It was a huge victory for Phillip Island. They'd gone it alone—illegally, if it came right down to it—and now the government had fallen into line.

There was an air of disbelief at the 1930 Australian Grand Prix.

A New South Welshman, an interloper, had won. Melbourne–Sydney rivalry, a national trait, was in full flight, even in motor racing. For a mere mechanic to win the Australian Grand Prix was unthinkable. For him to come from New South Wales was even more so.

To the Victorians, Bill Thompson defined the stereotype. He was a 'garagiste'—a derogatory term applied in the 1950s by Enzo Ferrari to describe what he saw as small, backyard British F1 racing organisations like Cooper and Lotus.

Thompson was super-fast, a thinker, and he was ambitious. His short-lived 1929 debut had taught him a lot. A grand prix is like no other race. It won't be won in the first five laps, nor will blind luck guide you unaided to the chequered flag. It demands planning and strategy.

First, the car. A naturally aspirated Bug wouldn't hack it. Thompson and his patron Burkitt ordered a four-cylinder Type 37A through NSW Bugatti agent Russell Taylor. They were most precise in the spec. Gear ratios and final drive, essential to get the most out of the car, were tailored to Phillip Island.

Thompson received the car early to properly shake it down. An untested car would never do—he'd learned just how unforgiving Phillip Island's surface could be. He replaced Bugatti's shock absorbers with ones purpose-built for the Island. Perdriau Rubber didn't construct carcasses especially for Phillip Island, but they worked with the team to hand-pick the casing that would best suit the circuit.

Thompson and Burkitt went into training to be match fit. They adopted kidney belts to keep their cores intact over 200 miles. They practised pit stops, even developed a centre-lift jack to raise the front or the rear of the car with one heave to make tyre changing quicker.

They shipped the car to Melbourne, giving it a sea voyage—the highway from Sydney to Melbourne was too rough to contemplate. At Phillip Island they were frugal in their practice laps, doing just enough to get used to the track and the extra speed of the supercharged car over last year's Bug. No point in wearing it out.

They put in place a small but effective secret weapon. The signalling pits were set up to notify drivers of their splits on the previous lap, which wasn't a lot of help over 10.4 kilometres. Thompson found a point where the field could be timed, and had the splits relayed to his pit board to give him near to real-time information. Genius.

Naturally, he won. It would have been a travesty otherwise. But it didn't come easily.

He led the first lap, but a lap later he was in the pits with fouled plugs. He rejoined, tenth in a field of 27, and began his relentless pursuit. Arthur Terdich responded. It's a delicate balance between extracting speed and demanding too much of the machinery. At half distance Terdich's Bug blew—a rod through the block. Reg Brearley sensed opportunity and drove out of his skin. His Type 37 was more robust than the supercharged version, but he flung it off the road at Hell Corner. It took more than a quarter of an hour to dig it out of the ditch.

When they chaired Thompson from the car—a form of celebration that long preceded the champagne shower—he was the only NSW entrant in a packed field of Victorians. And the winner.

Three months later, Reg Brearley and his riding mechanic, Bert Elliott, were dead.

The notorious city-to-city record runs were about to be banned. In the same month as the Australian Grand Prix, 27-year-old Sydney draftsman Don Robertson set out to be the first, and he hoped last, person to speed over the 920-kilometre distance in under ten hours. His 25-horsepower (18-kilowatt) Graham-Paige took 10 hours 5 minutes elapsed time and 9 hours 16 minutes driving time, an average speed of 99.28 km/h. To save weight, he drove solo—a massive effort.

Brearley and Elliott saw ten hours neat as a challenge.

At 5 a.m. on Monday, 9 June, they sped away in the dark from Sydney's GPO in Martin Place in their Grand Prix Bugatti. They planned to be in Melbourne for a late lunch. Three hours later they were already approaching the Hovells Creek bridge, nine miles (14.4 kilometres) from Gunning in southern New South Wales. It was winter and the sun had only risen at 6.55 a.m. Likely it was low and in their eyes. There may have been a blackspot of frost. Their Bug left the road, hit a ditch and rolled several times. Brearley, 23, was found dead at the scene. Elliott, 19, succumbed later that day.

The Great Depression was not kind to motor racing.

Just fifteen cars faced the starter of the 1931 Australian Grand Prix. Six finished.

The VLCC was struggling for entries, and that meant struggling with budget. They came up with a big idea: a handicap race to give mid-ranked starters an equal chance. Handicaps are difficult to manage, unreliable in their conclusions and invariably controversial.

Handicappers awarded the win and the trophy to an Austin 7; it was 1928 revisited. Then they took it away and gave it to a Bugatti. The result remains contentious almost a century later.

Bill Thompson didn't defend his championship. He'd sold his winning 37A to fearless Sydney racer Hope Bartlett, a specialist on the high-banked Maroubra speed bowl.

The Bugattis of Bartlett and Arthur Terdich would be off scratch. The recently imported Austin 7 of Cyril Dickason, colleague of Arthur Waite and a senior employee of S.A. Cheney, would have a twenty-minute advantage.

Dickason had kept it a bit quiet: he'd imported the engine that won the 1930 Brooklands 500 and installed it in his Austin 7 Ulster. The little car was a rocket ship. The scratch cars had to wait several laps until they could give chase.

Bartlett was electric. Any thoughts of a measured plan were gone. He lapped faster than anyone had ever done. Even when Terdich's car failed, Bartlett kept his pedal to the metal. Two laps from home his crew had him in the lead, confirmed by others. They signalled him to ease back and conserve the car. But Bartlett kept his foot down, simply not prepared to relent. Trust a handicapper? Would you?

One lap away from the chequered flag, his Bugatti blew up.

Mild-mannered Carl Junker, not even close to being a racing driver let alone a grand prix ace, had cautiously entered his country's national grand prix only at Terdich's urging. Now he cruised his Type 39 into what he thought was second place. Very pleasing. A lovely, spirited afternoon's drive—not bad on debut.

Officials and the media acclaimed Dickason the miracle

winner. He'd crossed the line first, so naturally he'd won. But then they checked. Their regulations awarded the win not to the car that was first across the line, but to the car that was fastest over 320 kilometres. Because of the handicap system, the two were not necessarily the same. Dickason had been 7 minutes 34 seconds slower than Junker, who'd also covered the full distance.

The compromise, announced the next day, was that Junker had won outright and Dickason had won on handicap. Dickason retained the trophy, anyway. Most likely the VLCC was too embarrassed to ask for its return.

Undisputed, though, was fifth place. Joan Richmond (Chapter 5), the first woman to drive in an Australian Grand Prix, had covered the distance at an average of 91.84 km/h. That was faster than Arthur Waite's 90.56 km/h when he'd won the inaugural grand prix.

Joan and her riding mechanic, Mollie Shaw, could have created a media storm, but it wasn't their style. At the prize-giving in the Isle of Wight Hotel that night, Richmond and Shaw, according to a report in *The Car* magazine on 15 April 1931, 'received a welcome that they very richly deserved'. There was no Ladies' Prize.

In 1932, Bill Thompson became the first person to twice win the Australian Grand Prix. He presented Bugatti with its fourth and last GP victory at Phillip Island.

Thompson's riding mechanic, Wal Warneford, was the hero. He held the disintegrating car together while Thompson shattered the lap record in their sprint to victory.

There's ample evidence that Thompson repossessed his Type 37A from Hope Bartlett—not nicely, but in a midnight raid on Bartlett's locked garage. And he spent an extraordinary amount of money, even in the middle of an economic depression, to bring the ageing car up to speed. It's an addiction. All race cars have a shelf life. The 35 series of Bugattis were reaching the end of theirs. Thompson saw value in one last shot.

The Light Car Club of Australia (LCCA)—as the VLCC had renamed itself—was smarting from the previous year's embarrassment. This year's rules were simple and ironclad. The cars would still be handicapped but first across the line would win—no arguments.

Bill Thompson and Arthur Terdich would start from scratch. The limit man, off 29 minutes, was Bill Northam—later Sir William, chairman of Johnson & Johnson, who at 59 would become Australia's oldest-ever Olympic gold medallist, winning a sailing gold at the Tokyo games in 1964.

This time the handicappers got it right. Raw speed favoured the Bugs, but age and unreliability made them vulnerable. Seven would start. Only three would finish.

Thompson's highly modified 37A sprinted away from Terdich's standard car, but two laps in the Thompson car sprang an oil leak in a braided line behind the dashboard. Warneford tied a rag around it, then pinched it shut with his fingers. For 29 laps he held back a tide of red-hot oil with his bare hands.

Thompson broke the lap record sixteen times. He left it at 4 minutes 49.4 seconds (82.6 mph/132.2 km/h). He passed Terdich's broken Bug stranded trackside, but Terdich had never been the target. It was the newer, more modern imports, aided by favourable handicap, that were his goal.

With just five laps remaining, Thompson passed 21-year-old Geoff Disher's French-built twin-cam San Sebastian Salmson to take the chequered flag. Disher held on to second. Northam, remarkably, was sixth.

It was the last national grand prix victory for the series 35 Bugatti anywhere in the world. Ettore Bugatti built the much more advanced Type 51, and it competed in Europe but not in Australia. Its successes, while heroic, were limited by the assault of the state-backed German racing teams—the Silver Arrows—which were essentially pre-World War II propaganda machines.

On 11 August 1939, Bugatti's son Jean was killed while road-testing a Type 57 close by the family's factory. Three weeks later, Great Britain declared war on Germany and production ceased.

Ettore died in 1947, aged just 65.

5

Heroes of the '30s

Bill Thompson—Our First True Champion

The white sandy seabed of Kwajalein Atoll, one of 29 in the Republic of the Marshall Islands, is the resting place of 25 World War II warships and 160 aircraft. Lying just west of the International Date Line, slightly north of the equator and 5000 kilometres from Australia, it is a recreational wreck-diver's paradise.

On 12 February 1945, Bill Thompson, Australia's greatest prewar racing driver, drowned in its deep-blue waters when the lumbering American-built Consolidated PB2Y Coronado flying boat on which he was hitching an unauthorised ride pitchpoled on landing.

Ten crew members survived. Two drowned. Squadron Leader

William Bethel Thompson was not part of the official manifest and was not immediately recognised as being on board.

His remains were interred at Carlos Islet, a small Marshall Island community, and finally brought home in 1947 to the Sydney War Cemetery, Rookwood. Thompson had forged his own permission to fly on the aircraft and it took some time to sort out the paperwork.

Bill Thompson was Australia's first professional racing driver, and for a decade its most successful. He raced in six Phillip Island Australian Grands Prix, winning three and claiming two second placings.

He was the Peter Brock of his time. You can overlay the similarities between both drivers: mercurial and irascible; immense talent sometimes flawed in its application; a powerful partner for the motor industry but careless in maintenance of the relationship; a larrikin and a self-promoter. A once-in-a-generation shining star.

Bill's mum Gladys was the shaker and mover. She bought and sold houses—not quite a property developer, but close. His dad, Bill Snr, was in the post office. They sent Bill to several good schools, never successfully. The last was Sydney Grammar on College Street, next door to the hub of the motor industry. Bill was kicked out of Grammar after riding a borrowed motorbike through the headmaster's assembly. He went to work on the magic mile of motors, joined the Royal Automobile Club of Australia (RACA) in Macquarie Street, and hung off the fence at Maroubra Speedway and met the racers. He'd found his calling.

Bill Snr and Gladys owned a British-built Crossley, for a time the car of kings. When the Duke and Duchess of York (later King George VI and Queen Elizabeth) came on their 1927 royal tour, the government imported twelve model 18/50 Landaulettes for the motorcade. You couldn't help but be impressed.

When the Crossley service centre in Sydney came up for sale, Bill Snr and Gladys funded their 22-year-old son's purchase of the business. Things moved fast. The small Redfern workshop opened its doors to wealthy car buffs.

On 30 June 1928, Bill made his racing debut in a Bugatti Type 37, in a butcher's picnic of time trials and hill climbs run by the RACA. He was in the same field as the heavies—Charlie East, Sid Cox, Hope Bartlett. He won his class and got their attention.

No one knew where the Bugatti Type 37 he drove came from. Bill just turned up with it and claimed it as his own. Here's a clue: Thompson's workshop was near the University of Sydney, an easy drive for mad-keen Bugatti fan and university professor Dr Arthur Burkitt. He could afford them. His family owned a sizeable part of Goulburn in the NSW Southern Tablelands. Burkitt brought his business to Thompson and became his patron.

Nine months later, Bill Thompson, with Burkitt as riding mechanic, raced in the Australian Grand Prix at Phillip Island.

It's arguable that Thompson was ever without sponsorship in his short eight-year career. In a sport populated by wealthy and entitled amateurs, he pioneered a new era of pay-to-play. He put a value on himself and, surprisingly, fielded offers. He followed the money.

When the NSW Bugatti distributor died in 1929, Thompson found the funds to buy the agency. When the Great Depression brought the Bugatti business to its knees, he became the paid professional race-team manager, and driver, for Empire Motors, the Riley distributor. When people failed to buy Rileys in sufficient volume, he jumped ship to Melbourne's MG distributor. He brought industry suppliers with him on the journey. Castrol (lubricants) and Champion (spark plugs) were rusted-on supporters. He joined Shell in Melbourne, ostensibly in sales but more likely as an ambassador.

Commercially, he was a role model. Fourteen-year-old David McKay met him for the first time just after Thompson's final grand prix. Young McKay, later Australian sports car champion and first touring car champion, based his powerful Scuderia Veloce ('Team of Speed') on Thompson's example. Both came from privileged backgrounds, but neither family held wealth enough to totally support their ambitions.

Success brought controversy. The Thompson versus Hope Bartlett court case in the wake of the repossession of the Bugatti Type 37A created headlines and caused people to take sides. The dissolution of his relationship with Melbourne's MG distributor was acrimonious. His patron Arthur Burkitt simply faded from the scene.

Thompson married twice, the first time in 1929 to Jean Anderson. He was 22, she was 18. They lived uncomfortably with his parents and had two boys. Phillip, born in 1930, was named for the location of Thompson's first grand prix win; William Riley was born in 1933, days after Thompson won the grand prix in a Brooklands Riley.

Shortly after William's birth, Thompson was surprised when Jean fled the shared family home permanently, leaving their sons in his care. In 1942, he married wealthy widow Franklyn Ironside. Franklyn bought Bill a Bentley as a wedding gift.

Bill Thompson made no announcement of retirement. He simply stopped. His last grand prix was 1935, his last speedway race shortly after. He'd fallen into a black hole, burnt himself out.

General (later Field Marshal) Sir Thomas Blamey was likely responsible for lifting him from depression. Blamey was a sometime resident of Phillip Island, and a keen fan. He enlisted Thompson in the militia and fostered his career in the Royal Australian Air Force (RAAF). As a founding member of the League of National Security, Blamey likely recruited Thompson into that too.

Thompson's official role in World War II was as procurement officer for the RAAF, but many thought he was a spy. He moved freely between American and Australian command, and the initial confusion over his presence on the sunken flying boat was consistent with clandestine activity.

He would have been almost 39 when Blamey and US General Douglas MacArthur jointly signed the Japanese surrender documents on the USS *Missouri* in Tokyo Bay. He may have been still young enough to have kickstarted a revitalised motor-racing career.

Joan Richmond—A Pioneer of Far More than Gender

Joan Richmond, the young heiress to the Haddon Rigg Merino sheep-stud fortune, had ridden her stallion Accrington in small country race meetings in Victoria. Accrington was a gun; he'd been second to Eurythmic in the Caulfield Cup. Joan used him largely as a hack, except every now and then they'd sneak out and win regional races.

But when she tried to enter a larger meeting at Euroa, Richmond was rebuffed. 'Women can't be jockeys,' she was told.

'I was furious and devastated. I couldn't see what being a man or a woman had to do with being able to ride a horse,' Joan told her biographer David Price.

That night at a dance she cried on the shoulder of young air force pilot Johnny Summers, an amateur racing driver. 'No such regulations in car racing,' he told her. So Joan's family chauffeur taught her to drive.

Her father and grandfather had both died. They'd sold the stud and left her 'a small legacy'. It became available, in increments, after her 21st birthday. Perfect timing.

She bought a little side-valve Citroën and took it club racing. When she won her class in a hill climb, Melbourne's Riley agent was waiting at the finish line. He persuaded her into a lightweight, fabric-bodied Riley Nine—not an Accrington equivalent but pretty lively.

Riley and Shell both offered her an ambassadorial role. 'Mother wasn't keen on me having a paid job,' she remembered. 'In those days it wasn't done for girls who'd been trained to be ladies to work for money and certainly not in the motor trade.'

Richmond accepted the job—just in time for the 1931 Australian Grand Prix. Her fifth place was an exceptional result. She parlayed that into an international career that shattered accepted conventions.

She talked Riley into letting her lead an overland expedition to the UK. It was only three years since Francis Birtles had made the first overland crossing. His journey had been epic. To be fair, Richmond took the easier route—her three-car women's team used ships to skirt the worst of the roads. But it still created records. To cap the journey, she entered the Monte Carlo Rally, covering 1788 kilometres from Sicily to Monaco in 51 hours to finish seventeenth in the small-car class.

Phillip Island hero Arthur Waite greeted her in London. At a gala welcome, he tapped Victor Riley, one of the four brothers who ran Riley, and said, 'She's the one.'

On 2 May, less than three months after arriving in the UK, Joan Richmond and driving partner Elsie Wisdom, one of Britain's foremost female competitors, won the inaugural British 1000 Miles Race at Brooklands in a works Riley Nine. Their victory was hailed by the British press as a breakthrough—the first win ever by an all-woman team in a major event. They beat some of the most prominent male drivers of the era and survived a near collision with world land speed record holder John Cobb.

The pair averaged 141.59 km/h on the combined banked and road circuit: 'I didn't know we were still leading until I saw Arthur Waite with the chequered flag,' Richmond said.

Richmond, tall and elegant, fitted in perfectly with the upper crust of Britain's racing motorists. As well as Riley she drove for Singer, Triumph, Aston Martin and HRG. She bought a fearsome three-litre Ballot open-wheeler from world land and water speed record holder Sir Malcolm Campbell and raced it with distinction. She was part of MG's three-car all-woman team at the 1936 Le Mans 24 Hour race. No other driver from Australia came close to matching her record or presence in pre–World War II Britain.

In 1937, Joan was in a works AC Ace in the Donington Park 12 Hour in Leicestershire, three hours north of London. Her co-driver was London stockbroker Bill Bilney. The night before the race, Bill proposed marriage and Joan accepted. Joan was the more experienced driver and took the start. She handed over to Bill in the rain: 'He tried to overtake a Riley Nine; the two cars locked wheels and crashed at full speed into a stone wall and Bill was killed. To this day I blame myself for asking Bill to drive with me,' she later wrote.

Richmond raced again, but not seriously. She was an important member of the British Racing Drivers' Club and was their liaison with Germany's Silver Arrows teams when they arrived on their crushing prewar propaganda tours. She competed in her seventh Monte Carlo Rally in 1939. It was a nice bookend that her co-driver was Elsie Wisdom.

Joan Richmond saw out the war in the centre of bomb-devastated London, working in procurement for the aircraft industry. She sailed for Melbourne on 27 March 1946 and took rooms at the Windsor Hotel. She entered the postwar revival meeting at Mount Panorama, Bathurst, in October 1946 but did not start.

Joan died in 1999, aged 94. For the second half of her life, she was known as 'the cat woman of Malvern'. She'd turned her home into a shelter for cats.

The National Museum of Australia holds Joan Richmond's trophies and memorabilia. Only recently was she inducted into the Australian Motorsport Hall of Fame.

6

Maintaining the Marriage

It was a tale told on Phillip Island that one of AKT Sambell's ferries, the English-built luxury yacht *Alvina*, had once belonged to the lovely Lillie Langtry, English actress and royal mistress.

The Prince of Wales, later Edward VII, had presented it to Ms Langtry; it was originally christened *The White Lilly*, which gave credence to the story. When their liaison ended, the yacht—and the actress—became superfluous.

The *Alvina* was part of the mystique of the island. The Roaring Twenties may have been losing momentum on the mainland, but on Phillip Island the party never stopped. Cowes was party central, a bubble of fun where reality was suspended.

If you'd booked ahead, you'd arrive from Stony Point on the *Alvina*, still sleek and beautiful even though she'd been stripped to carry 250 passengers.

You'd stay at the Isle of Wight Hotel. There'd be a floor show, dancing and a banquet. If the mood took you, you could wander out to the garages to view the best of the competitive vehicles under preparation in the hotel's courtyard.

Architecture on Phillip Island relied on lightweight, easily transportable materials. Walls tended to be thin. Sometimes there was a need for discretion. It was all part of the fun.

It was such a strong relationship, the marriage between Phillip Island Shire Council and the Australian Grand Prix. Both were big winners. The grand prix had become the flagship of Australian motor racing, a world leader. It had brought cachet to the island. Everyone was riding the growth curve.

In 1930, AKT Sambell opened his Summerland golf links to acclaim. Twelve professionals played 36 holes, four times around, for a £50 purse. *The Sporting Globe* proclaimed: 'Without exaggeration this course could become one of the most popular in Victoria.' Sambell presented the cheques and spruiked his plans for a grand clubhouse.

In 1931, motorcycles returned. Three in a marriage? The partners welcomed them. The Victorian *Highways and Vehicles Act* had given the bikes permission to race with impunity.

And if there was any residual concern about the use of public roads, then Victoria's chief of police and friend of the Island, the war hero General Sir Thomas Blamey, was able to help. Blamey had befriended Bill Thompson. When a local constable determined that race cars needed to be registered to be driven to and from the circuit, Thompson petitioned Blamey, who penned a handwritten note overriding the policeman and granting permission.

The Auto Cycle Council of Australia scheduled the Victorian TT for 26 January 1931. It was a momentous date—the first

Australia Day. Victoria gazetted the name first and by 1935 all other states had followed.

The bikes had learned hard lessons from 1928. This time they used the car course. Twenty-five-year-old Jimmy Pringle, a young star of Melbourne's murderous Motordrome, won the 200-mile (322-kilometre) Senior TT.

Pringle was the two-wheeled version of Bill Thompson. He went on to win the Senior race at Phillip Island three years in succession from 1936 to 1938. His works 500cc Manx Norton was the gold standard. In 1933 he made headlines with a huge crash in the TT. Like any grand prix rider, he brushed it off—a mere flesh wound.

The bikes claimed the Australia Day date as their very own. As long as the Island was running, they'd be there.

In 1931, the VLCC upgraded its name to the Light Car Club of Australia (LCCA), in celebration of its incredible success. It was akin to granting itself a knighthood. At the same time, the club bought a two-storey building in East Melbourne near St Vincent's Hospital. On Friday nights, the most marvellous sporting cars in Melbourne would be parked in Brunswick Street as club members inside easily circumvented liquor and licensing laws. Freehold ownership, a first for a car club, was an outstanding achievement.

It's sometimes hard to pinpoint the exact moment a relationship begins to break down. There's a lack of thought here, a delayed response there—not one big thing.

There'd been concern over a serious incident in the 1932 Australian Grand Prix. Albert Edwards, in a supercharged front-wheel-drive Alvis, had rolled upside down into a water-filled drain. The crew was okay, but they'd hit an onlooker standing in an unauthorised area. He was a fellow club member, trials driver Dick Wilkinson, and he lost his leg in the impact.

The debrief put it all down to dust. Edwards had been blinded by billows of dust and swerved hard to miss Carl Junker emerging from the pits.

It was time to talk seriously to the council about road sealing, and, for that matter, to take a deep dive into the club's own safety and marshalling procedures. But it was tough to propose public works in an economic downturn. The Melbourne and Metropolitan Board of Works was struggling to raise funds for essential projects on the mainland. Even if the Phillip Island Shire Council tried terribly hard, it would be difficult to contemplate them getting priority.

In 1933, Bill Thompson surprised everyone, even himself, by winning his third Australian Grand Prix.

The Great Depression had decimated his Bugatti business. He'd swiftly seized the lifeline presented by Sydney's Empire Motors to become their competitions manager. They were agents for Sunbeam, Rover and, most importantly, Riley.

Empire Motors used Thompson's credentials to convince the Coventry factory to build a Brooklands race special. Racetrack victory, they said, would sell more road cars. In the 1932 race, handicappers positioned the dual champion in the middle of a brace of Bugattis—three behind, five in front. He'd be off eight minutes. Bill Lowe precipitated the second spectator crash in two years. His supercharged Lombard went through a wire fence and hit five onlookers. Three were treated at the scene; two were hospitalised. Lowe checked them out, then rejoined the race to finish fifth. Through the prism of contemporary race protocol, it wasn't a good look.

Thompson relentlessly, never recklessly, hunted down the field. Handicappers had favoured veteran Harold Drake-Richmond, a Bugatti-driving LCCA committee member. But Drake-Richmond hesitated, lost the lead and spun in pursuit. The dust had been so extreme they'd been sighting the road by looking up at the tree tops.

Thompson won the prize but lost his job. Sometimes a win on Sunday doesn't sell on Monday, and the promised surge in Riley sales didn't happen. Thompson reached for his next, and last, lifeline. He relocated to Melbourne to join MG distributor Lane's Motors.

The Light Car Club of Australia was open in its avidity. They'd found another partner: a scenic road around Albert Park Lake, right on their doorstep in central Melbourne, was there for the taking. A confluence of circumstances prompted them; lack of road sealing was a big issue, but so was geography. A race circuit in the middle of Melbourne and on a sealed road? They didn't want to turn their back on Phillip Island but what choice did they have?

The Victorian Government was planning major celebrations in 1934 for the state's centenary. A race would lift the spirits of the population. Chocolate maker Sir Macpherson Robertson was funding an air race from London to Melbourne, the Centenary

Air Race—a huge deal, with £75,000 in prize money. The LCCA, now elevated in its stature, felt an obligation to match it with the Centenary Grand Prix.

They were excited. It would be, they said, the biggest, and by definition the best grand prix ever held in Australia. So much for 'love the one you're with'.

Discussions with Albert Park began in May 1933. Not In My Backyard objections arrived in June. Pretty clearly, this wasn't going to be an instant win.

The LCCA went back to Phillip Island, perhaps a little cap in hand. They'd maintain their March date for the 1934 Australian Grand Prix after all. And, as something of a makeup, they'd run another shorter meeting on New Year's Day.

Their Albert Park intent, however, remained steadfast, and they planned to run the standalone Centenary Grand Prix around the lake later in 1934. Surely by then they'd achieve permission? As it turned out, they wouldn't. The final irony was that Albert Park didn't want racing wheels tearing up its brand-new macadam surface.

On New Year's Day 1934, the LCCA attracted 8000 paying customers to Cowes for its 100 Miles Road Race, a bonus for the local economy. They knew how to run a motor race.

Jack Williamson's Riley won. Bill Thompson provided the excitement. He'd not yet found a buyer for his old red Bugatti and he flung it at the course, cutting the apex of Heaven Corner, jumping a drainage ditch, grazing the heavy timber straining post of the wire spectator fence, peppering those closest with splinters and even spinning before the Bug cried, 'Enough!' and stopped. The thick white dust had been extreme. Once more, Thompson said he'd been sighting by the tree tops.

Ten weeks later they were back for the Australian Grand Prix. Thompson's works MG K3 Magnette arrived by ship from the UK with just four days to spare. Even in an untried car, they made him scratch man with a near impossible 35-minute deficit to the limit men.

The dust was worse than ever. On a baked-hard surface, Johnny Summers rolled his MG Magna—same engine as Thompson's, just unsupercharged—and his riding mechanic Bob Heffernan was hospitalised with broken ribs.

The last lap was epic. Thompson entered it in second place, 1 minute 24 seconds behind limit man Bob Lea-Wright's Singer. It was the handicappers' perfect scenario. The grand prix seemed certain to be decided on the last corner of the last lap. And that's how it happened.

They were together at Hell Corner. Thompson had only to bide his time, straighten up and outdrag the slower car to the finish. Instead he made a lunge. The MG half spun; Lea-Wright held his nerve, and Thompson crossed the line twelve seconds behind. No elite competitor in any sport can rationalise second place. He was mightily pissed off. So, you'd imagine, was car owner Robert Lane. You don't pay Australia's top professional to make a rookie error.

On 4 June, the King's Birthday weekend, they were at the Island again. What was going on? The once-exclusive Island was being used up.

The Winter 100 was a failure. Crowds were way down. The longest and deepest downturn in Australia's economy was still in play. Who could afford another trip to the Island? Fifteen cars started, eight finished. Les Jennings won in an MG Magna. Bill

Thompson left his heavily handicapped K3 in the workshop and entered a stock MG from a midfield starting position. It broke down.

Johnny Summers, friend of Joan Richmond, was disturbed that his club, the LCCA, was not paying attention to its principal constituents, the drivers. Squadron Leader J.H. Summers proposed the formation of a breakaway. He called it the Australian Racing Drivers Club. Its purpose was to 'unite' racing drivers—and also, it turned out, to run the Centenary Grand Prix at Phillip Island. The LCCA was not to be the promoter. Johnny Summers and his Australian Racing Drivers Club had got under their neck.

On 30 August 1934, the Melbourne *Argus* announced the Centenary Grand Prix for 27 October. In truth it was a speculative call: 'The club hopes that all leading Australian drivers and several from overseas will compete,' *The Argus* reported. 'It is hoped that within the next few days the Centenary Council will include the race in its official programme.' And tellingly: 'the club has not previously conducted a sporting event'.

Undaunted, the Australian Racing Drivers Club pushed ahead. The Victorian Centenary Grand Prix, they promised, would be the longest and richest road race ever held. Prize purse was £300. Distance was 35 laps of Phillip Island—230 miles (370 kilometres). It would be time-certain; to be classified, it was necessary to finish within 25 minutes of the winner. Most importantly, the grand prix would be the first for 'all powers'. The cubic capacity limit imposed by the LCCA would not apply.

That last rule led to the most extraordinary entry in any grand prix, and to the most amazing victor. It's a true story, perhaps a little embellished in its retelling, but true.

Mick Smith was in love. The young pilot from upmarket Camberwell in Victoria sought the hand of local girl Rhoda Gardner. According to the convention of the day, her father questioned his prospects: could he afford a home, or at least a deposit?

By Smith's logic, the grand prix presented a solution. He'd never raced before, but he'd driven quickly on the road and his mates said he was a genius. That gave him confidence. He entered under a false identity—the name 'Gardner' seemed appropriate. No first name—just 'Gardner'.

The missing link was a car. He had a plan for that. His parents had just bought a '34 Ford Roadster, 221 cubic inches (3.4 litres) of Australian-built American V8 muscle. He'd run it around Albert Park a few times at night, illegally of course, to see if he and the flathead Ford might have what it takes.

No way would his folks let him race it. But they didn't have to know. Coincidentally, they'd be away from home over the grand prix. Smith and his mate Lin Terry waited until the front door closed, then they got to work. They stripped the Ford of its mudguards, bumpers, roof stays, rumble seat and lights. They fitted an aero screen and beefed up the shock absorbers.

It took so long that they missed practice and arrived on the SS *Killara* on the morning of the race.

They were no fools. They knew they were up against two Australian Grand Prix winners and a stellar field of 22 racing cars. Lin had a modicum of experience. He'd been a riding mechanic in Merton Wreford's Type 39 Bugatti in the '33 grand prix. They'd failed to finish.

Smith and Terry's plan was to stop, point, squirt. Corners are where you crash. They'd use the superior torque of the rumbling V8 to win on the long-rutted straights.

The first few laps were frankly frightening. It was corner entry that bamboozled Mick. How slow was too slow? How quick was inviting disaster? He had a few near misses and skidded a few times, though hardly flat-spotted the tyres on such a loose surface.

By the time he got into his rhythm, the grand prix had turned into the ultimate cliché: a race of attrition.

Bill Thompson was out. So was Jack Williamson's Riley, which had won in January. Stalwarts Barney and Bess Dentry, who'd raced in every grand prix, looked finally set for victory, then they faltered too. Fourteen cars failed to finish.

The flathead Ford took the flag first, then ran out of fuel 200 metres past the finish line. Smith and Terry covered the distance in 3 hours 7 minutes 56 seconds, an average of 73.49 mph (118.27 km/h).

Smith's cover was blown. He accepted the £125 winner's share of the purse under his real name—that of a tyro racing driver who'd never race again.

Melford's, Melbourne's Ford distributor, did a deal to put the winning car on display, offering a loan car to his dad and mum.

According to Lin Terry's daughter Lee Vautin, interviewed many years later, Mick and Rhoda married.

By 1935 Phillip Island's race days were numbered. Three deaths in two races sealed its fate.

On New Year's Day 1935, driver Campbell Graham, aged 37, and his riding mechanic Alfred Peters, 40, both from Warrnambool, Victoria, died instantly when their MG P-type Midget crashed overtaking a slower car at the Needle's Eye between Gentle Annie and Hell corners.

They were competing in the Centenary 300, the LCCA's response to the Centenary Grand Prix. It was called the '300' for the distance—302.17 miles (486.29 kilometres), the longest race ever held in Australia.

Bill Thompson also crashed. Eleven laps into the 46-lap race, and on maximum attack, he'd just set a new lap record when he jinked left to pass a slower car at Heaven Corner. His K3 rolled, momentarily trapping Thompson and riding mechanic Bill Balgarnie beneath a car leaking fuel on a hot exhaust.

The race was so long that winner Les Murphy, in a tiny MG P-type, had started 53 minutes 40 seconds ahead of the scratch man.

Three months later, at the Australian Grand Prix, former motorcycle racer Les Cramp, 24, of Brighton, Victoria, was killed on his second practice lap. His ex-factory Ballot 2LS had been part of a one-two class victory in Sicily's 1922 Targa Florio. It was well past its competitive best. The Ballot left the straight between Young and Jacksons and Gentle Annie corners. Cramp's riding mechanic, Reg Leslie, was 'badly injured by concussion'.

It was the end of the road for the Australian Grand Prix at the Island.

Les Murphy was its last grand prix winner, claiming a perfect double with the Centenary 300 in 1936. Bill Thompson was desperate to win. The previous year's loss had been a total frustration. But at one-third distance, his K3's spark plugs fouled. His well-drilled pit crew got him back out in less than a minute. Still, he lost to Murphy's tiny P-type by 27 seconds. The two were teammates, and Lane's Motors won the teams' prize.

Thompson would leave Lane's shortly after. You can only speculate. Were there team orders disobeyed? Thompson was the superstar. Should Murphy have been given a slowdown? Drivers have spat the dummy for a lot less.

It was the beginning of Thompson's end, too.

The 1936 Australian Grand Prix was conducted on Boxing Day on the Victor Harbor road circuit, South Australia, forward dated to become the 1937 grand prix in the record books. In 1938, the grand prix moved to the new purpose-built scenic road circuit at Mount Panorama in New South Wales. It would never be held again at Phillip Island.

The Auto Cycle Council of Australia vacillated between calling its premier event the Tourist Trophy, a very Isle of Man appellation, or the Australian Grand Prix. It settled on both, pretty much in alternate years.

In many ways, the motorcycle fraternity was far more adventurous than their car equivalent. They used Phillip Island as a springboard to international endeavour. Experience at Phillip Island was deemed to be preparation for the Isle of Man TT, the most daunting road course in the world.

Heroes were made on Phillip Island. In 1933 Harry Hinton, senior of the Hinton racing dynasty, claimed his first TT victory. It was his only win on the island. The Hinton family—Harry Snr;

sons Harry Jnr, Eric, and Robert; and Eric's sons Tony and Peter—between them amassed 33 national titles. They were as close as it comes to motorcycling royalty. Harry Snr was blind in one eye, the result of a motorcycle road accident in 1932, but it just made him harder to pass. You snuck up on him at your peril.

George Hannaford, a multiple winner on Phillip Island, claimed the 1935 Australian TT on his Rudge, then sailed to the other island for its June classic. He crashed in practice and fractured his skull. Back in Australia he won the 1939 TT at Phillip Island in the Junior and Senior divisions.

The internationals reciprocated. In 1936 Stanley Woods, the greatest of his day, with 29 grand prix wins and 10 Isle of Man TT victories, raced at Phillip Island. It was supposed to be a sales promotion for Velocette. But the Irishman was deadly serious. He won the Junior TT on his 350 Velo from Jimmy Pringle.

Phillip Island was fast turning into a goat track. Even a 'short' 3.3-mile (5.28-kilometre) triangular course adopted after 1935 as an alternative to the car's Grand Prix track was increasingly becoming rutted and strewn with loose stones. Woods' 500cc machine ingested a pebble and he was forced to ride his 350 in the Senior race. He came home a close third.

In 1938, the spies turned up. German champion Ewald Kluge raced for DKW, one of the four brands that comprised Auto Union. There wasn't a big market for DKW in Australia, and he certainly wasn't in the country for sales promotion.

With war looming, his manager, Baron Klaus-Detlof von Oertzen, had sinister intentions. His mission was to photograph sensitive Australian military installations (such as they were), and also to transfer large sums of money from the Nazi treasury to sympathetic local organisations.

Neither was strictly illegal, but it was definitely poor form. Motor racing provided the perfect cover. Kluge raced proudly with a swastika on his helmet, a little obvious.

The Allies were onto them. They'd even assigned a British car racer, Alan Sinclair, to shadow them.

Kluge won the Lightweight (250cc) TT and placed third in the Junior race. Then the Germans fled the country.

Frank Mussett, who had won at Phillip Island for the first time in 1934, was at the Isle of Man in 1939. He placed tenth in the Junior TT, got out before England declared war on Germany. He brought his two ex–Stanley Wood Velocettes home with him. On 30 January 1940, he rode them both to victory in the Victorian Senior and Junior TTs, the last motorcycle races ever held on the Phillip Island road circuit.

On 11 December 1940, the light on the Cape Woolamai headland, the nearest point on the island to Bass Strait, was turned off. It had taken a while, but Phillip Island was on war alert.

It was Saturday, 26 September 1936, and page 27 of Melbourne's *Argus* newspaper carried a single-column story:

> The death took place yesterday at his home, in Moonga Road, Toorak, after a long illness, of Mr. A. K. T. Sambell, who had been president of the Shire of Phillip Island since its inception nine years ago. Mr. Sambell, who was aged 57 years, was born at Violet Town . . .
>
> In 1912 Mr. Sambell took up land on Phillip Island, and he established the ferry service between the island and the

> mainland. He helped to make the island into one of the leading holiday resorts in Victoria.
>
> Mr. Sambell has left a widow, four daughters, and two sons . . .
>
> The funeral will take place at the Necropolis, Springvale, at 3.30 p.m. today.

Sambell had died without seeing his Summerland dream fully realised. Nor was he there to defend it when his achievements were torn down.

In the history of Phillip Island, Newhaven boatman Richard A Grayden is credited with leading the push that built the bridge Sambell had sought. On 27 April 1937, Grayden founded the Bridge League, with 388 members ready to petition for permanent connection to the mainland. There were some who didn't want it, who treasured their isolation. But Grayden persevered.

On the evening of 11 November 1938, Victorian premier Albert Dunstan visited the Phillip Island Shire Hall on Thompson Avenue to hear the results of the Bridge referendum. The yes vote got up. The first pile was driven in April 1939, and on Friday 29 November 1940, 5000 people saw Mrs Jessie Dunstan cut the opening ribbon. Construction had cost £62,000.

Sambell's Summerland development would have benefited mightily, but he wasn't there to drive it or protect it. At its peak, his grand Summerland estate boasted 183 houses, golf links, one hotel, a shop, and its burgeoning penguin colony.

In 1985, the Victorian Government launched its Penguin Protection Plan. It began buying back houses located within the breeding colony. All houses were removed from Summerland by 2010. What remained of Sambell's golf links became part of habitat restoration by Phillip Island Nature Parks. You walk over it, on raised metal footpaths, on the way to the Penguin Parade.

Part Two

A Permanent Circuit 1956–1962

7

The New Phillip Island

It was too good an idea not to happen.

Before World War II, Phillip Island was 'known' for motor racing. Ask anyone its key attraction and it probably wouldn't have been penguins—not then, anyhow. The island's prewar economy had motorsport at its very foundation. It brought the big crowds and, for local businesses, the big money.

Postwar, the island was struggling. Tourists were dribbling in, enabled by the new bridge, but there was no influx. Local businesses were longing for the days of yore.

In 1950, a group of small-business operators who didn't want to get any smaller got together and kicked around the idea of rejuvenating the grand prix circuit. It took a while—a long while, actually—but heading into the New Year of 1956–57,

Phillip Island held its first motor race on a purpose-built circuit, sitting proudly on its own land.

It was a triumph beyond expectation.

Lex Davison, soon to become four-time Australian Grand Prix winner and the inaugural winner of the Australian Drivers' Championship (the Gold Star), won the first race on the 'new' Phillip Island circuit, driving not his bellowing 4.5-litre Ferrari but a tiny car he called 'the mechanical mouse'. The tiny, spindly, supercharged Cooper-Vincent was his specialised hill-climb car.

On Saturday, 15 December 1956, the first race on the brand-new three-mile (4.82-kilometre) track was for racing cars under 1500cc, and it was too good an opportunity to miss. It was raining and Davison, wearing an oilskin jacket and an aeroscreen visor jutting out beneath his Herbie Johnson crash helmet, slipped and slid his way to lead from start to finish. His bum was never more than six inches from the ground.

Later, Jack Brabham won the feature race, the aptly named Bill Thompson Memorial Trophy. Ken Rumble, who went on to become a Motocross legend, won the first bike race. The one-day meeting was a 2+4 (two wheels for bikes, four for cars).

The opening of the circuit went largely unnoticed by the metropolitan media. Timing was everything. The race meeting occurred just two weeks after Stirling Moss had won the Australian Grand Prix at Albert Park, and just one week after the Olympic Games had concluded at the Melbourne Cricket Ground. By comparison, Phillip Island didn't rate.

It should have been a big deal: it was Australia's first permanent grand-prix-sized circuit and it had been enabled by a bunch of enthusiastic amateurs.

It wasn't as if there was a shortage of motorsport in postwar Australia. Little-used airstrips and tiny towns provided pop-up solutions. Lex Davison, well heeled and dedicated to his sport, competed in 21 events in the same year he won at Phillip Island. Postwar, the Australian Grand Prix was decided on dead-flat, non-cambered airbases at Melbourne's Point Cook and Queensland's Leyburn, or precariously around the houses at Nuriootpa in Adelaide's Barossa Valley, Narrogin in Western Australia's wheat belt, at Southport in Queensland (behind what would become the Gold Coast), and ultimately at Albert Park.

Only Mount Panorama offered a semi-permanent solution, and it required a decree of parliament with stringent police permission each time it was put to use.

In Sydney, the Australian Sporting Car Club challenged the NSW Government and its risk-averse police for the use of Parramatta Park, and succeeded in racing there for three years. Melbourne did likewise on the old Commonwealth Aircraft Corporation airstrip at Fishermans Bend where World War II–era Wirraways were manufactured.

A grand attempt was made to float a small but permanent track at nearby Altona, with grand prix ambitions, but it sank into the swampland within a year. In Sydney, landowner Belf Jones carved the 'permanent' Mount Druitt circuit out of one of his paddocks, then ploughed it under again in 1958 in a fit of pique after an argument with regulatory authorities.

Hill-climb tracks—smaller, more manageable, but definitely for one-vehicle-at-a-time sprints—proliferated, and the big guns of motorsport competed. Lex Davison won three national hill-climb titles in succession.

On 13 October 1952, the Australian Automobile Association (AAA), the peak body for the state-based automobile clubs, determined it would no longer administer motorsport. Until then, the AAA had acted as an umbrella administrator for all things motoring—political lobby, road service, insurance and motorsport. It was big business but not yet demutualised, and had often found itself at the mercy of high-maintenance car-racing enthusiasts. Now the entire Australian motorsport community was to be spun off.

An extraordinary rescue operation was mounted. Thirty-one-year-old Maurie Monk, owner of a successful engineering business, and a winning trials navigator alongside Stan Jones (father of F1 world champion Alan), led the charge. Monk recruited a fellow trials competitor and all-round pedant, Donald Kingsley Thomson, to help draft a constitution for a new motorsport organisation.

Thomson was a book editor and he presented himself as a man of towering intellect. At least he could write. They went to work on the kitchen table of Thomson's home in Beaumaris, and by 15 December they'd put together articles of association, complete with terms of reference. They'd even given the new organisation a name, the Confederation of Australian Motor Sport, or CAMS—a neat acronym, which existed right through to 2019 when it was rebranded Motorsport Australia. Monk became the first president. Thomson, always a polarising figure, was initially passed over as secretary, but by the end of 1953 had seized the role.

Monk's family, rightly, regards him as the father of CAMS. But Thomson was the power. His twenty-year reign, until he was deposed, spanned ten presidents. He was an important constant, with an uncanny ability to see the big picture and still sweat the small stuff.

Phillip Island wasn't on his radar to begin with. There was no reason it should have been.

Winston Maguire, beloved son of a Presbyterian minister who passed away on Phillip Island in 1948, had become proprietor of an upmarket coffee lounge and licensed billiard hall at Cowes. By 1950, eager to attract greater custom, he was up for good ideas to promote tourism.

Bernard Denham—Bern to his mates—and Herbert Watchorn ran a bus service on the island. Their specialty was penguin tours with a side show of mutton birds (once a thriving industry; now the birds are protected).

The coming of the bridge in 1940 had been both good and bad. Built to a budget, it had a load limit of just five tons. Sometimes bus passengers had to get off the bus, walk across the bridge and reboard on the other side—not good for tourism. The car-ferry service ceased in 1948. Getting there was no longer half the fun.

In the cafe, Maguire, Denham and Watchorn reminisced about the days of old when thousands of daytrippers would arrive for the car races and many would stay and spend their money.

How good would it be if they could reopen the circuit—not the road course, but a new, dedicated, purpose-built racetrack?

PD Whitlock, a cafe regular and island farmer (he presented his cattle regularly at the Royal Melbourne Show) had the answer. He had land that he was prepared to give up for a reasonable sum: 300 acres (121 hectares) for only £6525. It was off Back Beach Road with views forever over Bass Strait, a little windy perhaps but majestic in its location. Whitlock was prepared to sign it over for a £100 deposit without, it appeared, a rigid payment schedule.

Whitlock owned Brighton Beach Motors, which had secured the highly lucrative Holden franchise. Locally manufactured FJ Holdens had claimed half the entire automotive market. There was no problem selling them, but it didn't hurt to have the island on side.

Win Maguire's cafe car club quickly grew. They even gave their group a name: the Phillip Island Motor Racing Club. Six of them raised the deposit to secure Whitlock's land. He was in no hurry to settle the contract.

More than anywhere else in Australia, in Melbourne the old school tie means something. Winston Maguire was an old boy of Geelong Grammar. Sir Keith Murdoch, proprietor of the Melbourne *Herald*, didn't go to Geelong, but his son Rupert did, graduating in 1949. For a time, Maguire's dad, the Reverend Tom Maguire, had been the Presbyterian pastor in Geelong, providing spiritual guidance to the school. So his son approached Sir Keith.

The Herald gave the fledgling idea some ink, exciting interest among the Melbourne smart set. On 26 March 1952, a large crowd of enthusiasts, all of them potential investors, arrived at

Melbourne's upmarket Savoy Hotel in Little Collins Street. The three founders had dressed up their proposal with a bit of razzle dazzle. The Savoy was showbiz central. Throughout the '50s and '60s it would host luminaries like Louis Armstrong, Nat King Cole and Ella Fitzgerald. It was a good place to make a pitch. They were busy, exciting times, way beyond motor racing.

In 1949, Melbourne had been controversially selected to host the 1956 Olympic Games, the first to be held in the Southern Hemisphere. In 1951, the city celebrated half a century of Federation with a massive street parade and a theatre production called *An Aboriginal Moomba*. Within four years, Moomba would morph into Australia's biggest annual street party. Queen Elizabeth II, crowned in 1952, would visit in 1954—a truly big deal. And to glue it all together, television was coming with its transformative change in communication.

In 1953, *The Herald*'s opposition newspaper, *The Argus*, backed a proposal to turn Albert Park into a part-time motor-racing circuit. Chairman of the Albert Park Trust, Pat Kennelly, later a federal senator, led the push. He enlisted the LCCA to run it and persuaded the newly minted CAMS to license it as the Australian Grand Prix.

On Saturday, 21 November 1953, Doug Whiteford (Lago Talbot) won over 64 laps (324 kilometres). Big-time motor racing had returned to mainstream Melbourne and everybody wanted to get on board.

Just one week later, Winston Maguire's group confirmed it had raised £13,000 in membership funds and it was signing up members at a rate of 80 a month. The founding fathers had devised a sensational joining offer. For £1 a year, paid ten years in advance, members would be entitled to free entry to all race meetings for the first decade. Subscriptions were so good that they'd been able to purchase PD Whitlock's land outright. A track was laid out and work got underway.

There was one major change. The Phillip Island Motor Racing Club (PIMRC) became the Phillip Island Auto Racing Club (PIARC). Two-wheel racers, keen to come on board, belonged to the Auto Cycle Council of Australia. 'Motor' had to go in favour of the catch-all 'Auto'. No worries.

The PIARC board was drawn from two- and four-wheel disciplines. The fifteen-person committee comprised five from motor racing, five from motorcycling and five from Phillip Island's business community. Their skills were respected and interchangeable. Phil Irving, for example, built the best Vincent motors ever—for cars or bikes. And Hedley Thompson was renowned as Melbourne's best welder. Whether you wanted a featherbed frame for your Norton or tweaks to your Formula Three car—Reg Hunt's was called the Flying Bedstead—Thompson was your go-to man.

PIARC were enthusiastic promoters. They sought endorsement from global stars like Stirling Moss and Peter Collins, and made them honorary members. They sold corner names before corners were built. They hit up big business. Charles 'Dave' McGrath, later Sir Charles, was managing director of Repco and also a landowner on Phillip Island. Repco was in. Olympic Tyres, chaired by Olympic swimming silver medallist Sir Frank Beaurepaire, signed up. Both companies would later offer bank guarantees to enable construction.

Members? The PIARC committee convinced them they had the best open-air clubroom of all: 250-odd hectares of Bass Strait real estate, unlimited camping rights and the opportunity—in fact, the obligation—to help build the track. Bridge loadings restricted heavy machinery, so they built the circuit the old-fashioned way, with picks and shovels, using lightweight road base with an icing of gravel.

PIARC ran its first event for members on 17 October 1954; a rally from the Botanic Gardens in Melbourne allowed 2000 members to drive around the still-unmade track. It was a PR imperative, devised to keep enthusiasm high.

A year later, with the track laid, they were back, this time on a more important mission. Constant low-speed laps by many members' cars would settle the delicate coarse-chip road surface and get it ready for racing. For the founding fathers, it was a long wait, fraught with frustration. Bernard Denham pulled out in September 1955, a hint of pique in his resignation. Winston Maguire was quick to make public that, 'as I have pointed out on many occasions, the original idea was yours'.

What do you do when your circuit designer has got it wrong? When he's created a clockwise track that just doesn't work?

Simple—you reverse the direction.

Alan Brown, a Melbourne surveyor and consulting engineer, wasn't Hermann Tilke, the renowned and somewhat controversial modern-day designer of circuits built to contain speed, control overtaking and optimise safety. Brown, a newcomer at circuit design, took an entirely different brief. He was to create a track that delivered as high an average lap speed as possible within its topography.

He loved the terrain. No matter where you stood in the natural lush green bowl, looking across the clifftops and the rolling breakers beyond, you couldn't help but feel your soul stir.

Brown took advice from the stars of the time—Reg Hunt, Stan Jones and Lex Davison. He also searched internationally. Just west of Amsterdam was Circuit van Zandvoort, at the time a 4.193-kilometre undulating track through sandhills on the shores of the North Sea. It had opened in 1948. Zandvoort gave Brown a benchmark. Apart from its proximity to the ocean, the major feature of the Dutch circuit was its long straight. Brown liked that: 'Generally, winding bends have been avoided where straights could be substituted,' he wrote in his design notes. 'This has been done so that the lap speed will be as high as possible. A track with never-ending curves could be most tiring on drivers. From a spectator's point of view, high laps speeds are important.'

For further guidance, Brown turned to the Melbourne and Metropolitan Board of Works. Even then, everyone knew that the three tenets of road safety are the car, the driver and the road. With road safety as their foremost consideration, the Board of Works was building corners with closing radii, having the corner tighten up on exit so drivers wouldn't be tempted to stand on the gas while not in a straight line. It's the exact antithesis of sound motor-racing circuit design, which encourages a slow-in-and-fast-out technique.

Brown followed Board of Works guidelines, and that's how he presented his first design.

PIARC was shocked. It wasn't going to work. They had money in the bank, certainly, but not enough to squander. A return to the drawing board was going to be expensive. Until someone said, 'What about the other way?'

It was an inspired solution. Anticlockwise, there'd be no grind, virtually vertically, from what is now Southern Loop up the main straight all the way to Lukey Heights, the highest point on the circuit. Taken in reverse, the whole section became a magnificent downhill plunge. It was otherworldly. As speed increased on the straight, you'd rush towards the cliff edge and feel you could soar above the ocean. Heart in mouth, you'd ease hard right, balancing on tiptoes, into the fastest sweeper in Australian racing.

In 1956 at the first open meeting Jack Brabham claimed the lap record for the exactly three-mile (4.82-kilometre) circuit, 2 minutes 20 seconds, an average of 124.15 km/h. At the 4.193 km Zandvoort's opening meeting, albeit in 1948, Prince Bira of Siam (Thailand) had done 2 minutes 0.2 seconds (125.58 km/h). Alan Brown could take satisfaction that he'd delivered pretty much to brief.

In November 1956, organisers of the Australian Grand Prix at Albert Park pulled off the most audacious piece of ambush marketing in the history of the Olympic Games. Three days after nineteen-year-old Melbourne athlete Ron Clarke lit the Olympic flame at the Melbourne Cricket Ground, burning his arm in the process, Stirling Moss won the Australian Tourist Trophy for sports cars, just five kilometres away at Albert Park.

A week later, mid-Games, Moss won the Australian Grand Prix for Maserati. Reg Hunt, also on a works Maserati, was the first local in fourth.

The Olympics and the Australian Grand Prix in the same week in the same city? Unheard of.

Both were live-telecast. Television had been switched on in Australia on 16 September. There'd been a lot of pressure to go live for the Olympics. The Grand Prix was a major beneficiary. On 8 December, International Olympic Committee president Avery Brundage declared the Games closed. Melbourne was exhausted.

Holding a race meeting a week later—just a fortnight after the Australian Grand Prix and ten days before Christmas—was not the rational act of a professional promoter. But PIARC had postponed the Phillip Island opening twice already in 1956. Another delay, for any other reason than a natural disaster, was untenable. The committee was under pressure to do something, and quickly. Phillip Island opened on 15 December.

Page five of the following Monday's *Argus* brought a sad perspective.

> Young, talented university student, Phillip Rothfield, of Toorak, had only one secret he kept from his devoted parents—that he was driving in sports car races.
>
> On Saturday the secret came out . . . because Phillip was killed in a race smash at the Phillip Island racetrack. Until they were told of the fatal accident, Phillip's parents had no idea their son had become a weekend racing car driver.
>
> The parents, Mr. and Mrs. Nathaniel Rothfield of Woorigoleen Road, Toorak, are well known in Melbourne's business and

social world. Mr. Rothfield is managing director of Rothfield and Co. Ltd., cotton and fabric manufacturing firm.

Phillip, 18, was a first-year commerce student at Melbourne University. He was given an Austin Healey sports car by his parents as a reward for matriculating from Wesley College last year.

It was in that car that he skidded and rolled to his death during the 12th lap of the 16-lap Bill Thompson [Trophy] . . .

Saturday was the opening day of the Phillip Island Auto Racing Club's new £54,000 circuit.

Phillip's only brother, Ronald, 16, saw the accident.

Phillip crashed on KLG corner [Turn 1]. His car appeared to get out of control half-way round the corner. It skidded first to the outside of the track, then slid inwards, crashed into the banking, and rolled over twice . . .

Phillip, although a committeeman of the University Car Club, was an inexperienced racing driver. He had raced only once before Saturday.

A close family friend said last night: 'The news of his death was a shattering blow to his parents. They knew nothing of his motor racing. On Saturday the parents were at Frankston. They did not even know Phillip and Ronald were going to Phillip Island, let alone driving in a race.'

It was not an auspicious start. But it would be 22 years before another death occurred at the circuit, and 39 years before the next competitor fatality.

PIARC felt it deserved to host the Australian Grand Prix. But it wasn't going to happen.

Donald Kingsley Thomson had done a deal with several devils. CAMS was on shaky ground; Thomson favoured federalised control but the states had minds of their own. In New South Wales, a breakaway group had even formed their own governing body, the Council of Combined Motor Clubs, and bypassed CAMS entirely. Thomson worked to bring them back under control. Part of the deal was the Australian Grand Prix. It would move in annual rotation to each state—a big concession to make the concept of federalism more palatable.

The kicker was that a representative of the state that held the grand prix would also become president of CAMS for the same year. Who could resist? Thomson, a masterful manipulator, kept his own position intact while he cycled through disposable presidents. The CAMS National Control Council, made up of representatives from each state, had become Thomson's shadow cabinet, his puppets.

He was, he liked to think, benevolent. In 1957 he instituted, mid-season, the Australian Drivers' Championship, whose winner would be awarded the Gold Star. It would be an open-wheeler series, decided over several rounds in several states, incorporating the Australian Grand Prix. Thomson had a special role for Phillip Island. It would host the final and, if they got lucky, deciding round of the Gold Star title. The offer appeared to be in perpetuity.

Lex Davison had won the first two races of 1957, including the Australian Grand Prix on the disused and deteriorating airbase at far-flung Caversham, fifteen kilometres from central Perth, when the Gold Star news broke.

The Gold Star changed Davison's perspective. Until then he'd raced for individual wins. This series provided the opportunity to be a bit more strategic. He was able to concede victories on three occasions—to Stan Jones, Arnold Glass and upstart Murray Trenberth in a 'mechanical mouse'—and still wrap up the championship before he arrived at Phillip Island for the grand final.

Winning the Gold Star and the Australian Grand Prix in the one year gave him permission to retire. He'd decided Phillip Island would be his last race.

The 34-year-old father of six (soon to be seven) was expanding his family's shoe-manufacturing business. He was in the second year of his presidency of the LCCA and faced increasing pressure over the continued use of Albert Park.

When he brought his Ferrari to Phillip Island after five consecutive weeks of motor racing, he was tired—like his machinery—but determined. The abrasive Phillip Island surface tore his tyres down to the canvas and any sensible man would have pulled to the pits. But he kept flogging his prancing horse and he won in front of Tom Hawkes in his home-modified Cooper Repco Holden.

Davison raced the Ferrari once more, in the New Zealand Grand Prix in January 1958. The bellowing motor blew, its first mechanical catastrophe, no doubt exacerbated by its workout at Phillip Island.

Then Lex retired, for the first time.

Alan Jones, who would one day be crowned Formula One world champion, was nine years old and mightily disappointed. His dad, Stan, had sent his long-time race engineer Charlie Dean to Italy to buy a real race car. Stan and Charlie had persevered for years with a Dean-built, Repco-engineered local masterpiece called the Maybach, constructed around a 3.8-litre six-cylinder German Maybach engine taken from a World War II Bussing-NAG scout car. Stan Jones had won the 1954 New Zealand Grand Prix with it and was leading the Australian Grand Prix on the Southport road circuit at year's end when the chassis broke, destroying the car and damned near killing Stan.

'My idea of an Italian race car was a Ferrari,' Jones told me from his Gold Coast home. 'Instead, when we went down to the Melbourne docks, it turned out to be a Maserati.'

But Stan had also briefed Charlie to pick up a kid-sized pair of light-blue Maserati racing overalls. Alan was a Maserati fan from that time on.

The bright-red car, with Jones' added white radiator ring, like liberally applied sunscreen around a cricketer's lips, had arrived with a 2.5-litre engine (hence 250F), but in the big box of spares was a 300S sports car engine. The extra 500cc would make all the difference.

Stan had turned Alan into a race fan. The kid knew all the circuits—which ones were goat tracks, which ones were mickey-mouse and which ones were to be admired. 'Turn 1 at Phillip Island,' he smiled. 'You just grit your teeth and go for it.'

In December 1958, twelve-year-old Alan was at the Island the day his dad won the Gold Star. Stan's style was belligerent: win or bust. It had won him a few races and cost him a lot more. Otto Stone and John Sawyer, his two mechanics, had done their best to get him to settle. He'd won one round at Fishermans Bend and taken three safe seconds.

He should have won the Australian Grand Prix at Mount Panorama, but four laps from the flag, while fighting for the lead, the Maserati was a smoking retirement. If Stan had cruised to second he would have won the Gold Star right there. Instead, the grand finale at Phillip Island was to be fought out by three contenders: Jones on 23 points, Len Lukey on 20 and Alec Mildren on 18.

Lukey was the first to falter. He crashed in a warm-up race and wrecked the suspension of his Cooper Bristol. He borrowed Frank Coad's Vauxhall Special and drove to a commendable sixth, but points were only awarded to the top five. Jones led Mildren home and won his Gold Star.

'The only time I got to steer the Maserati back then was when we pushed it to the grid,' Alan said. 'But I did drive it only a few years back at the Goodwood Festival of Speed. The old man had sold it to a Western Australian for something like four thousand quid and he thought he'd got it well away. Years later the car was rescued and given to me to drive up the hill climb. By then it was worth three or four million.

'It was pretty well impossible to drive. The brakes kept pulling it to the right. It was a relief to get to the top.'

Len Lukey, the businessman-driver who would figure so heavily in Phillip Island's future, won the Gold Star at the circuit in 1959.

The series featured twelve separate races—more than there were suitable racetracks in Australia. So they ran it twice at

Mount Panorama, Port Wakefield and Lowood Airfield in Queensland, and ran the final two over two months at Phillip Island. It was a marathon for teams, costly and time-consuming.

Lukey and Alec Mildren did them all. Stan Jones used up four cars trying to defend his Gold Star title.

By the time they reached Phillip Island the second time around, Jones was out of contention and Mildren led Lukey by a slender three points. It was winner take all.

Lukey was in big trouble. He'd blown his final drive in practice and a replacement had arrived from Sydney but without time to fit it. Then young Bob Jane rolled his Jag in a touring car race and needed to be transported to hospital. The delay worked in Lukey's favour, providing time enough to fit the part, and in the race he worked Mildren over: twelve points for a win, seven for second. Lukey won the Gold Star by two points.

Jack Brabham drove again at Phillip Island in March 1960—the first time a reigning Formula One world champion had raced a car in Australia—and he highlighted the chasm between local enthusiasm and international experience. In December, while thrashing Mildren, Lukey had set a new lap record of 2 minutes 11.6 seconds. The following March, Brabham eased to victory in 2 minutes 2.6 seconds.

His Cooper T51, the chassis with which he'd won the 1959 world title, was at the vanguard of a trend. Everyone had to have one. Alec Mildren won the 1960 Gold Star without even needing to show up at the Island. He'd fitted his Cooper T51 with a Maserati engine—which, against all odds, turned out to be reliable—and scored sufficient points to make entry in the grand final redundant. Melbourne car dealers Bill Patterson and Bib Stillwell, already on their way to mega-wealth from their franchises, used their T51s with Coventry Climax engines, like Brabham's, to fight over the minor placings.

CAMS had promised Phillip Island would have the Australian Grand Prix in 1962, its turn in rotation. That wouldn't happen. In fact, the 1960 Gold Star finale was the last race of that era to be held on the island.

8

The Racer and the Gentleman

Lex Davison was a Gentleman Racer. Jack Brabham was a Racer.

One raced to live; the other lived to race. It sounds like a simple distinction but it's not. It's a lot more complex than that.

Lex Davison tried three times to quit the opioid of motorsport. At each attempt he failed, and he died at the wheel of a race car aged just 42, never regretting a moment of the journey. Jack Brabham retired just once, aged 44, and spent the second half of his life—another 44 years—lamenting his decision to give it away.

Brabham stopped at the urging of family and friends, later resenting their influence. Davison ignored the advice of his family and his doctor. His son Chris puts Davison's obduracy down to his fourth Australian Grand Prix victory. 'He'd been racing a big front-engine Aston Martin, tilting at windmills against the tiny Coopers,' Chris told me. 'Then when it was trapped on a boat from England and wasn't available, he leased a T51 Cooper Climax from Bib Stillwell and won the 1961 grand prix at Mallala. He'd never raced a Formula One Cooper before, just derided them. It gave him a new perspective. If he hadn't borrowed that car, and won, he would have retired.'

Davison was the son of a bootmaker. Brabham was the son of a grocer. Both statements are a bit disingenuous. A.A. (Alec) Davison owned Paragon Shoes, a substantial manufacturing operation. Tom Brabham was a wholesale grocer of size and substance.

A.A. Davison was opposed to his son racing. Tom Brabham actively supported Jack.

When Lex's father died, Lex cut the body off the family's Alfa Romeo 6C touring car and replaced it with a pretty open sports tub, which he and his bride Diana drove to Mount Panorama on their honeymoon so that Lex could have his first race. It was an 'Up you, Dad' moment.

When Jack Brabham showed talent, true grit and unbounded determination, his dad put up 50 per cent for the purchase of the first Cooper Bristol to be brought into the country, and found his son a sponsor for the other half.

Could Lex and Jack have ever swapped roles? No way, though Alan Jones reckons his dad Stan could have given Brabham a run for his money. 'In his day, he was faster than Jack,' Alan says proudly today. But it takes more than speed.

Brabham's skill as a designer, engineer, fabricator and ultimately driver was unique. He is the only person to win the world championship as a driver and constructor, and under the structure of motor racing today that record will forever remain unbeaten.

Davison loved his racing cars. Brabham saw them as commodities.

Counter-seasonal Australia gave the English factories the chance to race and test all year round. Even though Jack had long since committed to the UK, he'd race Down Under each Australasian summer.

'We would always try to sell our cars in Australia,' Brabham said of his early days with Cooper, for whom he won his first two world titles. 'We would come out with a race team and go home with a bag of cash . . . and maybe a trophy. I sold my first car, a Cooper, to Bib Stillwell, but I had to give the money to John Cooper when I got back to the UK. That got me thinking about starting my own team.'

It's estimated that Brabham and his long-time collaborator Ron Tauranac built and sold 392 Brabhams, sometimes multiple times, during their eighteen-year ownership of Motor Racing Developments; that grew to 720 after Jack's departure.

Lex Davison had a passion for the provenance of each of his racing cars. His Ferrari 500/625 was very special. It was the first Ferrari to win a world title—chassis number 5, the Formula Two Tipo 500 that delivered Alberto Ascari his two world championships in 1952 and 1953.

Lex's good friend Tony Gaze, a World War II flying ace and Australia's first Formula One driver, had acquired the car from Enzo Ferrari in 1954 intending to contest the world championship. It was only the second time Ferrari had sold a works car to a privateer. But Ferrari reneged on an agreement to upgrade it to current spec, so Gaze brought it to Australia, finished second to Stirling Moss in the New Zealand Grand Prix and sold it to Davison. Davison won the Gold Star and two Australian grands prix, and kept it well beyond its use-by date.

'In 2012, the Ferrari returned to Australia for the Phillip Island Classic Festival of Motorsport,' Chris Davison said. 'Its owner, Kevin Wheatcroft, had faithfully restored it to its F2 spec in which it won the 1952 world title. It was proudly the star of his collection, called the Ascari-Ferrari. We filled him in on its Australian success. When it returned to England, it had become the Ascari-Gaze-Davison Ferrari.'

Gentleman Racers can afford to think differently. Davison was happy trapped in the bubble of the front-engine '50s. Brabham burst the bubble and led the charge into the rear-engine '60s. In 1959, Brabham's Cooper Climax vanquished the dinosaurs in the world championship, and they'd never win again. Jack taught Enzo Ferrari new tricks.

Perversely, Davison ordered a front-engine Aston Martin DBR4 Formula One car to replace his Ferrari. Aston entered F1 for only two seasons, in 1959–60, and was an anachronistic failure. Davison was their only bright star.

In 1960, Davison lost the Australian Grand Prix on the last corner at the Lowood Airfield when Alec Mildren's nimble Cooper nipped under him. 'If it had not been for my clottish forgetfulness on the last corner we would have had an international Grand Prix win to our credit,' he wrote to John Wyer at the Aston factory. Four months later, at Phillip Island, the three-litre Aston was overwhelmed by Coopers.

When Davison won the Australian Grand Prix in 1961 at Mallala, in the borrowed Cooper, the deal was sealed. Davison joined the ranks of what he had until then referred to as 'anti-Climaxes'. At the victory celebration that night, he said: 'I feel like a man who in middle age takes a young mistress.' The Cooper, he said, had given him a new thrill, and he ordered one from Brabham. When Brabham started his own show, Davison faithfully followed. He'd agreed to buy Jack's Brabham BT11 at the end of the 1965 Tasman Series.

Brabham's three sons followed him into racing. 'It's not genetic, it's a disease,' the oldest, Geoffrey, joked. 'You catch it from exposure. I used to fly with Dad in his plane to European events. I only realised it was unusual when they asked me at my new school what I'd done on the weekend.'

The Brabham boys' international exposure delivered them global success. Geoff was a multiple American IMSA-series sports car champion, Gary a British F3000 champion, David a British F3 champion. Geoff and David have won the Le Mans 24 Hour. David and Gary attempted F1 careers.

Lex Davison died in a practice crash at Sandown International Raceway in 1965. His children raced in his memory.

Jon, aged seventeen when Lex died, raced F5000 and managed the Sandown circuit for two decades. Richard became Australian F2 champion. Until recently, Chris owned a brace of Formula Ford cars under the family's racing umbrella Ecurie Australie, hired out to keen overseas racing-tourists to experience the Phillip Island Classic.

Both families boast third-generation motor-racing success.

'I'm going to die without an enemy in the world,' Sir Jack Brabham, motor racing's first knight—before Stirling or Jackie—told me, as we shouted at each other, knee to knee to overcome Brabham's chronic deafness, just weeks before his death. 'I'm going to outlive the bastards.' It's an old line, but it gave him a chuckle because he knew in his case it wasn't true.

He'd garnered heaps of enmity in his time. And he had no regrets.

When Lex Davison was killed, the press was full of love. Two thousand mourners, it was reported, gathered under the grand Gothic spire of St Patrick's Cathedral (later conferred the title of minor basilica by Pope Paul VI). The rector of his old school, Xavier College, lauded the Gentleman Racer for far more than his motor-racing prowess. He was a business and community leader and a patriarch.

Brabham was at Davison's funeral service. He'd won the Sandown International Cup the day after Lex's crash. Death in motor racing at the time was a tragedy that was stoically acknowledged. There was no counselling. It was perhaps not even considered.

Pragmatically, Jack now had to find a new buyer for the BT11. The following year, he won the world title—his third—in its successor: the BT19.

'I do need to apologise that this service is a little bit late,' Geoff Brabham told mourners at his father's funeral on 11 June 2014. 'Matthew and Sam [Jack's grandsons] had racing commitments overseas and I know Dad would have got out of his coffin and kicked our arse if they missed a couple of races for him.'

Gentleman Racer vs Racer. There's probably no better insight than that.

When Geoff embarked on his racing career, Jack took him aside and gave him a piece of advice. 'There are people who *drive* racing cars,' he told his son. 'And there are people who *race* racing cars.' Blunt, perhaps even a bit disparaging, but in context it goes some way to explaining the racer's mindset.

9

The Making of World Champions

Kel Carruthers, the 250cc world motorcycle champion of 1969, wasn't overly impressed with Phillip Island when he rode it for the first time. 'It was short—not like the classic road-racing tracks overseas,' the 85-year-old Carruthers told me from his home in Murrieta, Riverside County, California.

'There was Assen, twice the length; Spa-Francorchamps; Nürburgring; Dundrod; and the Isle of Man.' Carruthers was being a bit presumptuous. He had been to none of them when he first rode Phillip Island. He was nineteen, working in his racer dad Jack's bike shop at Gladesville in Sydney.

Kel's benchmark was Bathurst. He'd won on Mount Panorama when he was just seventeen.

'It was a Junior B-grade race. They put me up to A-grade after that, with the really good guys, and I couldn't beat them—not for a while. Bathurst was special, head and shoulders over the rest.'

One month short of his twentieth birthday, Carruthers raced in the Ultra-Lightweight (125cc) TT at Phillip Island. He was on a Lambretta, a scooter, and he came second to an ex-works MV Agusta ridden by Bob Brown, third placegetter that year in the Senior TT at the Isle of Man. 'It wasn't really a scooter,' Carruthers explained. 'It had bigger wheels, about midway between a scooter and a bike, and it had a full fairing. You held it pretty much flat all the way around.' Its lack of pace served to disguise the attributes of the classic grand prix track. 'Perhaps,' Carruthers concedes finally, 'the best of all circuits.'

Judged by today's standards, Carruthers said, 'Phillip Island is a classic' because other tracks 'have come back to its level'. It's not a totally disparaging remark. He's not a fan of modern track design where the action happens on tight turns in the infield. 'The beauty of Phillip Island is that it's built around its perimeter, with maybe two short infields cut into it. The new racetracks are the opposite, with very little perimeter and lots of twists and bends within. On a perimeter track you can enjoy fast corners.'

In the 1950s, Australian motorcycle racers were so much more advanced than their car-racing equivalents. The Auto Cycle Council of Australia and its state constituencies set up formal funds to send teams to Europe. They'd fly out of Australia—or go by ship—wearing green-and-gold blazers like cricketers and they'd race in their national colours for their country.

There was a lust to race the great tracks of Europe. Some would stay on, chasing the dream. Others would return to influence the next wave. A few would perish in the attempt.

'I was inspired by those guys,' Carruthers said. But he was in no rush. His dad and mum, Lil, had instilled in him an almost innate sense of 'hurry up and wait'. Now he's a world champion, and first-wave inductee into the Australian Motorsport Hall of Fame and the Australian Sports Hall of Fame, he can make a claim unique in motorcycle racing: 'I've never been hurt, never gone to hospital, never fallen off.' Although he started keeping records only in 1961, he claims 148 wins and 22 second places from 181 domestic starts before he began his international career.

The key to international success is progressing slowly, learning your limits.

The motorcycle members of PIARC had high hopes for Phillip Island.

In 1955, with the circuit still just pegged out, Phil Irving had driven six-time world champion Geoff Duke, in Australia on a whistlestop race tour, to the island to get his views. Duke was motorcycling's first superstar. A busload of members of Melbourne motorcycle clubs turned up. The clubs saw Phillip Island as a track that could springboard Australian racers to world-championship contention. And, just as importantly, it was a venue to showcase world-class talent in their own backyard.

Maurie Quincey, fifth in the 1956 Isle of Man 350cc TT and then severely injured in the Senior event, used Phillip Island to make his return. He won the Junior and Senior events in mid-1957. After his riding career ended, he bought a Formula Two Elfin and went car racing on the Island.

Ken Kavanagh, the first Australian to win at the Isle of Man (the 350cc in 1956) and the first to win a round of the world championship (the 350cc Ulster GP in 1952), raced for the last time in Australia at Phillip Island and won the 125cc TT. In an act of amazing generosity, he donated his treasured Isle of Man trophy to the Hartwell Motorcycle Club to present as their annual Most Outstanding Road Racer award.

Australia's first world motorcycle champion, Keith Campbell, crashed his works Moto Guzzi 350 in the first practice session for the first race meeting on the PIARC track. Rain penetrated his goggles during a relentless squall, and he misjudged the Repco hairpin (Turn 4) at the back of the pits. The crash dislocated his shoulder and mangled his motorcycle. That year, 1957, Campbell had two big wins. He claimed the 350cc world championship and he married Geraldine, sister-in-law of Geoff Duke.

In 1958, he died in a non-championship 500cc race, the Grand Prix de Cadours in France. Oil had been spilled in a preceding sidecar race; his bike skidded on the oil and crashed and he fractured his skull. As a result, officials mandated that sidecars would only ever compete after the solo races had finished.

Tom Phillis, 125cc world champion in 1961, won the Senior event at Phillip Island four years in succession.

'I didn't have a lot to do with Tom,' Kel Carruthers mused. The two Australian world champions grew up only half a dozen suburbs apart: Phillis in Marrickville in Sydney's inner west, Carruthers in middle-suburban Gladesville. There were four years between them, Phillis the elder. 'We just moved in different circles,' Kel said.

Four years is a lot when you're ambitious. Phillis sold up everything and, with wife Betty, shipped out to England in 1958, aged 24. 'I was still young Kel at the time,' Carruthers said. 'I wasn't winning a lot of races, especially against the guys who came back from Europe. They'd been racing every weekend, sometimes two or three races at every meeting. When you do that, everything comes automatically.

'Safety was something you didn't really think about, but I didn't want to get hurt. There were guys getting killed, wholesale, on bikes and in cars. I was learning how to ride up to my potential, not over it. I was teaching myself how to ride ten-tenths and not go beyond.'

In 1959, after his first European season, with a Manx Norton he hoped to sell locally, Phillis engaged with fellow Australian international Eric Hinton. Their Victorian Senior GP on Phillip Island was the race of the year.

Phillis took the lead; Hinton had a bad start and tigered up on him, passing on lap seven of ten. Phillis stuck to Hinton's rear wheel, stones flying from the loose surface. On the run to the flag down that long, long straight he timed his run perfectly to pull out of the slipstream and win at the flag.

He did it again in 1960. This time Hinton crashed chasing him.

In 1960, Phillis and Carruthers were hired by Honda. In Europe, Phillis would race in the 125 and 250 classes. It was a big deal; he was the first non-Japanese rider on the Honda team.

Kel Carruthers' involvement was domestic and complex. There was to be a Japanese motorcycle sales push against the entrenched British bikes. The local Honda distributor, Bennett & Wood, asked Kel's father Jack, renowned engine tuner, to evaluate their first 250cc road bike, the Dream, to see if it was suitable for Australia. His report was positive, and Honda went on to local market leadership.

As both promotion and reward, the company imported one of their six state-of-the-art, four-cylinder, in-line racing bikes—a world-championship-level 250cc machine. It was for young Kel. 'It was an evil-handling bike,' Kel recalled. 'The engine and drivetrain were nice but the frame was horrible. We did a lot of work on that bike.'

When Phillis returned at the end of the European season, Honda asked Kel to give Tom the bike for his Australian program. 'What were we to do?' Kel mused. At Phillip Island, Phillis won the 250 and 350 grands prix and took ten seconds off the lap record. Then he swapped to his Manx Norton and won the Senior GP too. It rankles Carruthers even now that some historians regard his Honda as the 'ex-Tom Phillis machine'.

In 1961, Carruthers swept the Australian field on the bike. Phillis, on a works 125cc Honda, won the world championship. He returned to Australia a hero—a civic reception, finalist in the ABC Sportsman of the Year (cricketer Richie Benaud won it), and a lap of honour on 'Kel's bike' at the Warwick Farm car meeting. In Melbourne, the Hartwell club made him a life member.

New Year's Day 1962 was to be huge. Honda had promised to ship a second Honda Four to Australia.

Carruthers and Phillis, finally, would go head-to-head in the Victorian GP at Phillip Island. It was a promotional bonanza. But the Honda didn't arrive.

Promoters quickly scrambled. They found a Ducati for Phillis to ride in the 125 race and a brace of Nortons for the 350 and 500 grands prix. Frustratingly for both riders, Carruthers was untroubled in the 250. Without the second Honda, Phillis did not have a competitive mount. It was an opportunity lost to test against each other on identical machinery.

Carruthers beat Phillis in the 125 grand prix. Phillis beat Carruthers in the 350.

Phillis won his fourth successive Senior grand prix in a four-way battle from Trevor Pound, Ken Rumble and Jack Ahearn. Ahearn would go on to place second to Mike Hailwood in the 1964 world championship.

At Phillip Island, they perched Phillis in an open sports car for a celebratory lap of honour. Sadly, it was his farewell. Five months later he was dead. He crashed at Laurel Bank on the Isle of Man, a fast, kerbed right-hand bend near Ballacraine. Phillis was cremated on the Isle of Man and his ashes scattered on the start line.

'Tom was a level above me [at the stage],' Kel said. 'But he was trying too hard at the Isle of Man. The crash should not have happened. You've got to know when you're going over your limit.'

Carruthers, still hastening slowly, would not go to Europe for another four years.

'You know, our son Paul and Tom's son Brad were born within

a week of each other [in 1961],' Kel said. 'Paul came first. Jan and I reckoned at least we'd beaten him one time.'

There would be no grand prix at Phillip Island in 1963. The Armstrong 500 took care of that.

10

The Race That Changed the Motor Industry

The Armstrong 500, first held in 1960, was more than a race. It was a public demonstration to give proof and legitimacy to the Australian automotive manufacturing industry, and it was initially to be held around the lake at Albert Park. Melbourne was the epicentre—the home of the Olympics—and Albert Park, with its grands prix, had cemented its name as a big-event venue. If the motor industry was going to showcase its local car-building prowess, it had to be in the most visible and, for that matter, accessible location in the country. The car industry deserved nothing less.

But it wasn't to be.

A concerted political campaign had consigned Albert Park to a fate akin to that of New York's Central Park and London's Hyde Park—a leafy place to exercise the dog, give the kids a run, and take the horse and carriage for a trot. Albert Park's loss was Phillip Island's gain—at least temporarily.

Within three years this most ambitious of all ventures, using motor racing to secure trust for the motor industry, had reduced Phillip Island to a goat track and caused its first closure.

By 1960, the national car park had expanded to more than 2.8 million, up from about 750,000 after World War II. That was one car for every 3.6 people—one for every family, give or take. A dedicated workforce of more than 40,000 was building new vehicles at a rate of 210,000 a year.

A massive industry had sprung up seemingly overnight, and the federal government had moved to make sure it was local. It imposed high tariffs on imports and enforced local content rules on domestic manufacturers. If you were going to build Australia's own car then it had better be truly Australian, or at least close to; 85 per cent local content equated to 100 per cent in the government's eyes.

British, European and American car makers rushed to oblige. In the case of the large-volume makers, General Motors and Ford, stand-alone operations were the way forward. For others, shared assembly made more economic sense. Vanguards were being assembled alongside Mercedes; Citroëns were cheek by jowl with Renaults.

A whole sub-industry grew around the car makers. Second- and third-tier suppliers—providing everything from fully made-up suspension systems to nuts and bolts—were manufacturing locally.

Keen to assert its local position was Armstrong York, makers of shock absorbers. Once proudly British (Gordon Armstrong had made his first shock absorber in Yorkshire in 1927) but now proudly Australian too, it challenged its PR company to come up with a big idea. The PR company was a one-man band.

Ron Thonemann—actually Baron Ronald von Thonemann, a hereditary title from Austria's Habsburg dynasty—graduated from Melbourne's Scotch College in 1952 to take a cadetship with Keith Winser's *Australian Motor Manual*, arguably the country's first car mag when it appeared in 1946.

Ron tested OPCs (other people's cars) for five years for the magazine, then left in 1957 to start his own PR company, Automotive Public Relations Pty Ltd. His client Jim Thompson, managing director of Armstrong York, was pursuing a greater share of the original equipment business. When a car came off an Australian assembly line, it needed to be fitted with Armstrong shocks.

Thonemann had been greatly influenced by the prominent REDeX Round Australia Trial, first run in 1953. Reg Shepheard, an ambitious importer of a lubrication additive, had pretty much created that concept. He was selling REDeX by the truckload.

'So,' Thonemann thought, 'why don't we create an event of our own?'

There were a few hurdles to jump. For a start, a race is a public thing. There's nowhere to hide if something goes wrong, not like a trial. And second, would the car makers want it? A 500-mile (804-kilometre) race would put a lot of strain on cars that in 1960 weren't particularly durable.

Thonemann thought fast. This wasn't just a race, he told media and manufacturers alike. It was a high-speed display of proficiency—a showroom on wheels. Only Australian-manufactured cars would be eligible, eliminating competition from imports like Jaguar, which had just won the first Australian Touring Car Championship. And there would be no outright winner: just five classes, so cars would race like for like, from under 750cc tiddlers up to large family vehicles over 3500cc.

Thonemann approached the Light Car Club of Australia to run the Armstrong 500, then he set out with Jim Thompson to convince the local manufacturers it had been their idea.

The LCCA couldn't deliver Albert Park. President Arnold Terdich, son of 1929 Australian Grand Prix winner Arthur, and past president Lex Davison had lost some influence. In a much larger political stoush, the *Herald* newspaper had run a successful vendetta against Labor politician Senator Pat Kennelly who was, incidentally, chairman of the Albert Park Trust. Kennelly was an advocate of motorsport at the venue and *The Herald* used the racetrack as a political football. The track, ultimately, was sacrificed and there was no turning back.

Instead the LCCA offered to dry-hire Phillip Island. They paid a peppercorn rental to PIARC, a recognition by the club that what was good for the motor industry was good for the Island too.

Armstrong bought it. Live TV was going to cover the event. The views over Bass Strait said 'Australia' as much as the Melbourne skyline at Albert Park. Jim Thompson became such an advocate he proposed at the prize-giving that Phillip Island should become a proving ground, accessible to all local car makers.

Market leader Holden was the first in. Three of its biggest dealers were motorsport stars—Bib Stillwell, Bill Patterson and Stan Jones. The three amigos entered under their dealership names, but everybody knows a works entry when they see one. A huge sales war was brewing. Holden released its FB in January 1960, and Ford was to follow with its first Falcon, the XK, in the third quarter. A Holden victory, even if there was no outright prize, would be a big boost.

Then, suddenly, Holden was also first out, its entries withdrawn. The FB was heavier than its predecessor and no more powerful. Private testing on the Island revealed alarming oil surge, which placed a cloud over engine life. Holden put an international spin on its withdrawal. Its Detroit master, General Motors, had a no-motorsport policy, it said. Never mind that a dealer entry was an easy workaround.

Just the same, support for the first Armstrong 500 was a huge success: 44 entries, 20 makes and models, and 9 manufacturer entries either directly or thinly disguised.

Norm Beechey, the self-promoting one-man Barnum & Bailey of the fast-emerging touring car scene, could not believe he was lying upside down in a ditch at Southern Loop. It would have been understandable if he'd been in his jet-black FX Holden, the tin tops' star car. Or if he'd been in his massive Ford Customline that won the touring car support race at the 1956 Australian Grand Prix.

But he was in a stock Standard Vanguard, assembled by Australian Motor Industries in Port Melbourne, testing for the Armstrong 500.

Stormin' Norman, 1970 Australian touring car champion and still the undisputed ringmaster of the touring car circus, had a flamboyant style. He'd throw a car at a corner, skidding it around and staying on the gas for as long as possible.

But here he was inverted, hanging (thankfully) from a three-point harness, appraising the difference in technique required to race a showroom stock family car over 500 miles. 'It was so soft,' he recalled 63 years later, still pin-sharp, black-haired and ready for tomorrow's adventure. 'The bolts on the tie rod ends were biting into the chassis. It just stopped steering.'

Beechey and co-driver John French, later to win the Bathurst 1000 with Dick Johnson, found a technical solution that was mainly legal, and stroked the Vanguard home in the race, second in class.

'It was serious right from the start,' Brian Foley, a works driver for the British Motor Corporation (BMC), told me from the fifteenth fairway of Moss Vale Golf Club where the sprightly 89-year-old plays twice weekly. 'There were no parties, no easygoing atmosphere.' Foley was one of a new breed of professionals. 'Professionals without pay,' he quipped.

He'd won the under-1000cc class of the inaugural Australian Touring Car Championship at Gnoo Blas, Orange, in February 1960, driving an Austin A40 Farina, beating Kevin Bartlett in a Morris Minor.

'I honestly don't recall if it was my car or if a dealer had given it to me,' he said. 'If you get to drive someone else's car, that's professional.'

Arthur Grogan, race manager of BMC on Sydney's South Dowling Street, made Foley part of his ambitious six-car, twelve-driver team for the Armstrong, the biggest entry by any manufacturer. They'd be driving Austin Lancers and Morris Majors. The driving roster was a who's who: Brian Muir, who went on to be multiple British touring car champion, along with Mini-king Peter 'Skinny' Manton, and Jim Smith, multi-franchised motor-industry icon.

Inaugural Australian touring car champion David McKay believed the VW Beetle team for which he was driving was a big chance. The three cars tested at the Island and went faster as the session progressed. Twice round-Australia trial winner Eddie Perkins, father of touring car ace Larry, was quickest. They handed the cars back to VW's Clayton factory. On race weekend, the VWs were 'several seconds' slower, McKay reported. 'The factory had completely rebuilt the engines. Any Beetle driver knows the older they are, the better they go. Now we would have to run them in all over again.'

There wasn't enough time to do that. They were swamped in class by the Australian-built French Simcas.

'There had to be commercial consideration in play,' Chris Davison laughed. His father Lex and Lex's great rival, Doug Whiteford, combined in 1960 to win the small-car class in a 600cc, 30-horsepower (22-kilowatt) NSU Prinz. Don't discount the skill needed to nurse a small car to victory. The grand prix champions led home a team of three identical cars assembled on the site of the 1956 Olympic Village at West Heidelberg. The manufacturer, Continental & General Distributors, was one of the most active of the multi-brand assemblers. It made Peugeots, Studebaker Larks, Citroëns and the mighty midget NSU, all down the one assembly line.

It took just 8 hours 25 minutes for Frank Coad and John Roxburgh to cover 167 laps (501 miles/806 kilometres) of the fast-deteriorating Phillip Island track to win their class and claim de facto outright first. Their 2.2-litre, six-cylinder Vauxhall Cresta, complete with tail fins but without the optional radio, was pretty well spot-on an average of 60 mph (96 km/h), more than respectable for a car with a top speed of 144 km/h and a 0–100 km/h acceleration time of 16.8 seconds.

Coad and Roxburgh were no amateurs, and this was no lucky win. They'd run a full race simulation on Phillip Island, and knew the strengths and weaknesses of the car and the circuit. They'd had a plan and they stuck to it.

Tasmania's Youl brothers, Gavin and John, had been hot favourites in a dealer-entered Mercedes-Benz 220SE, assembled at Australian Motor Industries, but according to Coad, interviewed half a century later, they hadn't properly respected the track. They fell victim to the loose surface and blew a tyre while leading; the car rolled.

Cars rolled at Phillip Island; they didn't simply crash. David McKay, in his report for Sydney's *Sunday Telegraph*, estimated sixteen cars had rolled in testing and practice, 'but only three in the race'. McKay said: 'It was more like a Round Australia Trial as the track broke up badly in the first hours and stones and dust were commonplace.'

Remarkably, only eleven failed to finish—or, to put a positive spin on it, 33 did finish, and that was a triumph for the motor industry. Armstrong would be back next year, and Ron Thonemann got to keep their account.

In 1961, Australia was in the grip of a credit squeeze, a 1960s euphemism for 'minor recession'. In 1960, federal treasurer Harold Holt had called for an abolition of import restrictions, a direct threat to cosseted local motor manufacturers. Employment had plummeted: 53,000 people were out of work at the end of 1960, 115,000 by the end of 1961.

Entries for the Armstrong 500 fell mightily. Just 26 cars would face the starter's flag. But they were quality entries. PIARC had leased the track to the LCCA in 1960 for £500. This time the entry fee was £2500.

Brian Foley would drive the first V8 in the race. 'David McKay had come to an agreement with David Shmith, owner of Sydney's York Motors, to race a V8 Studebaker Lark and he invited me to co-drive,' Foley said. Shmith's father, Maurice, one of the pioneers of the Australian retail motor industry, had been an entrant in the 1928 Australian Grand Prix on the island.

'David [McKay] suggested we go to Phillip Island to test,' Foley recalled. 'He said, "You drive, I'll fly and I'll meet you there." David was a huge devotee of the Pirelli Cinturato tyre. We did just five laps before the steel bands were showing through the right-hand front tyre. That caused us to do a quick calculation:

a pit stop every five laps [over] 500 miles was disastrous, and we knew we needed another solution.'

The pair switched to Michelins, made four scheduled stops, consumed six front tyres and 40 gallons (151 litres) of fuel, and they were two laps in the lead when they got nervous and decided to change the rear tyres as a precaution.

Bob Jane and Harry Firth had entered a Mercedes-Benz 220SE in a different class and they charged past to claim unofficial first. 'David's first wife Betty was lap scoring and she reckoned we'd won anyway,' Foley said, still injured after all these years. But as there was no first place on offer, there was nothing to protest. The Lark won its class a full lap clear of 1960 winners Coad and Roxburgh in a Vauxhall Velox, a stripped version of the Cresta.

The race had become more professional. General Motors was unofficially back. Stan Jones Motors entered an EK Holden, with John Lanyon, a major figure in the future of PIARC, and Ian Strachan as drivers. Holden's engineers had 'shown interest' in the car, even developing a race-first fuel-freezing system to stretch the time between pit stops. Lanyon took the class lead just 40 laps from home, then he lost a wheel and was out.

Manufacturers were prepared to bend rules to win.

In March 1961, BMC introduced the first Mini Minor to Australia. It was presented to technical checkers with twin SU carburettors, not the single carb specified in the owner's manual. A telegram from the BMC attested that a special run of 100 conversion kits had been produced. The race's long tradition of homologation wars—a euphemism for cheating—began right there. Scrutineers rejected the claim.

In 1962, the LCCA pulled out of its involvement in the Armstrong 500. In hindsight, it was a grave error.

The LCCA was fully committed to a new era of motorsport, one that involved world F1 champions in open-wheeler cars, racing on new circuits being purpose-built for the occasion. Surely that was the future. Touring cars—tin tops—were, the LCCA thought, a sideshow.

PIARC put up its hand to fill the void. That, too, was folly. The club was cash-strapped and the Phillip Island surface was in need of restoration, not just repair. In Sydney, the Australian Racing Drivers Club (ARDC)—not the prewar organisation in Victoria, but a NSW version inaugurated in 1952—could sense blood in the water.

They scheduled the Bathurst Six Hour Classic for production touring cars and production sports cars at Mount Panorama. It would be held on 30 September 1962. The Armstrong 500 at Phillip Island was slated for 21 October, three weeks later. Harry Firth and Bob Jane, who would set the gold standard for early long-distance racing, contested both.

Ford contracted Firth in 1962 to be their official works team leader. Ford put their ambition proudly and precariously on display, even entering as 'Ford Motor Co. of Australia'. It was a big commitment. Their Falcon looked sensational, but it needed performance credibility.

It was no help when Firth rolled the car at Hell Corner in the Bathurst Six Hour in full view of TV cameras. The XK Falcon's rear brakes seized, the car inverted and, without a roll cage, its roof was flattened to the door sills. 'I wore a seatbelt with a dual cross-over on each shoulder,' Firth said. 'That saved me, but it took a while to get the belt undone and find a way out, all the time with petrol leaking.' Firth made his escape through a small gap in the rear window. It was his second rollover in several weeks. He'd upended a Falcon in a Victorian rally, too.

Phillip Island would debut the new XL Falcon with the up-powered 170 cubic inch (2.8 litre) Pursuit engine. On the Thursday before race day, Firth rolled it during official practice at the Island.

History presents Firth as invincible. But he wasn't. His long-time mechanic Ian Tate told me: 'He was shaken. His brother Norm brought the car back to Melbourne for a new body and rebuild. But Harry stayed on the island.' He needed to rebuild his nerve.

On Sunday, he and Bob Jane won the Armstrong 500—the first major victory for Ford. Confusion abounded. Officials gave the chequered flag to the car that came second. Timekeepers and lap scorers took several days to ratify Ford's win. It was a huge fillip for Firth. He'd built a car that Phillip Island couldn't break.

Instead, the cars broke Phillip Island.

'We'd spent a really happy day in the Bathurst Six Hour, driving around to come fourth in class,' Brian Foley reminisced. Foley was paired with NSW Citroën distributor Bill Buckle in an air-suspended Citroën ID19, locally made by Continental & General in Melbourne. Buckle was another son of an industry pioneer. To learn the brand, he'd even been sent by his family's firm to Slough in the UK where Citroëns were assembled for the British market.

The Australian-built version was a down-specced version of the classic French floater, stripped of a lot of its luxury. To compensate, local dealers had given it PR panache, christening it 'the Parisienne'.

'We came to Phillip Island expecting another trouble-free run,' Foley said. But the Citroën, of all cars, fell to pieces beneath them. David McKay's Scuderia Veloce had put the team together for Continental & General Distributors. Its drivers included Norm Beechey. 'It was a fascinating car,' Norm recalled. 'It had brakes you wouldn't believe. You'd stand on them and all the air would go out of the suspension, and it would sit down and stop.' Foley went one step further: 'You wouldn't start braking until the officials at the side of the track began to scatter because they thought you had no chance of making the corner.'

Constant, heavy rain had damaged the flimsy track surface before the race. The incessant pounding of the cars did the rest. The race, truly, became a test of endurance.

'We saw Billy [Buckle] stopped over on Siberia,' Foley recalled. Siberia is the double-apex corner closest to the sea cliffs. 'They gave me some tools and I started to run towards him. It's a long way. Just as I came near, he got it fixed and drove off. But then Greg Cusack, Norm Beechey's teammate, went by, and the back door fell off. Just fell off. He stopped, got out, dragged the door off the track, shoved it in the back and headed to the pits.'

Standing there, abandoned, Foley became aware that not many drivers were trying to negotiate Siberia. The track had broken up so badly that they'd gouged an alternate cross-country route to avoid the potholes.

'George Reynolds in the VW just went bush' Foley said. 'During my next stint in the Buckle car, the rear mudguard fell off. This time we didn't try to reattach it. We just drove to the finish with the rear wheel exposed.'

Reynolds won his class, and Beechey and Foley were third and fifth in theirs.

In 1960 at the first 500, Lex Davison had told reporters the potholes were so deep that the little NSUs needed their headlights on to find their way out. It had been a joke then. Now it wasn't.

The Phillip Island circuit had delivered for Armstrong, and for the motor industry, but at a cost to itself which seemed irreclaimable.

In early 1963, Bathurst BMC dealer Barry Gurdon flung his racing Austin A90 around the public road known as Mount Panorama with executives from Armstrong York on board: no helmets, no seatbelts and no road closure. Gurdon was a prominent member of the ARDC and the Bathurst Light Car Club, and his mission—a successful one, as it turned out—was to bring the Armstrong 500 to Bathurst.

On 6 October 1963, the Sunday of NSW's Labor Day long weekend, Harry Firth and Bob Jane guided a locally developed Cortina GT to win the inaugural Armstrong 500 at Mount Panorama.

Armstrong withdrew from sponsorship in 1965, arranging for the Federation of Automotive Products Manufacturers to step up to maintain a strong presence for the industry in its race. Irish tobacco company Gallaher captured the attention of the Australian Racing Drivers Club with eye-watering sponsorship money, never quite understanding what it had bought. It wasn't a good fit. In 1968, local brake manufacturer Hardie-Ferodo seized the race back for the motor industry.

Ron Thonemann joined General Motors' local advertising agency, McCann Erickson, to work on the Holden account. His last job in Australia was as motoring editor of what was once Sir Keith Murdoch's Adelaide *News.* The paper closed in 1992. Thonemann moved to India's happy place, Goa, and ran a luxury beachside hotel.

11

The End of the World

'*On the Beach* is a story about the end of the world, and Melbourne sure is the right place to film it.'

Actress Ava Gardner, Academy Award nominee in 1953, wife to Mickey Rooney, band leader Artie Shaw and finally Frank Sinatra, and apparently consort throughout of Howard Hughes, was quoted while starring alongside Gregory Peck and Fred Astaire in the apocalypse movie of 1959. The Phillip Island motor-racing circuit had been the movie's set for two days as director Stanley Kramer mocked up his version of the Australian Grand Prix, an essential part of the plot.

PIARC earned £150 a day leasing the track to Kramer. He bought three days and used two. The movie makers had gone there at the insistence of Neville Shute, the screenwriter and author of the book on which the film was based. Shute, an

English immigrant and author of *A Town Like Alice*, was an amateur racing driver. He lived just across Western Port Bay and raced his brace of Jaguar sports cars (XK140 then XK150) at the Island. He'd been in the field of the opening meeting in 1956 under his full name, Neville Shute Norway.

On the Beach envisaged a world destroyed by nuclear holocaust. Phillip Island was also doomed, and its initial capital-raising business model was its downfall.

Subscribers to the ten-year £10 membership offer had been promised free entry for the duration. They were turning up every time there was a race, but paying customers weren't. Cash flow was negative and with the track badly breaking up there weren't sufficient funds to effect repairs, let alone make improvements.

PIARC had lost two of its most influential supporters. Sir Keith Murdoch had died in 1952. Then Sir Frank Beaurepaire—one of the underwriters of the circuit's construction through his Olympic Tyres, and the driving force behind Melbourne's Olympic Games—died suddenly in May 1956. Repco's Dave McGrath remained as the circuit's sole conduit to the big end of town.

Winston Maguire, hands-on founding president of PIARC, was also gone. Business had taken him to Portland on the western end of Victoria's Great Ocean Road. It was 500 kilometres away, too far for him to continue as president. His place was taken by a true hero.

John Pryce was a Red Beret commando who flew his glider behind enemy lines into France on D-Day. He emigrated to Australia, became president of the Austin 7 Car Club and was a welcome member of Donald Thomson's CAMS kitchen cabinet of supporters. In 1956 when oil company BP broke a cartel agreement not to openly sponsor motorsport, Pryce became BP's motorsports manager. He deftly balanced commercial agreements with statutory responsibilities. Pryce was a man on the inside, but he saw no conflict of interest—only mutual interest.

PIARC, however, was another matter. The financials did not look good.

The estimated cost to build the Phillip Island circuit had been £30,000. Total construction had been north of £50,000. The original committee had forecast overheads per race meeting at £200. So far each event had cost £600. Cash-flow forecasts had been predicated on 7000 attendees per race meeting. The missing link in that computation was the membership offer of free entry. It skewed the total calculation.

The committee had been relentless in its pursuit of funds through subscription. They'd also been a bit cheeky. A press release issued on 8 June 1955 was an obvious retail ploy: 'Late in May the club announced that it would not accept any further Foundation Members after 30 June. All those who had been thinking about it had better do something definite or miss the benefits and concessions of Foundation Membership.'

On 7 July, a follow-up proclaimed: 'A flood of new members received during June was far greater than expected, and for the month we banked £6,100 representing 610 new members. Foundation Membership lists have been closed with a total of 2,730 members.'

The club had been promising its early foundation members a race meeting since late 1953. Bad weather in 1954 had been understandable but by 1955 the promise had worn thin.

The 7 July release continued: 'Our contractor has assured the Committee that we will definitely have the track completed and ready for racing on October 22 [1955].' It took another eighteen months for the first rushed meeting to occur. The result, financially, was not good.

In February 1957, a circular to foundation members from Winston Maguire noted: 'The opening meeting on December 15 was seriously affected by heavy rain and resulted in some loss. The second meeting on January 28 was much better attended—but of the 7,200 adults who were there, 3,400 were members and their friends who entered by means of their free passes.'

The bottom line: 'With some reluctance the committee has now decided to make an immediate levy of £2 on each member in respect of the current year and to request a similar levy of £2 in advance in respect of the following year.'

That didn't go down well.

On 10 May, Maguire got tough: 'It is my duty to state that non-payment of this levy will involve suspension of membership.'

Many members simply left.

Poor John Pryce. What had he bought into?

The club was clinging to viability by its fingertips. In his first circular, Pryce proposed an equitable solution. Foundation members would pay 2 pounds, 2 shillings per year as a subscription. New members would pay a joining fee of 5 pounds, 5 shillings and an annual subscription of 3 pounds, 3 shillings.

He followed up with a begging letter: 'It would be magnificent if all 2,900 Foundation Members were to pay the proposed annual subscription, but we must face facts; many of the original members are no longer with us. There are probably only 2,000 left.'

Pryce countenanced the obvious alternative: 'To wind the club up and lose the circuit would be a downright tragedy for motor sport. If you fail to save the club, not only would the two great Australian companies which guaranteed our bank overdraft so generously lose heavily, and the club wind up in very bad odour, but no public company could ever be expected to again lend such support to motor sport.'

Pryce tried every avenue.

PIARC leased its property to a nearby farmer for grazing. He paid £100 for agistment. The contract required him to sweep the track clear of droppings before race meetings. It didn't specify the condition of the infield.

A letter to the editor of *Australian Motor News* asked: 'Imagine what the Italian factories would say if they knew that a 250F Maserati and a Super Squalo Ferrari had got bogged in the spongy marsh referred to as the Competitors' Paddock.'

Dissatisfaction was mounting. Criticism had begun as early as the 1957 Gold Star round: 'a double line of cars four miles long took an hour and a half to move the last half mile up to the entrance gate where, although there was room for cars to enter three abreast, officials allowed only one car at a time. Several thousand missed the first half of the program.' Food outlets copped a serve: 'Catering facilities on the pit side of the track consisted of one small boy selling peanuts!' The complainant concluded: 'I suggest an immediate CAMS investigation.'

Early in 1958, the LCCA cancelled its planned circuit hire in March. It cited a problem of tyre wear, which still appears to persist in the minds of some competitors.

Authorities weren't helping. Phillip Island had become a test case for the tax office. The tax commissioner hit up PIARC entertainment tax—almost £700. It was a try-on and PIARC objected. They turned to their advisers Flack & Flack, a division of Price Waterhouse. Tax law offered exemption to non-profit organisations 'established for the encouragement or promotion of an athletic game or athletic sport in which human beings are the sole participants'.

A leading driver (unnamed by the tax department but later confirmed to be Australian Grand Prix champion Doug Whiteford) debated the definition of 'athletic' sport: 'Even sprinters use spikes or blocks. The Olympic Games involve the use of substantial machinery or equipment for cycling and rowing.'

The chairman of the review board demurred: 'In my opinion where motor car and motorcycle racing is concerned, the important factor is the capability of the car or the cycle. I find it difficult to find that motor car and motorcycle racing can be regarded as an athletic game or athletic sport. I do not deny that the driver or rider must have considerable ability. I would uphold the Commissioner's decision on the objection.'

Flack & Flack rendered their invoice for £75.

In 1961, the Shire of Phillip Island demanded an immediate upgrade to ablution facilities. The organisation representing the community that stood to gain the most from crowd attendance seemed to have turned against PIARC. Or perhaps it had a genuine case. Either way, without Winston Maguire there to run defence, PIARC's position was weakened.

The elite competitors decided to pay for their own racing. With the track in such poor condition, on 3 November 1960 Bib Stillwell, Stan Jones and Bill Patterson presented PIARC with a cheque for £1000. 'Spend it on surface improvements,' they said, 'specifically for the upcoming Gold Star race on 11 December.'

It was a small price to pay compared to the havoc the damaged track could wreak on their cars, or their chances.

Phillip Island was fighting for survival on all fronts.

Suddenly, other permanent circuits were being built. It was a four-year epidemic. Hume Weir on the border of Victoria and New South Wales opened on 2 November 1959, at first 1.2 kilometres unsealed and soon lengthened to 1.8 kilometres sealed. It was nestled in a disused quarry made redundant after the building of the massive Hume Weir.

Baskerville outside Hobart opened in early 1958. Its 2.01-kilometre sealed surface set a very early standard for amphitheatre tracks. The slightly longer Symmons Plains near Launceston followed in 1960.

In Sydney, the all-powerful Australian Jockey Club had decided to optimise the use of its subsidiary horseracing track, Warwick Farm in the city's south-west. It modelled its 3.6-kilometre racetrack on Aintree in the UK, and it brought out Aintree's deputy clerk of the course, Geoffrey Sykes, to design and run it. Its first race was in December 1960. Warwick Farm would set new, high standards.

In Melbourne, a bunch of Holden-car nuts had carved a track in a paddock near Diggers Rest in the city's north-west. The Australian Motor Sports Club's 1.6-kilometre bitumen track opened in January 1962 as Calder Park.

The Benalla Auto Club in Victoria began planning a regional track in 1958 and opened its 2.028-kilometre Winton circuit on 26 November 1961. Many years later, five-time Australian touring car champion Dick Johnson described driving Winton as 'running a marathon around your clothesline'.

The Queensland Motor Sporting Club, of which Johnson was a member, opened the 2.25-kilometre Lakeside track north of Brisbane on 19 March 1961.

The ARDC, in association with the Blue Mountains Sporting Drivers Club, ran Catalina Park in the heart of Blue Mountains at Katoomba. Authorities relocated an Aboriginal community to enable the 2.1-kilometre track to be built. It opened on 12 February 1961.

The 1.6-kilometre Oran Park was built by the Singer Car Club near Camden, south-west of Sydney, and opened in February 1962.

Famine had become a feast. A motor-racing community bereft of a place to race had, almost overnight, been oversupplied. Circuit owners and promoters needed to make their investments profitable. There would, ultimately, be a sorting out.

PIARC's major threat was close to home.

Albert Park was gone as a racing venue. Journalist and later lord mayor of Melbourne, Peter Costigan, knew why. In a story published in *The Age* years later, he pointed to the premier Sir Henry Bolte: 'Bolte told me he closed the race because "I owed Jack Williams [proprietor of the Melbourne *Herald*] a few favours at the time, and he was a determined bugger."' Williams had wanted the track shut. Simple as that.

But there were deals to be done. A report in *The Herald* on Monday, 11 May 1959, read:

> The president of the Light Car Club, Mr. Lex Davison, will see the Minister for Lands, Mr. Turnbull, next week to discuss finding a suitable motor racing course to replace Albert Park.
>
> The club had asked the government for permission to hold the Melbourne Grand Prix at Albert Park later this year.
>
> But the Parliamentary Liberal and Country Party (LCP) decided last Tuesday that motor racing would never take place there while the LCP remained in office.
>
> Mr. Turnbull said that the Government would be happy to discuss any proposals to develop a circuit at another site for car races of international standard.

PIARC volunteered its services. On 12 May, it wrote to the lands minister:

> We are very interested in press reports of the Government's willingness to assist in the development of a motor racing circuit in Victoria, as this club owns a three-mile circuit on the club's own 300-acre property at Phillip Island.

The letter proposed Phillip Island as the 'logical and ideal venue of motorsport in Victoria'. It was a long letter, with plenty of twists and turns.

On 26 May, Minister Keith Turnbull replied, briefly:

> The final decision as to the most suitable venue for the holding of Car Races of an International Standard will probably rest with the Light Car Club of Australia which has been assured that any suitable location chosen by that body as a suitable location will be investigated by the Government with a view to

> giving all the assistance and co-operation possible. I therefore suggest that your approaches should be to your sister club.

The fix was in.

Sandown, a standalone, permanent, world-class circuit, had been conceived.

In September 1959 John Pryce had told PIARC members 'it is practically impossible to develop or build a new circuit within a short distance of Melbourne'. He was wrong.

Jon Leighton, a friend and early teammate of four-time Australian touring car champion Allan Moffat, was a member of the Leighton Construction family. He put a persuasive argument to his dad, Stanley, to build the track John Pryce said couldn't be built. A company, Sandown Park Motor Sport Pty Ltd, was formed and work commenced on a 3.1-kilometre track. Sandown was at Springvale, conveniently located on a rail spur 25 kilometres from the CBD.

On 11 March 1962, Jack Brabham won the inaugural Sandown International Cup by 0.4 seconds from John Surtees, both in Cooper Climaxes.

Initially the circuit was managed by the Victorian Sporting Car Club (VSCC), an ambitious organisation that promoted hill climbs and rallies, and observed trials. Donald Kingsley Thomson was closely associated with the VSCC, directing the club's Sun Rallies. But Sandown was a step too far. It stretched the amateur club's ability and its finances.

In 1966, the LCCA issued a 'we're back' statement. It had taken control of Sandown. 'We will show the press, the trade, and the public that we still pack the punch we did when we organised events at Albert Park,' new president Ron Dearie

No champagne showers in 1928. Wellwishers chaired Arthur Waite to his victory celebration. (Primotipo.com)

Overnight preparation at the Isle of Wight Hotel, with Captain Waite's Austin 7 on makeshift blocks. (Chevron)

Lillie Langtry's yacht, the *Alvina*—an elegant reminder of a gentle age, and firm favourite of the 'smart set' that attended the pre–World War II races. (Phillip Island and District Historical Society)

OFFICIAL PROGRAMME

Victorian Light Car Club

100 Miles Road Race

THE FIRST IN AUSTRALIA

VICTORIAN LIGHT CAR CLUB

AT

Phillip Island, on MONDAY, 26th MARCH, 1928

By permission of the Woolamai and Phillip Island Shire Council

Price 6d.

The 100 Miles Road Race program, with no mention of an 'Australian Grand Prix'; that would come later, after the success of the first race meeting. (John Smailes)

AKT Sambell, developer of Summerland golf links and influential supporter of motorsport on Phillip Island. (Phillip Island and District Historical Society)

Even in 1929, the concept of an Australian Grand Prix was an afterthought (see bottom left)—a tenuous probe at making a grandiose claim. By 1931, the grand prix was the headline act, postdated to 1928. Arthur Waite's 1928 winning car is exaggerated here. (Primotipo.com)

Motorcycles raced in 1928, then not again until 1931. Jimmy Pringle's career spanned the entire pre–World War II period, here flashing past the manual scoreboard shared by car and motorcycle competitors. (Hartwell Motorcycle Club)

As a committee member, Arthur Terdich tested the road track after the deluge prior to the 1928 Grand Prix. It was obvious racing could not occur on the first planned date. (Primotipo.com)

First Bugatti win. Terdich and Jack Raybould take the flag in 1929. The pits are crowded with spectators. (Chevron)

Arthur Terdich (right) toasts victory with riding mechanic Jack Raybould, 1929. (Primotipo.com)

Bill Thompson's first win of three was in 1930, driving a Type 37A Bugatti owned by patron Professor Arthur Burkitt. In 1932 Thompson would win with riding mechanic Wal Warneford—Bugatti's last win at Phillip Island. (Chevron)

Reg Brearley and Bert Elliott crashed in the 1930 grand prix. Three months later, both were killed attempting the Sydney–Melbourne speed record. (Primotipo.com)

In 1932 Albert Edwards crashed his front-wheel drive Alvis on lap two, avoiding a car emerging from the pits in a cloud of thick dust. Spectator Dick Wilkinson was severely injured. (Primotipo.com)

Joan Richmond and Mollie Shaw were the first female crew to contest the Australian Grand Prix. They finished a creditable fifth in 1931, in Joan's Riley Nine. (Australian Motorsport Hall of Fame)

The day a hot rod won. In 1934, the Australian Racing Drivers Club hosted the Victorian Centenary Grand Prix over 230 miles (370 kilometres). Tyro driver Mick Smith won in his parents' 1934 Ford Roadster—and never raced again. (Primotipo.com)

The wide-open spaces. In 1935, Bill Thompson hustled his MG K3 Magnette to a frustrating second place just 27 seconds behind teammate Les Murphy in the last Australian Grand Prix to be held at Phillip Island. (Primotipo.com)

Jimmy Pringle used an ex-works 500cc Manx Norton to win the Phillip Island Senior grand prix in three successive years from 1936. (Old Bike Australasia)

Lex Davison won the first race on the new Phillip Island circuit in 1956, driving a Cooper-Vincent with the engine specially prepared by Phil Irving. Davison won three hill-climb championships in the tiny Formula Three car. (Davison Collection)

Lex Davison (Ferrari 625) briefly leads Jack Brabham (Cooper Bristol) in the feature race of the first meeting—the Bill Thompson Memorial Trophy. Brabham went on to win. (Davison Collection)

World 125cc champion Tom Phillis won the 1961 Victorian Grand Prix on Honda's breakthrough four-cylinder machine. The following year, world 250cc champion Kel Carruthers would win the same race on his version of the same Honda. (Old Bike Australasia)

The most basic of podiums. Tom Phillis, microphone in hand, acknowledges the crowd. Phillis died in 1962 on the Isle of Man. (Hartwell Motorcycle Club)

Kel Carruthers on 'his' Honda Four. He rode it at the Island over almost a full decade, and won on it for the last time in 1969 in the Australian Grand Prix in both the 250cc and 350cc categories. (Old Bike Australasia)

The fields of '57, part 1. In March, PIARC's Formula Libre race over eight laps was won by Lex Davison (Ferrari no. 9) from Stan Jones (Maserati 250F no. 2) and Tom Hawkes (Cooper Holden no. 3). Ted Gray (no. 1) in the middle of the front row, in his Tornado Ford, did not place. (Bob King Collection)

The fields of '57, part 2. In May, Hartwell Motorcycle Club leased Phillip Island for the first time and Maurie Quincey (no. 8), recovered from injuries at the Isle of Man, won both the Junior (350cc) and Senior (500cc) races. (Old Bike Australasia)

Sidecars in a class of their own. In 1957, Lindsay Urquhart and 'swinger' Ray Kelly (no. 54) round up Jim Hocking and Max George (no. 3) in the Australian Tourist Trophy. (Hartwell Motorcycle Club)

Phil Irving, a Phillip Island regular since its inception (foreground), with Lex Davison. (Davison Collection)

Stan Jones' number one fan was his son Alan, perched on the right-hand wheel behind his dad. Alan would win the 1980 world F1 championship. (Primotipo.com)

The last Armstrong 500 on Phillip Island, 1962. The small car class for vehicles costing up to £900 gets away on an already deteriorating surface. Class 'D' was won by George Reynolds and Jim McKeown in a works VW Beetle. (Chevron)

Touring car legend Norm Beechey rolled his Vanguard in practice for the inaugural Armstrong 500, but with co-driver John French finished second in class and seventh outright. (Beechey Collection)

Ford Falcons claimed three of the first four places in the 1962 Armstrong 500 on debut, split by a Studebaker Lark in second place. Harry Firth and Bob Jane won. Yachtsman Syd Fisher was third. (Chevron)

John McCormack won the first F5000 race at Phillip Island, here being tended by John Lanyon, the Island's manager and Elfin team manager, with Phil Irving standing far left. (Chevron)

A small field for the 1973 Gold Star. Kevin Bartlett (Lola T330 no. 5) on pole with Johnnie Walker (Lola T330 no. 25) alongside; second row John McCormack (Elfin no. 3) and John Leffler (Elfin no. 7). Coming onto the third row is Elfin owner Garrie Cooper alongside Western Australian Howie Sangster (McLaren). Johnnie Walker won. (Chevron)

Kevin Bartlett (Lola T300), first to break the 100 mph lap average in 1973, leads John McCormack (Elfin MR5) in the 1972 Victorian Road Racing Championship. (Primotipo.com)

Talented youngster Bruce Allison negotiates the concrete patchwork of Phillip Island in the Gold Star Championship of 1976. Vibrations broke his rear-wing struts while he was leading the race, dropping him to fourth in the title. The following year, Allison won Britain's Grovewood Awards for the best driver from a Commonwealth country. (Chevron)

In 1968 Peter Brock made his Phillip Island debut in his homemade Austin A30 Holden. He won his class. Brock and Colin Bond joined the fledgling Holden Dealer Team in 1969. (Chevron)

The only driver to win the Australian Touring Car Championship and the Australian Rally Championship, Colin Bond was a master of the rough surface. He won the Phillip Island 500 three times out of seven, on the 'old' circuit more than any other driver. (Chevron)

Gregg Hansford (02), once Bruce Allison's brother-in-law, leads Greg Johnson on the concrete line around Phillip Island in the Tom Phillis Memorial Trophy race in 1977. (Old Bike Australasia)

After the Armstrong 500 destroyed the track, it became grazing property. Even after Len Lukey saved it, his sheep continued to graze at will. (Hartwell Motorcycle Club)

Bob Barnard rebuilt the circuit to international standard and secured the 1989 Australian Motorcycle Grand Prix. (Barnard Collection)

wrote. Ultimately the LCCA, too, would be bankrupted running it.

PIARC was in deep trouble, and it knew it. In 1961, John Pryce stepped down from the presidency. John Lanyon, a gifted graphic artist, enthusiastic competitor in the lower grades (he had a stove-hot MG TC) and visionary, seized the baton. The top job had become a relay. One of the first letters Lanyon received as president was from Len Lukey. It wasn't congratulatory: 'Would you please accept this letter as my formal resignation from your committee.'

Lukey had become a major investor in the Hume Weir motor-racing project. 'I have spent a considerable amount of time organising the Brabham meeting at Albury,' Lukey wrote to Lanyon. 'I now find that my business commitments leave me no time for outside interests.'

There was a subtext to his resignation. Lukey had wanted to bring world champion Jack Brabham to Phillip Island. He planned to hire the circuit, run the event, assume the risk and reap the profit. PIARC imposed a rental fee Lukey considered unreasonable. So he took his big idea to far-flung Hume Weir in Albury. Distance killed the Brabham meeting. He made a loss.

CAMS was suspicious of Phillip Island's ability to deliver. It allocated race dates to other emerging tracks, not to the Island. PIARC wrote a strong letter of protest.

Club culture was at its lowest ebb. PIARC had no clubroom. Twice in 1962 it had promised its dwindling membership a suitable location in Melbourne. That was in stark contrast to the LCCA, which had moved to new enlarged premises at 46 Queens Road, opposite Albert Park, complete with roof garden, liquor licence and a staffed dining room. The premises were leased from the Melbourne Cricket Club and part of the deal was that LCCA committee members also became members of that prestigious club. The distinction between the haves and have-nots could not have been greater.

The 1962 Armstrong 500 was Phillip Island's swansong.

Part Three

The Circuit Revisited
1967–1978

12

Funland: Len Lukey Saves the Circuit

On 27 November 1962, just a month after the Armstrong 500 destroyed Phillip Island's playing surface, Australia's prime minister Robert Menzies announced Victoria would become home to the country's biggest and best international airport.

The federal government had acquired 5300 hectares of grassland in rural Tullamarine, north of Melbourne, to build a new gateway to the city, the state and the nation. It took another two years for the first sod to be turned, and another five after that before the first touchdown.

It couldn't come soon enough for Len Lukey, as he stood in a long queue waiting to board his propellered flight at crowded Essendon just up the road. Len was a busy man, impatient with delay. Essendon was overcrowded; its runways were too short to handle the new jet aircraft that promised to slash travel times, and if you wanted to fly overseas you were directed to an overflow terminal in a northern hangar.

Len travelled frequently to Japan. He loved the place, and he had interests in steel production there—all the better to feed his growing automotive muffler business, which had begun to explore offshore markets. Len was a man on the move, except in a boarding line.

In 1964, that's where he ran into George Coad, brother of Frank Coad who'd won the inaugural Armstrong 500. The Coads were a motor-racing family. George Snr revelled in building specials—bikes and cars. He restored a magnificent HRD with his mate Phil Irving. The Coads' passion was Vauxhalls. They even owned a Vauxhall franchise. George Snr and his two boys built a Vauxhall sports car, had Harry Firth fabricate the chassis and successfully took on works cars imported from the Italian factories. Frank in the Vauxhall Special and Doug Whiteford in an ex-works Maserati 300S staged a wheel-to-wheel duel at Phillip Island and came away with a joint lap record for sports cars.

It's popularly held that Coad told Lukey the Phillip Island circuit was on the market, and most likely for a bargain. That's hard to believe. Lukey was as switched on as they get. He would have known. But Coad opened the door for Lukey to be approached as a potential suitor, rather than him taking the initial step. In negotiation, it's all about tactics.

There was a third party involved. Dave McGrath's largesse had brought Repco into play as a guarantor. It was in for £10,000 and it was in McGrath's best career interests that the company of which he was managing director exit with at least that amount. Beyond that, he was a true enthusiast, a good mate of Jack

Brabham, and if he could help to broker a deal that advantaged all parties, then he was up for it.

That same year, Len Lukey bought the Phillip Island Motor Racing Circuit for £13,000. PIARC had wanted £17,000 to clear their debt. Instead they were offered a deed of arrangement which promised so much more. Lukey would develop the rundown property. His plan was to turn it into a holiday destination, a theme park, a waterskiing park (a German inventor had just devised cable waterskiing), a golf course and a place of tranquillity with its very own Japanese gardens. The motor-racing track and its facilities would be leased to PIARC for £1 a year. They would be responsible for track restoration and maintenance, and they would have to guarantee they would run four race meetings a year. Len was going to call the whole project Funland.

At first it seemed like mission impossible.

Even PIARC president John Lanyon, like Lukey a person who saw only positives in any situation, was flummoxed. The once mighty PIARC was down to the bare bones of its membership. Of more than 3000 members on the books, just 40 were financial.

Lanyon and his brother Russell were dreamers. Some called them schemers, but not in an unkind way. They ran a successful graphic art business in downtown Carlton—the creative end of town—and they spent their lives jumping happily from one big idea to the next. No doubt, they did their SWOT analysis—Strengths, Weaknesses, Opportunities and Threats.

'What have we got that others covet?' Answer: Phillip Island.

'What have others got that we want?' Answer: members, clubrooms, cash flow.

Solution: Simple—find and amalgamate with another club.

The Southern Sporting Car Club had clubrooms in the old Prince George Theatre in Church Street, Brighton. It was an easy task for smooth-talking John Lanyon (he was the mouthpiece) to successfully propose a marriage. Naturally PIARC retained its name.

Russell Lanyon was the money man. In 1966, as his brother and Len Lukey continued their collaboration to rebuild the Island, Russell was intrigued as the Victorian Government introduced a Co-operative Housing Society program. It allowed non-profit organisations with projects in the public interest to sell shares in a Co-operative Society for ten per cent of their par value. They could source low-interest bank loans against the full value, with the loan guaranteed by the government. What a deal. And what was more in the public interest than a motor-racing circuit?

Russell formed PIARC Co-Operative, prepared spreadsheets and cash-flow projections, practised on a few banks (which knocked him back), then presented his proposition to the National Bank of Australasia's Stock Exchange Branch at the big end of town. He came away with a $40,000 loan. It was the kick-start that fulfilled PIARC's end of the bargain with Len Lukey.

Russell's son Mike, who chronicled his dad's dealings, said not one PIARC member ever requested their money back, although 'occasionally in later years PIARC would receive calls from the executors of deceased estates who had found the share certificates and wondered if they might be worth something'.

Phil Irving MBE, by any measure one of the world's great designers of racing engines and a high-performance deity, camped at

Phillip Island like any mortal. He drank flagon red wine and had a party trick. 'He was the only man I ever knew who could smoke a cigarette down to the butt and never spill the ash,' grand prix ace Reg Hunt once told me. 'He'd be bending over your carburettors with a red-hot engine and petrol flowing, and his ash dangled precariously.' Did he ever get it wrong? 'One day he arrived at my new home and spilled ash all over the new carpet,' Hunt said. 'So he stamped on it with his foot.'

Irving was the spirit of the Phillip Island Auto Racing Club.

Phillip Island was never going to recover by conventional means. There were never going to be sufficient funds to pay contractors. PIARC, only months before in disarray, was galvanised. 'It was so much fun,' Henk Duncan, who would later succeed John Lanyon as president, recollected. 'Working bees were the only way.' They started as soon as the Lukey contract was signed. But it didn't seem like work. 'We were building a circuit.' It was a higher cause.

And not just that. They were working hand-in-glove with Len Lukey, creating his dream.

They'd come in through the north gate on a Friday night and set up camp: swags, tents, caravans if they were lucky. No permanent structures. John Pryce 'discovered' a stock of green overalls in a storeroom at his employer BP and distributed them freely. When Phillip Island reopened they became uniforms, and the people wearing them were the Jolly Green Giants, the go-to officials charged with making the Island fan-friendly.

For young Henk Duncan—full name Cornelius Hendrikus van den Dungen—who was then a junior at Myer department store in Melbourne, PIARC was a massive influence.

'We'd sit around the campfire with Phil Irving and listen to his stories. He used to draw engine plans with a stick in the dirt. At his home in Warrandyte, Repco would sometimes send people along to photograph them.' The same year Henk met Phil (1966), the Irving-designed Repco engine won the world F1 championship for Jack Brabham.

Duncan went on to become national clerk of the course for the Australian F1 Grand Prix and in 2022 was named Global Official of the Year by the Fédération Internationale de l'Automobile (FIA).

'Phil would tell stories of earlier working bees at the Island,' Duncan recalled. Like when there was a massive explosion in a caravan next door and the first person to rush in warned that there was gore all over the walls and two bodies on the floor. Except it turned out that a can of spaghetti had exploded in its pot and the two bodies were too inebriated to notice.

Then there was the car that kept doing late-night laps and refused to stop. The campers gave up trying to arrest its progress and went to bed, and the next morning found a car upside down at Siberia, its owners nowhere to be seen.

'John Lanyon was a great leader,' Duncan said. 'He seemed to work at the club full-time.' He got Len Lukey's attention. What had started as a challenge became a collegial effort.

Lukey transformed the venue. He re-grassed the entire 300 acres (121 hectares), installed ten large water tanks and built a half-sized Olympic pool. Lukey loved water. He built a massive dam in the centre of the property, intended to become a cable-waterskiing park. He surrounded the property with a high cyclone fence and planted the perimeter with olive and cypress trees. He built two grass airstrips—one manageable, the other to be used by experienced cross-wind pilots, only at a pinch.

He was also happy to lend his equipment. 'I was on Len's grader when it blew up,' Henk Duncan laughed. 'I was at the top of Turn 12, facing downhill with no brakes, no steering and no power and it just kept going faster. Peter Nelson [soon to be an influential motorsport official] had his car parked in my way. His wife Marcia moved it just in time.' The grader ground to a halt.

'Len saw our relationship as a two-way street,' said Geoff Bull, another of the early volunteers who went on to become a PIARC president. 'You'd turn up and he'd demand your attention urgently to come and help with a cow that was calving.'

'We'd built a new pit wall,' Duncan remembered, 'and he saw it as an ideal place to hang drinking troughs for his sheep. The problem was that, during later race meetings, the sheep droppings would dry on the track when the sun hit them. They'd shrink and take the track surface with them when you swept them away.'

PIARC built a mound of sheep poop. Dry, it looked just like soil. 'There was a girlfriend of one of our volunteers who was a bit up herself,' Duncan recalled. 'Once, when she wanted to know where her boyfriend was, we said, "Just climb up there, you'll see him from the top." She got halfway before she sank.'

John Lanyon developed the art of the scrounge.

He bought the redundant control tower, for a song, from the Commonwealth Aircraft Corporation (CAC) at Fishermans

Bend, then persuaded mates in the transport business to move it to the island. Disassembled, it was lightweight and came across the San Remo Bridge. Len Lukey had worked at the CAC during the war and met his wife Helen there. He may have given Lanyon an inside run at the tender.

The clubhouse on Church Street in Brighton became the source of seats and a generator. The club had been given notice the theatre was to be redeveloped, and stripping it seemed too good an opportunity to let slip by.

Sandown Racetrack, surely a competitor, became an unwitting donor. 'There was a concrete factory nearby and we got their offcuts,' Henk Duncan said. 'We'd pick them up in a trailer. I learned how to fire a detonator. There'd be a big bang and we'd have two pieces we could use.'

Len Lukey's plans were on a grand scale. And they didn't come off. He'd gotten the Phillip Island Shire Council offside.

'Dad was building his Japanese garden. To source rocks of the right size and shape, he cut a road down to the beach between what is now Turns 2 and 3,' Keith Lukey, Len's son, told me from his home in South Gippsland, 75 kilometres from the Island. What was the fuss? Len was only taking the rocks from below the waterline. 'The council was horrified. They ended up in the Supreme Court in Melbourne and Dad copped a fine.'

Len's vision was for a luxury hotel perched above what is now Lukey Heights, looking out to sea. It wasn't modest. He had a bunch of Japanese investors lined up at a time when the Japanese bubble economy was reaching its zenith. But the council wouldn't budge.

In the longer term, as Japanese investment waned, Lukey may have dodged a bullet. But he didn't feel that way. 'Dad secured a whole heap of land in Surfers Paradise on a hundred-year lease,' Keith said. But nothing came of it.

Lukey and Lanyon, together, were super promoters.

In March 1966, Lukey invited world champions Jack Brabham, Jim Clark and Graham Hill to a quiet day at his country property. Then he ambushed them with a heap of media. Brabham, a friend and business associate of Lukey's, flew his F1 colleagues in a twin-engine Beechcraft Bonanza. The media travelled by road. It was the week between the Sandown round of the Tasman Series and the grand final at Longford in Tasmania.

According to Mike Lanyon, the internationals were a bit taken aback by the media presence, but the Tasman was a relaxed affair and it was a fun day: a round of golf, swimming, waterskiing (albeit short) on the lake, an Aussie barbecue. Lukey had trucked in sand to turn his lake into a far more attractive beach. Brabham and local driver Bill Patterson did a few passes in their aircraft, even staging a mock dogfight along the cliff face. 'Jim Clark got his nether regions caught in the trampoline,' Keith Lukey remembered.

A month later at Phillip Island, on the Easter weekend, John Lanyon hosted what could well claim to be the world's first outdoor rock festival. It wasn't as big as Woodstock (15 August 1969), Glastonbury (19 September 1970), or even the Fantasy Fair and Magic Mountain Music Festival in California's Marin County (10 June 1967) that is often hailed as the world's first.

The acts weren't as big, and the promotion not as great. But Lanyon did secure rock superstar of the time Normie Rowe to headline twenty entertainers in a Battle of the Bands. The stage was on the main straight, backstage was the control tower and several thousand fans bopped on the grassy knoll opposite. There were Bathing Beauty contests (big in '66), dance competitions, even a strongest man tournament.

PIARC self-catered and oversupplied the event. And after unsuccessfully offering its leftovers to local charities, it ended up dumping them in a ravine behind Siberia.

Rowe was as big as it gets—number one on repeat. Two years later he was in the army, a conscript in the unwinnable Vietnam War. Many years on, the singer alleged to interviewers he'd been a political draftee, called up as 'Australia's Elvis Presley' to alleviate anti-war sentiment. Today he's honoured, rightly, at the National Vietnam Veterans Museum at Newhaven, at the entrance to Phillip Island.

Timing is everything.

If Lukey, Lanyon and PIARC had delayed their ambition by three years, they would have been able to build a super-circuit. The 1940 bridge connecting the island to the mainland was crumbling. Even before the first Armstrong 500, a new bridge was considered an inevitability.

In April 1966, a contract was raised to build a bigger, better bridge parallel to the existing one. That was too late for Lukey and Lanyon.

PIARC was well advanced on rebuilding the racetrack the old-fashioned way.

There had been no way to economically move heavy road-building machinery onto the island. Hot-mix asphalt, the chosen technique for a smooth, high-grip and relatively low tyre-wear surface, was simply out of the question. The equipment to lay it wasn't able to get across the old bridge to the site.

Volunteers removed the surface and prepared it for re-laying. They would use a cold-mix asphalt—not recommended for permanent pavement, but the best they could do. It would be protected by an emulsified spray seal.

'It was good for country roads, basically a mixture of tar and crushed rock,' Henk Duncan explained. 'On the road, constant movement of traffic would bed it in. At Phillip Island, it was okay for a while with treaded tyres, but slicks ripped the hell out of it.'

It took two and a half years from the time roadwork began for PIARC to run its first race meeting. There'd been three false starts. On Sunday, 24 September 1967, after a chilly five-degree dawn, the sun rose on a perfect rain-free day and PIARC members competed in a closed club race meeting. Their cars were peppered with stones, fired at them with shotgun intensity off the track surface. A hardy bunch of warriors had successfully, perhaps even miraculously, built a racetrack.

PIARC had become one of the largest car clubs in the country—it would be second-largest within a year—and it was populated by people who'd soon take their places as major influencers in the development of the sport.

13

The Man in Pink

On a stacked clothes rack in a well-kept storeroom of the Phillip Island Motor Racing Museum, there's a crumpled pair of pink overalls, more King Gee than Nomex. Even crammed among the garish suits of grand prix racing leathers, some worn by the greats of the sport, they stand out.

Len Lukey had the touch of the showman about him. When he chose shocking pink as the colour for his driving suit, it helped that he was colourblind.

Lukey came to the sport late and left it early. In a racing career spanning just seven years, he won the Australian Drivers' Championship, set land speed records and pioneered touring car racing. Yet his legacy is that of a simple device that became part of the soundtrack of Australia in the '60s.

Acquiring a Lukey muffler, an aftermarket exhaust

enhancement, was a rite of passage for any young owner of a hot Holden or even a 'G' (MG). Lukeys growled and occasionally roared, upset the neighbours and served as a cop-magnet. Young bucks would kid themselves that they were buying a through-flow performance part, designed to ease exhaust back pressure and add multiple horsepower to their 179 cubic inch EH 'Red' engines. But they were really buying street cred.

Sound trumped fury any day. Len Lukey single-handedly sparked an acoustic revolution.

On any main street on any Saturday night, your exhaust note was your mating cry. You'd do multiple laps until the snap, crackle, pop, growl and rumble of your tailpipe attracted the right attention. And even if that was a bit crass, there was a certain assurance in the thrum of the exhaust beneath your floorpan. Holden did the dating world a disservice when it introduced bucket seats.

Len Lukey was a welder. His dad, Frank, had raced motorbikes in the 1920s and '30s and Len initially learned his craft from him. When World War II broke out, young Len applied to the air force to become a pilot. That's when he learned about his colour blindness and the navy took him instead as a fitter and turner. He returned from the Pacific with a souvenired Japanese rifle that he hung proudly in his later workshops.

Len worked at the Commonwealth Aircraft Corporation postwar. His side hustle was making metal bathtubs. Ceramics were in short supply; scrap metal wasn't. There was good money in tin tubs.

'One day a mate said he had a dodgy exhaust,' Len's son Keith told me. 'It was a simple fix, but it got him thinking.'

By 1952, with a £100 loan from his dad, Len had a small factory making mufflers. It's easy to characterise Lukey as a simple bloke who got lucky, but he was a lot more than that. He was in the right place at the right time with the right contacts, huge ambition and a creative mind that never stopped working.

'He was the first to design electric mirrors,' Keith said proudly. 'He supplied them as OEM [original equipment] to Jaguar and Volvo.'

Len was 32 when he caught the racing bug, and even then he did it initially to promote his products. His first race car was his workshop's utility, a Ford Mainline, a massive barge of a truck festooned with Lukey signage. It captured the attention of regulator CAMS for two reasons—first, the advertising, which at the time was banned; second, it was just so beyond their expectation. People raced saloon cars, not industrial vehicles.

He swapped it out for a Ford Customline sedan, no less of a barge. At the landmark 1956 Australian Grand Prix meeting at Albert Park, he and 24-year-old Norm Beechey struck a hugely positive blow for touring car racing, sliding sideways, tyres smoking in a massive battle, in stark contrast to the open-wheelers. Beechey won the support race to the grand prix, Lukey was second.

Lukey clung to the Cusso even as he progressed through open-wheelers. In 1957 at the Australian National Speed Records, held on a ribbon of country road outside Coonabarabran on the edge of the Warrumbungle National Park, he set a new two-litre racing-car record of 147.4 mph (237.2 km/h) in his Cooper Bristol, and a 'sports car' record of 123.3 mph (198.4 km/h) in his Customline. He'd sealed the panel gaps with masking tape to enhance aerodynamics, and climbed in and out through the window.

Lukey retired from driving before he turned 40. He'd won the Gold Star in the 1959 Australian Drivers' Championship, in the ex-Jack Brabham T45 Cooper Climax, through sheer perseverance. The punishing twelve-event series took him to every state—no bad thing for a man actively promoting his mufflers. He beat Alec Mildren, another businessman-racer, by just two points.

But he never stopped motor racing.

'I first met him when I beat him at the Hepburn Springs Hill Climb,' smiled Norm Beechey, 1970 Australian touring car champion. 'He came up to me and said, "Son, if you continue to drive that car with one hand, you'll kill yourself."'

Beechey was king of the big tourers. In 1962 he imported a pillarless four-door Chevy Impala. They helped promote Beechey's growing chain of speed shops—a mecca for motoring enthusiasts. The Impala was a massive beast to fling around. Lukey, aware of the publicity value but also just attracted by the challenge, bought a new R-spec Holman-Moody Ford Galaxie to match Beechey, and because he'd retired, he hired (politely requested, actually) Lex Davison to race it for him. It was no contest.

'Davison hated me. I was from the wrong end of town,' Beechey said. 'But he couldn't drive the big Ford. He was all straight-line, and brake-then-turn, like an open-wheeler driver. He kept crashing it. I'd just hold it sideways.'

Lukey replaced Davison with Beechey. 'He invited me out to his farm on Phillip Island for a chat'—a home on Back Beach Road, bought before he acquired the circuit. 'He was picking blackberries when I arrived.' Beechey agreed to drive the Ford at Sandown. 'I was two seconds a lap quicker,' he smiled. It was an easy matter to dispose of the Chevy. Norm had specified the race car with electric windows so it would be more attractive for resale.

Beechey admired Lukey. He was no-nonsense. 'I was racing my EH Holden and Len came up to me and said, "I'd like to build you a new exhaust." I thought, "Beauty, it'll be done by his boys." Len was, after all, very successful even then. Instead he and his offsider Jack Wilson turned up at my place in dirty old overalls and did the job themselves.'

That led to a business relationship. 'When I had the speed shops, Len said, "You should be selling my mufflers. I'll send a couple of thousand dollars' worth around."' That was Lukey's style.

He'd befriended Jack Brabham early in both their careers. The 1966 and 1967 Repco Brabham engines, designed by Phil Irving and used by Brabham to win the world championship in 1966, used Lukey exhausts. His carefully crafted swirl of tuned pipes were an intrinsic component of the success of the Repco Brabham engine. It wasn't product placement or a PR stunt. Lukey innately knew how to extract exhaust from a racing engine.

Len Lukey died on 28 October 1978. He'd hidden a melanoma-induced cancer from family, friends and associates. 'He was in Queensland when he fell really ill,' Keith Lukey recalled sadly. 'Bib Stillwell sent a Learjet to pick him up. He went straight to the Mercy Hospital where he died.'

For more than 25 years, Lukey's Gold Star-winning Cooper T45 was displayed in the Phillip Island Motor Racing Museum and occasionally raced by Keith: 'I have the scar on my face from where Stirling Moss threw up a stone during a historic race.'

Then it passed to Ron Walker AC, initiator of the Melbourne-based Australian F1 Grand Prix and the Australian Motorcycle Grand Prix, according to Keith 'on a handshake promise it would remain in Australia'.

The car was sold overseas, the cause of some acrimony, which rankles with Keith. 'Happily it has now come back to Western Australia,' he told me. 'But it's different, no longer original.'

Lukey Mufflers has also passed through several owners. In a world of environmental restraint they comply, naturally, with Australian Design Rules, limiting emissions and restraining decibels. But their sales pitch, still, is: 'If it growls, it's a Lukey.'

14

Lukey Unmuffles PIARC's Potential

David Yates was going as fast as he'd ever been—upwards of 200 km/h—on Phillip Island's main straight. It was Saturday, 21 October 1967, official practice for the first open meeting on the 'new' track and his pretty little Nemesis Ford, a special made in South Australia, was tucked into the slipstream of Hoot Gibson's Lotus 15 Le Mans.

'Suddenly there were brake lights in front; everyone was slowing,' Yates, now 83, recalled with great clarity. 'A VW special had blown its engine and dumped oil all over the track, but I didn't know that until I went for my own brakes. Then it was too late. I was sliding off the track, still doing close to 200 [km/h].

'There were two figures in white right on the verge of the track. They were flag marshals, standing unprotected, maybe ten metres out from the spectator fence. I can recall the collision when I hit them and then I was 100 metres further down the straight before my car stopped. My fuel lines had torn loose and there was petrol pumping and the smell of fuel, and I bailed out quickly.

'That's when I saw the guys lying in the grass. I started to run to them, but we were right opposite the control tower and the officials from there got to me as I got to the marshals. They held me back, put me in a car and drove me away.

'One flaggie spent six months in hospital, the other three. I wanted to help then and later, but I was advised not to. It would be an admission of liability.'

Yates went through hellish uncertainty, and was even served with a summons, but he was not called, and he was told nothing more. 'I later learned there'd been a settlement. I heard a figure of $9000, a lot of money in 1967. But I don't know for sure.'

Noted motoring writer Chris de Fraga gave the incident coverage the next day in *The Age*. 'Both marshals, Brian Ellery of Windsor who was a member of the Victorian Amateur Drivers' Club, and Darryl Minter, of South Yarra, a member of the Huntingdale Auto Club, were in the Alfred Hospital yesterday in a satisfactory condition,' he wrote. 'They suffered leg injuries.' Not a great way to open Phillip Island's new era.

Yates raced on. 'At the next meeting, the announcer pointed out new marshal barriers, built to give them some security. Then he pointed to me on the grid and said, "This is the guy who made it happen."' David took it as a positive.

David Yates had his last race aged 71. He'd won the 1970 Sandown 250 teams' prize with Allan Moffat and Bob Holden in a brace of Fords, taken a two-decade break to raise a family, then, well past 50, he joined his sons Timothy and Cameron to race HQ Holdens.

'Motor racing is dangerous.' It's a disclaimer on every entry ticket. For the eleven years of Len Lukey's ownership, and John and Russell Lanyon's stewardship, Phillip Island had a dream run. It was only at its last open meeting in January 1978 that a fatality occurred, attributed to a heart attack as a consequence of a crash.

John Lanyon was ambitious. Phillip Island had been built by club members for club sport, but the track deserved so much more. It was truly a grand prix circuit, fast, flowing, challenging and—uniquely—visually compelling. From certain points of its landscape, spectators could watch most of the action all of the time.

Lanyon went for broke. He applied to CAMS for rounds of the touring car title and the Australian Drivers' Championship series. He began a dialogue with what became Motorcycling Australia to bring the grand prix and their Tourist Trophy (the Senior title of the two) to the Island.

He came up with a big idea. The Phillip Island 500 was reborn. The Island's reputation had been built on the success of the Armstrong 500. For all the open-wheeler and two-wheel motor racing—even at its peak domestic level—it was the long-distance production-car race that had captured the nation's attention. Australia's Great Race had been PIARC's gift to Mount Panorama, which built on the foundation.

In 1971, CAMS inaugurated the Australian Manufacturers' Championship, a title run separately to the Australian Touring Car Championship and intended to reward the car, not the driver. Lanyon seized the opportunity. The Manufacturers' Championship (Manchamps) would be run over five rounds, including a sprint race at Bathurst at Easter. The formats would alter slightly over the seasons but the Phillip Island 500 would be the longest and toughest.

Eighteen-year-old Colin Bond watched the first Armstrong 500 from Lukey Heights. Bond and his schoolmate Andy Frankel had driven down from Sydney on a whim. 'We were in my supercharged bug-eye Sprite,' Bond recalled, his trademark smile and raucous laugh not far from his lips. 'I was an apprentice at Grenville Motors, under the Harbour Bridge, and it was nothing on a Friday night for Andy and I to leave from there to go to a race meeting, somewhere.

'We got as far as Albury before we ran out of petrol with everything shut up, so we slept the night in the car, not comfortable in a tiny two-seater. We got to Phillip Island in time for the race start, watched a couple of hours, then headed back home again so we wouldn't be late for work.'

The Sprite wasn't quick, but it made it in time. 'There were no open-road speed limits,' Bond cackled. 'You knew you were going good from the look on the faces of the people coming towards you.'

Round trip—2200 kilometres. Expenses: as much as a £5 apprentice's wages could afford. 'I was earning an extra three guineas [three pounds, three shillings] playing for a local soccer club,' he said. 'I always knew I wanted to be in professional sports—I just didn't know which one. Soccer and golf didn't cost a lot. Motor racing did.'

The Phillip Island sojourn tipped the balance. 'My one major recollection was that there were a lot of VW Beetles racing, and they were affordable.' He entered a Beetle in the 1964 Round Australia Trial. Along with Frankel and another young mate, George Shepheard, son of Reg, the instigator of the Round Australia adventures, they came fourth in class and won the Young Guns award.

Bond captured the attention of outright winner Harry Firth. Within a decade, driving for Firth's Holden Dealer team, he'd win Bathurst (1969), three Australian Rally Championships (1971, '72 and '74) and the 1975 Australian Touring Car Championship, becoming the only competitor ever to claim both the race and rally titles. In 1971, he was on the front row for the inaugural Phillip Island 500.

Bond was king of the Torana XU-1s. Holden had been in an arms race with Ford: the Monaro 350 GTS versus a succession of Falcon GT-HOs. But as Ford built bigger, more powerful Falcons, General Motors went the other way. The Torana XU-1 was smaller, lighter, more nimble and much kinder to its components.

'Harry Firth came up with the XU-1,' Bond recalled. 'The Monaro's brakes were never good enough for the big car but put them on the lighter Torana and they worked really well.'

Bond won on debut in Firth's straight-six-cylinder XU-1 at Warwick Farm in late 1970, using his better brakes to pass one car per lap down into Creek Corner. He beat home Bob Jane in a Monaro GTS, 'who kept trying to punt me off', then spent 1971 dominating the Australian Rally Championship, along with the long-distance Dulux Rally and the Southern Cross Rally. 'It was a better rally car than a race car,' Bond claimed.

In 1971, Phillip Island was part racetrack, part rally stage. Three years into its new iteration, the track was already becoming a patchwork quilt. As the spray-sealed surface inevitably broke up, the only option was to apply temporary repairs. The chosen material was concrete.

'We were still carrying debt from resealing the circuit,' PIARC's Geoff Bull said. 'We couldn't afford to reseal it again, even though the new San Remo Bridge now allowed heavy machinery onto the island. Our only solution was a permanently temporary one.'

The club effected emergency repairs only the night before practice. Teams rolled out onto a carpet of stones, which needed to be cleared off the racing line. It was good news for Bond but bad for rival Allan Moffat, whose Falcon GT-HO would suffer tyre wear.

In the race, Harry Firth accentuated Moffat's woes. He sent his second driver, young Peter Brock, to harass Moffat while he held Bond back to cruise home after just one stop at the halfway point. Moffat suffered a calamitous blowout and came fifth. Bond won by eight seconds from Brock.

The plan had been perfect. Holden won the manufacturers' title by two points from Ford.

'I liked Phillip Island a lot,' Bond reflected. 'It was a fast, flowing circuit, and I liked the concrete. The corners had grip. It was a bit like a rally. You'd head for the grip amongst the holes.'

Phillip Island suited the Torana. 'The Fords were better on stop–go tracks. We were much lighter and easier on tyres.' But tyres were hard to come by. The trick was to get in Harry Firth's good books. 'He'd sometimes have only one set [of good ones] and you had to be a bit cunning to get them from Brock.' Bond worked out it was best to provide Firth with autosuggestion, to make it his idea.

In the seven years of the Phillip Island 500, Bond won three times to Brock's two. Allan Moffat and Allan Grice won it once each. One Ford, six Holdens.

It was never without drama.

In 1972, Bond was on the front row, alongside Moffat, when his XU-1 jammed in first gear. 'I had a different start technique to most people,' Bond said. 'I'd wait until about fifteen seconds to the flag before I'd put it in gear, then I'd gently let up the clutch to make sure I was okay.' But he didn't check the shift to second. At the flag, the lever wouldn't move. His quick reactions saved him from a rear-end collision. Moffat won, Brock was second, Bond scrambled to fifth.

In 1973, Allan Moffat had what was then the worst crash of his career.

Moffat rated Phillip Island 'the most challenging of all Australian circuits. Nothing, not even Bathurst, matched that track in its requirement for absolute precision and preservation,' he told me for his autobiography *Climbing the Mountain*. Allan, sadly, is an Alzheimer's sufferer, a brave ambassador for Dementia Australia. In 2017, before the condition had totally gripped him, I sat with him as he recalled his terrible moment.

'Peter Brock and I staged a monumental battle for twenty-three laps before I just had to stop for new tyres, dropping to eighth. I'd worked my way up to fourth by lap fifty-one when I needed two new front tyres, again.

'I got back to second, but I knew it couldn't last. Eighty laps into the 102-lap race, the wheels started to wobble, so badly it felt terminal. I screamed into the pits and looked up at team manager Howard Marsden on the pit box and asked him to check for flat spots, those points on the tyre that make it out of round and difficult to drive. Worse, they can cause a tyre to blow out. He looked at them in a cursory fashion and waved me away. "Go!" he called, not wanting to lose any more time.

'It seems he didn't check well enough. The vibration was worse, and I was contemplating murder when the tyre blew. At just under 200 kilometres an hour, I was off into the long grass at the side of the track, then I hit a ditch and rolled. The impact was so great that my belts stretched, and my sternum cracked. I staggered from the wreck and then collapsed. I was struggling for breath and the pain was immense.'

Ford announced its withdrawal from the sport in January 1974, but Moffat returned, heading a Ford dealer team. His co-driver for 1977 would be Colin Bond.

In 1974, a plane crash stopped the Phillip Island 500.

'We were pulled up on the grid, ready for the start, and we heard it first before we saw it,' Colin Bond recalled. His brand-new V8 Torana SL/R 5000 had claimed pole position for the Holden Dealer Team. Robyn Bond, Colin's wife, took up the story. 'It was a plane landing with the wind behind it. It was going too fast, trying to take off again and trying to clear the dam,' she said. 'But he needed more power. Instead he dropped tail-first into the dam. It was just behind the pits. All the mechanics left the grid and ran across. It was a plane full of Mazda executives. And it was upside down and underwater. They got them out safely, and we got on with the race.'

It was just as well Robyn was there. The electronic timing equipment had developed a mind of its own, recording too fast and then too slow. Robyn, along with other motor-racing wives and partners, carried a bank of stopwatches, so they determined grid positions. Colin Bond won that year.

Brock won in 1975, independent of the Holden Dealer Team; he had left at the end of the '74 season. Then Bond won again in 1976, in his last drive for the Holden Dealer Team. In two years, Harry Firth lost his two stars.

According to Bond, 'Brock left because he was married to Miss Australia [Michelle Downes] and thought he was Mister Australia.' It was maybe not as unkind a comment as it seems. 'Brock had become frustrated with Harry and tried to convince our sponsors to support him instead. That wasn't going to happen—at least not with Holden's agreement.'

Bond left for money. 'When he joined me it was for more money than he'd ever earned at Holden—the whole house, not just half of it,' Allan Moffat told me. After their classic 1-2 finish at 1977 Bathurst, when Bond yielded to his team leader, the accuracy of Moffat's assertion failed the test, at least in the eyes of the Bonds. They pursued him for bonus money owed. The Bonds' later reconciliation with Moffat, financial and personal, took some years.

In 1977, post-Bathurst, Bond was the sole representative of the Moffat Ford Dealer Team at the Phillip Island 500. The pair had sewn up the manufacturers' title and Moffat was loath to race for no purpose. Bond was leading with six laps to go, managing his tyre condition, when his front right tyre blew. He limped to fifth.

'That was the race Peter Janson won,' Robyn Bond recalled, tongue-in-cheek. The Bonds used to stay with the outrageous 'Captain' Janson at his 'towers' in Melbourne, not by choice but because Harry Firth billeted them there cheaply. Janson was the sport's most colourful character. In decor, his home was part bordello, part Madame Tussauds. The scar on his cheek, partly concealed by his black beard, was from a race crash, or a slash in a swordfight, or a misplaced mallet in a game of polo in India. Take your pick.

Janson was a personality and a pain in the neck for Phillip Island. 'He'd send down a double-decker London bus as a hospitality centre, then drive down in his Rolls-Royce for a bit of show,' Mike Lanyon, Russell's son, happily recalled.

'But he had a major problem abiding by the rules,' Lanyon added. 'At one meeting, we kept track of his misdemeanours. The list totalled seventeen by the end of Sunday. For the next meeting we sent him a list of the seventeen conditions under which we would accept his entry. Knowing Peter, he probably framed it and pinned it on the back of his toilet door.'

You couldn't help but love Janson. For all his unconventionality, he was a highly competent racer who deserved a victory. In 1977, the timing gear failed again, and they gave him the win on national TV. He responded with an ebullient acceptance speech. Everyone cheered. It was only later that timekeepers discovered the real winner had been Allan Grice. 'PIARC officials were relieved and appreciative of the stoic manner in which Grice accepted the incident,' Lanyon observed.

Janson kept the trophy.

'We used to stay out at San Remo, because it was cheaper for the team,' Robyn Bond said. 'But the parties were at the Isle of Wight Hotel.' Those were the days when there was still time for congeniality. Even as the teams celebrated Janson's win, there was already speculation they were gathering for the last time at the Island.

15

Hear the Thunder

Kevin Bartlett, already twice winner of the Gold Star in a brace of sweet-handling Formula One cars, pointed his massive and comparatively ill-handling Formula 5000 Lola at the fastest corner in motorsport—and kept his foot flat.

It was a moment of extreme bravery, maybe foolhardiness, and certainly self-confidence.

Max Stewart, Johnnie Walker, John McCormack, and John Leffler were in the pits, their engines shut down. Only Bartlett—'KB', as he was universally known—was live. The thunderous roar of his five-litre Chevrolet V8, building to 8500 rpm as he amassed speed down the main straight, was the signal of his determination to do what no driver had achieved before.

'It was practice for the Gold Star round in 1973,' Bartlett said from his home in leafy Maleny, in the backwoods of Queensland's

Sunshine Coast. 'We'd been going to Phillip Island for three years by then, each time with cars that were a little better and a little faster, and every time knowing a bit more about the track.

'I said to my crew chief, John Anderson ['Ando', who would become one of the greatest-ever crew chiefs in Indy 500], "I reckon I can take Turn 1 flat," and he looked at me with a glint in his eye and he said, "S'give it a go."'

The boys—the band of drivers who adopted and committed to the most awesome customer-based open-wheeler formula the world had ever devised—had been talking about Turn 1 all day. In past years taking it without lifting had been unattainable. Around Phillip Island, the more places you could stay flat the better.

'You could do Turn 3 flat—there was a lot of time to be made up there. And at Siberia you needed to be flat on the second apex,' Bartlett recalled. But Turn 1 remained the so-far-unachieved unknown. It wasn't just a case of whether it could be done. There was also the question of what benefit it would bring.

'We didn't have electronics or rev limiters or traction control,' Bartlett said. 'Every gain you made [on track] depended on the intelligence of the driver. Phillip Island was a fast-flowing circuit. You had to look at it in its entirety, rather than one corner at a time like on a stop–go circuit.'

In his lexicon of circuit descriptions, Bartlett's image of the Island is New Age poetic: 'Phillip Island allows a driver to express themself.' It did for him. Someone had to be the Turn 1 pioneer. There was a strong argument that he was best suited for the job.

For his entire career, Bartlett carried the epithet 'Big Rev Kev'. He hated it. He saw himself as a stylist. It's just that his style was oversteer, tail hanging out, correcting the slide. 'You'd turn into a corner smartly, not violently, and by the time you hit the apex you'd be on full throttle with your nose pointed down the next straight.' He relied on the flighty brilliance of the Weismann locker differential to enhance his technique. The locker governed delivery of power to the drive wheels. Applied precisely, it was his friend and ally. Get it wrong and it would bite with instantaneous loss of control. 'Luckily my reflexes were pretty good,' he smiled.

Phillip Island, though, presented a conundrum.

Two forces keep a race car on the road at maximum speed—aerodynamics and mechanical grip. Aero-induced downforce could help settle a car under braking and stick it to the ground in the corners. But the more downforce your wings created, the less speed you'd get down Phillip Island's long straight.

In 1973, aerodynamics in motor racing were rudimentary. There were no cockpit controls to change wing angles, no drag-reduction system. Yet to get through Turn 1 flat a certain amount of downforce to keep the car glued to the track would be handy. It was a question of balance.

Bartlett was the master of mechanical grip. He had a natural feel for the adhesion between the contact patch of his tyres and the Island's jittery surface. He backed himself.

'For a quick lap you had to come out onto the straight as hard as you could,' Bartlett recounted. 'I came onto the straight in fourth, then snatched fifth a third of the way down and watched the revs build until it was maxed out before the turn in point,' he recalled of the moment. And then, nudging 300 km/h, he eased into the fastest right-hander on any Australian track.

He never lifted.

The thunder of his exhaust remained constant, way down into Turn 2, and then he was out and accelerating away towards the hairpin.

The boys in the pits, especially Ando, exhaled.

'When I got back, the boys all said, "Bastard! If you can do it, so can we." I never told them that while I'd got through [Turn] one flat, it set me up horribly for [Turn] two. I missed the braking point and had a big moment.'

One by one they all learned for themselves—all except McCormack, who'd already worked out the futility of the attempt and didn't try.

Phillip Island was made for Formula 5000.

They were the hot rods of open-wheel formula racing. A genuine, purpose-built tub, initially designed for global Formula Two, with a five-litre small-block V8, usually a Chevy, bolted behind and weighing something like 240 kilograms—way too heavy if you were a stickler for conventional design. It was a case of Formula One meets NASCAR. And on the wide-open spaces of Phillip Island, a driver could give a Formula 5000 car its head.

F5000s sat on tiny wheels with a 13-inch (33-centimetre) diameter—as wide as they were round at the front and even wider (17 inches/43 centimetres) at the rear. They developed so much power that they were still wheel-spinning at 220 km/h. It took heroes to drive them.

Australia adopted F5000 as its national F1 category in 1970. It replaced the purist 2.5-litre formula that served the early Tasman Series. Back then, European world champions came to Australia in the off-season, hoping to sell their redundant last-season cars to the locals. But Australia had fallen out of sync with Europe's fluctuating F1 rules. F5000, gaining traction in America and as a second-tier formula in Europe, was the obvious but not necessarily popular replacement.

The impossible dream, promoted by purists at CAMS, was a unitary F1 car, chassis and engine built to act as one. It was expensive, and unsustainable in far-flung Australia. F5000, using a stock-block motor that could power your Speedcar, speedboat or even tow car, was the achievable compromise.

The tipping point was money from big tobacco. In the '70s, motor racing was a high-speed billboard for the cigarette industry. Rothmans not only funded F5000 but pretty much took over its promotion. When it came to attracting international entrants to the Australasian series, the tobacco company's sports marketing team, headed by former sports journalist Jim Shepherd, was in charge of acquisition.

For almost a decade, F5000 was a runaway success. It spurred a local industry. For every English-made Chevron or Lola (largely designed by Australian Frank Gardner), there were matching Matichs (Sydney), McRaes (New Zealand), Beggs (New Zealand) and Elfins (Adelaide). For a time, F5000 became Australia's largest motor-racing export opportunity.

Danger was the norm. In early versions, especially of the British-made Lola, the pedal box, inside which the driver's feet danced between brake and accelerator, was forward of the front axle. In a nose-first collision, a driver's feet, ankles and legs became unintended shareholders in devastating energy absorption. They shattered on impact. The so-called 'Lola limp' was an all-too-prevalent outcome, a sometimes crippling disability that afflicted the driver for life. Australian Grand Prix winner Warwick Brown, New Zealand Grand Prix winner Graeme Lawrence and Kevin Bartlett all still suffer.

The A-cars, so-called because that's what they were known as in the United States, kept open-wheel racing relevant well past its use-by date. Touring cars were taking over—everyone knew that—but in their time, the F5000s were thunderous dinosaurs that faded before our very eyes.

John McCormack won the first F5000 race on Phillip Island. In another seven attempts, he never won again. But he did use the Island strategically to win three Gold Stars and become, by that measure, the most successful domestic open-wheeler driver of the F5000 era.

His win in the 1971 Victorian Road Racing Championship was a victory on debut for the Elfin MR5, designed and manufactured by South Australian enthusiast builder Garrie Cooper.

Elfin had been in business since 1959 when Cooper and his father, Cliff, a former racer, set it up in Conmurra Avenue, Edwardstown, a southern suburb of Adelaide. Garrie, a good but not great racer, had already used his lesser-formula Elfin to win the 1968 Australian Formula Two (1.5-litre) championship, and he'd travelled to Singapore to win that country's grand prix too, on the old and dangerous Thomson Road street circuit.

In all, Elfin would win 29 national titles and become Australia's most successful domestic manufacturer.

McCormack was the most unlikely of racers. The Tasmanian garage proprietor, a married father of five, sold up and moved to the mainland to pursue his motor-racing passion. He was three-time Tasmanian champion and already pushing 30. 'I made sure I put enough aside that I had investments which would deliver us a basic living,' he told me. That was Johnny Mac, the most measured man you'd ever meet.

He formed an alliance with Garrie Cooper to go F5000 racing. 'I was never his partner, only ever his customer,' McCormack said. But he was a customer with a lot of sway. At Phillip Island that first time, he introduced Garrie Cooper to John Lanyon. 'We wanted to contest the upcoming Tasman Series [in Australia and New Zealand],' McCormack said. 'And we needed money. John Lanyon was a smooth talker, so we asked him to help.'

The Lanyon brothers had organised, as only they could, a sidebar event at Phillip Island—a Fashions in the Field contest. It was part-sponsored by Ansett, Australia's second major air carrier at the time. Lanyon and McCormack put a proposition to Ansett's senior management. 'We were only after $1500 for air travel, and they agreed,' McCormack recalled. 'But Lanyon hyped it up. We became Ansett Team Elfin and, as far as anyone externally knew, it was a huge deal. We got so much publicity.

'I never met Sir Reginald Ansett, but I heard he told his board it was the best promotion they'd ever done. They came back to us and said, "How much do you really want?"'

A conservative person by nature, McCormack was concerned for the airline's reputation. 'I was fearful of having Ansett's name on our wings, and what would happen if we ended up in a fence.'

McCormack's first win on the mainland had been at Phillip Island in an Elfin Formula Two car, fitted with a 2.5-litre Repco Brabham engine. He won the Victorian Road Racing Championship. 'That was my first test of myself. I knew I could be competitive with the best in the country. I could win if I chose to win, and if I didn't then I knew there was a reason.'

McCormack had a good rapport with Repco's engine development manager, Malcolm Preston. McCormack's first MR5 F5000 was fitted with the five-litre Holden-based Repco engine.

F5000 had been promoted as an affordable Australian National Formula One (ANF1). In practice, that was open to some debate, exacerbated by the rise in popularity of touring car racing. McCormack's Elfin had a retail value of some $15,500—still a lot, but that was key money. Operational costs chewed up a lot more. Increasingly, the big money was going to touring cars. It took a brave heart to pursue F5000.

Kevin Bartlett had won two Australian Drivers' Championships under the patronage of Alec Mildren, the 1960 Gold Star and Australian Grand Prix winner. Max Stewart had won the Formula Two (1.5-litre) title for Mildren. The bright-yellow Mildren cars—one, naturally, dubbed the Yellow Submarine—had been a prominent force in the closing days of the previous ANF1 category. But Mildren had baulked at F5000. 'He just lost interest,' Bartlett said. 'He gave Max and I a lot of notice, then bought a bigger boat and went fishing.'

Bartlett and Stewart pursued F5000 as privateers. Struggling financially, they pooled their resources, moved into shared premises just off the beach at Manly on Sydney's northern peninsula, and attempted to find some economies of scale.

In 1972, Bartlett, with some backing from Rothmans' brand Chesterfield and Shell, brought his newly acquired

Lola T300 to Phillip Island for the Victorian Road Racing Championship, which was not a round of the Australian Drivers' Championship that year. He put it on the front row, next to John McCormack's pole-sitting Elfin.

On the warm-up lap, Bartlett suffered bird strike. Fortunately it was seagulls. 'The [Cape Barren] geese are bigger, but they're more car aware,' Bartlett semi-joked. 'You can see them pecking at the side on the verge, but they don't come onto the track. They're either super intelligent or super lucky.'

When the gulls struck, Bartlett ducked: 'That's all you could do.' One grazed his helmet and disappeared into his air cooler. The start was delayed as his crew removed the remains and restored the engine's air passage.

The race between Bartlett and McCormack was a seesawing classic. Bartlett took the flag by just 0.2 seconds and claimed a new lap record of 1 minute 40.4 seconds (168.8 km/h).

His defence of the title in 1973 highlighted the parlous state of the F5000 privateer. Max Stewart was at Phillip Island for the first time. (Four years later, he would be killed at the wheel of his F5000 car.) Stewart blew his engine in the first practice session, borrowed a replacement from Bartlett but damaged that on Saturday. In Sunday's warm-up, the repaired replacement caught fire. Simultaneously Bartlett broke his engine. With just hours to go, the pair built one car out of two, with Bartlett to drive. The engine lost its coolant and Bartlett drove it to a stuttering fourth.

Two months later, John McCormack endured two engine failures in practice but finished second, a lap down on South Australian Johnnie Walker, just enough to claim his first Australian Drivers' Championship by a mere three points. It didn't come easily. He, Walker and Bartlett were locked in an intense battle for the lead. 'There was so much wind buffeting,' McCormack said. 'My right-hand side mirror disintegrated. It was like losing an eye. I didn't know where the others were, and it was highly dangerous. I couldn't operate like that, so I backed off to see what would happen. Sure enough, they both went off.' Walker recovered to win. McCormack hung back and strategically claimed his Gold Star.

He won it again in 1975 and 1977. By then, controversially, he'd moved on from Elfin.

He'd become dissatisfied with Elfin's F5000 package. He was looking for a winning advantage. 'I was having dinner with Phil Irving at Barry Street, Carlton, John Lanyon's business premises, and old Phil said, "Have a look at the aluminium Rover engine." It was on display at the nearby Melbourne Motor Show. It was the engine fitted to the Leyland P76 Force 7. Lanyon arranged a meeting with Peter North, managing director of Leyland. North said he wanted it developed at a professional level, so we dropped Phil Irving's name. That did the trick.'

For McCormack, there was a problem with the Elfin chassis. McCormack contended that Garrie Cooper should have used more robust construction. 'Garrie and I were like brothers,' he conceded. 'But he wasn't capable of driving the chassis hard enough to find its breaking point. F1 cars use chrome moly; Garrie was using mild steel. If you find it cracking, you pack it up and take it home. If it fails at the wrong place, you're dead.'

McCormack went in search of an F1 tub. He found it in South Africa: the McLaren M23 in which Peter Revson had won the 1973 British Grand Prix, and which was then used by Dave Charlton to win the South African domestic series.

The McLaren-Leyland was a rocket ship. McCormack used the combination to win his third Gold Star.

'It didn't have the power of the Chev V8s, but it was aerodynamically balanced and sensitive,' he smiled. He'd even been tempted to emulate Bartlett's rush into Turn 1. '"She'll go through there flat without lifting," I thought, but then I said to myself, "Wake up, dickhead."'

In 1977, McCormack qualified a startling 2.2 seconds clear of a packed field of four purpose-built Lola F5000s, and his 1 minute 34.3 seconds (183.24 km/h) was the fastest lap ever around that iteration of the Island. In the race, the M23 lapped the field. Then it expunged its coolant and lubricant. With two laps to go, McCormack pulled to the pits, waited, then took the flag in third place, enough to claim his third title by three points. Typically strategic.

Phillip Island management was cock-a-hoop. They'd been granted the Australian F1 Grand Prix for 1978. It would coincide with the 50th anniversary of the first-ever grand prix, held on the island's road course.

But it didn't happen. McCormack's Gold Star victory, and John Leffler's win in the same race, was the last time F5000 cars would compete at Phillip Island. Kevin Bartlett (three wins), Johnnie Walker (two), Alfredo Costanzo, John Leffler and John McCormack (one each) would be enshrined as the Island's F5000 victors.

In seven seasons, even on a spasmodically disintegrating surface, the F5000s had lowered the lap record from 1 minute

49.11 seconds (158.37 km/h) in 1971, to 1 minute 36.5 seconds (179.07 km/h). Both were set by John McCormack.

Formula 5000 was on its way out. In 1982, the category was replaced by another Australian National Formula One—for 1.6-litre, four-cylinder cars complying with Formula Pacific, a derivation of Europe's Formula Atlantic. In 1989, Australia's domestic category morphed into Formula Holden, then Formula Brabham, using 3.8-litre Buick V6 engines. From 2005 to 2014, the Gold Star was decided in Formula Three cars, then abandoned as the field dwindled. CAMS (which changed its name to Motorsport Australia in 2020) determined it did not want to see its Gold Star devalued, and placed it in mothballs. In 2021, a newly minted series, S5000, using an F3 tub and a 5.2-litre, four-valve V8 motor, became the new Australian Drivers' Championship. Phillip Island was included on the race schedule.

16

New Year for Bikes

Kel Carruthers was back. His dad Jack had resurrected their eight-year-old grand prix Honda Four for one last crack at the Island at the 1969 Australian Motorcycle Grand Prix. The Honda had been under dust sheets at the back of Jack's Gladesville workshop since it had last raced in 1966. It was New Year's Day—the start of the year in which Kel would win the 250cc world championship.

He'd been in Europe for three years, knocking on the door. He'd not yet won a grand prix, although on points he'd claimed third in the 1968 350cc world title, riding as a privateer on an Aermacchi. The Italian firm was so impressed that they'd offered him a works ride for 1969. He was on his way up. The Phillip Island crowd greeted him as a hero, as if he was already their world champion.

Almost 10,000 people showed up, the biggest crowd the Island had seen.

Motorcycles weren't a major part of the Phillip Island revival. The accent had been on cars, weighted heavily towards tourers and F5000s. The Hartwell Motorcycle Club, home of road racing, secured one annual slot: a combined car/bike meeting, the 2+4, each January.

The bikes' hard-fought racing during the Lukey era cemented the Island's reputation as a motorcycle super-circuit-in-waiting.

'In Europe, I'd become used to riding on bad surfaces, sometimes paved with cobblestones,' Carruthers said. 'We'd race around the houses where the next corner was unsighted. Phillip Island was a bit similar. There was a big, long, fast corner onto the straight and it was lined with trees, and you couldn't see around them. The concrete patches were really pretty easy.' Carruthers' report was telling: it was just a year since PIARC had begun its restoration of the track, and already it was becoming a patchwork quilt. There was no shortage of bikes for Kel. The Hartwell club entered him across the card.

His first race was a wake-up call. He was leading the Ultra-Lightweight (125cc) race on a Bultaco borrowed from enthusiastic patron Jack Gates when he 'kind of fell asleep'. Well in the lead, Carruthers let his mind drift and backed off the pace. Young motocross rider Graeme Smith broke the lap record on the last lap, nicked into Kel's slipstream, then leaped out at the last moment to win by half a bike's length.

The locals had come a long way in three years.

The old Honda Four was up against current works-specced Yamahas and Kawasakis in the 250cc and 350cc GPs. Never perfect, it was still 'shaking its head off' over Lukey Heights. Carruthers put his head down, aware the crowd had come to see not only him but to see and hear his world-shattering bike at full noise. He won both events, smoked them, although Victorian Dick Reid's Kawasaki was fast closing towards the end of the 350cc GP. 'It would have been a huge letdown if it didn't win,' Kel, said, still relieved.

In Carruthers' absence, Sydney builder Ron Toombs had assumed the mantle of top local racer. Toombs was a hard man and, at the same time, one of the great stylists. 'He was so precise,' Kel recalled. Toombs was on a locally tuned Matchless G50 with a four-valve head devised by its Sydney owner Tony Henderson. The G50 had dominated from the time Kel went away. For the 500cc race, Carruthers was on a borrowed Norton.

The pair raced wheel to wheel in the 500cc and Unlimited GPs. Toombs won the first, after a mechanical failure on Kel's bike—a pity, because there should be no excuse. In the Unlimited, they traded the lead several times each lap. Carruthers prevailed by centimetres. Queenslander John Warrian, trying to stay with them, set a new lap record of 2 minutes 4 seconds (139.35 km/h), then crashed.

It had been a huge race. 'I recall [Kawasaki race boss] Neville Doyle saying years later it was the first time he'd heard anyone take Turn 1 wide open,' Kel said, still a bit proud. 'I might have gone back a gear,' he added.

Carruthers returned to Europe, and won the Isle of Man 250cc TT and the 250cc world title.

The most abiding memory Victorian Grand Prix winner Mick Hone has of the inaugural 2+4 meeting in 1968 isn't of a motorcycle. 'It was a blue Austin A30 with a big bum,' he told me. 'When you looked at it from behind, the rear wheels were so wide they almost touched in the middle.'

The A30 belonged to a long-haired roughie from Hurstbridge, a rural community north-east of Melbourne's expanding suburban boundary. Peter Brock was debuting at Phillip Island and having only his second race meeting in his home-built A30 sports sedan. It had a 179 cubic inch straight-six Holden engine shoehorned into the engine bay.

Naturally, he won his class and claimed the class lap record.

'I didn't meet Brock then,' Hone recounted. 'That came much later when I was knocking around with [Brock's teammate and associate] John Harvey.' Brock and Hone were mates for 30 years. 'He was interested in anything that moved.'

They lived in parallel universes, both of them perpetually inquisitive, both seeing poetry in mechanical endeavour. Then, in 2006, Brock asked Hone to join him in a couple of Targa road rallies—nothing serious, just a bit of fun. 'It was out of the blue, unexpected,' Hone said. 'He knew me as someone who could organise, who could make things happen.' Hone was sitting alongside Brock as his navigator when the driver regarded as the most successful and most revered of his generation went off, mid-stage, into a tree at Gidgegannup, 40 kilometres north of Perth, and died instantly.

Hone was sixteen in 1968 when he went to Phillip Island for the first time. 'I was there with John Maher, who worked as a tractor driver for my dad,' Hone recalled. Maher was a capable

A-grade rider. He was happy for Mick and his brother Martin to tag along.

Gordon Hone ran a machine-hire business. The Hones were into bikes. 'I was never going to race cars,' Mick said, recalling long road trips, aged five, with his parents in his dad's sidecar outfit. Gordon tuned bikes for guys on the edge of the sport, outliers like the outrageous A.D. Pimm, who drove a Cadillac convertible and raced a featherbed Vincent called The Beast.

In 1969, aged seventeen, Hone 'was on a 125cc Yamaha road bike, midway through Southern Loop, thinking I was travelling at world-record pace, when Ron Toombs came by me on the Matchless G50. He was whistling. I'd never seen anything so quick.'

Hone developed into a more-than-competent racer: winner of the Victorian Grand Prix at Phillip Island in 1977; winner of the Australian TT; winner of the Castrol Three Hour; for a time, the production-bike lap record holder at Phillip Island by eleven seconds; then onwards to become one of the sport's most successful team owners and promoters of young talent as a Suzuki expert.

Looking back, his honest (if harsh) self-assessment is that he wasn't Brock, gifted beyond the skills of a mortal. 'There were blokes going faster, easier,' he mused. 'But being in the field was the best way to watch races.'

For Hone, the 1970s were the golden era of motorcycling, and Phillip Island and Mount Panorama were the citadels. The era was also the most lethal.

In 1968, his hero Ron Toombs threw the Henderson Matchless away after just two laps leading the 500cc grand prix, caught out by surface gravel at Siberia. South Australian Bill Horsman—so impecunious that he travelled, slept and lived in and out of his utility, relying on the kindness of race promoters to provide basic ablution facilities—won by a whisker.

At Phillip Island in 1973 Toombs won every solo race from the 125cc to the Unlimited. It was a first, and no one has repeated the feat since.

On the strength of that dominance, Neville Doyle hired him to head Kawasaki's new team. Toombs' three-cylinder, air-cooled, two-stroke H2R ingested a stone from the circuit first time out, in the December 1973 meeting. It was a bitter pill, but the Kawasaki dealers stuck with Doyle. The next year, Toombs won. It would be his last win at Phillip Island. He retired in 1975, handing the Kawasaki ride to the next generation.

But he couldn't stay away. In 1979, in a comeback, the 46-year-old crashed at Mount Panorama and was killed.

Back in 1970, South Australian youngster Kenny Blake had used a 730cc Triumph Special to beat Toombs in the Unlimited Australian TT at the Island. To be fair, Toombs was on a 350cc Yamaha. Blake was a member of the Phoenix Motorcycle Club, formed by a few friends in 1964. Growing up, they'd spent their weekends racing over a 300-kilometre course they'd mapped out on the Fleurieu Peninsula, swooping by cars and tractors on the road, taking advantage of low police presence.

Brothers Les and Deane Jesser built the Triumph out of the remnants of Blake's road bike. Phillip Island was a big win. He went on to claim eleven national titles, and the coveted Tom Phillis Memorial Trophy, the most treasured trophy of Island motorcycling.

In 1981 Blake was killed at the Isle of Man, just like Phillis had been. His hometown of Strathalbyn commissioned a statue, welded from mechanical parts. It stands in the main street.

Sydney rider Bryan Hindle was third in the 1970 Unlimited TT behind Blake and Toombs. He crashed heavily at Mount Panorama and, for the sake of his family, decided not to chance the odds and retired. He took up the much safer sport of ultra-light flying and died at an air show in regional New South Wales when his engine stalled.

Sidecar riders operated on a different planet.

At the inaugural meeting in 1968, billed the Victorian Grand Prix, South Australian Alex Campbell had the Sidecar GP in his grasp—until his fuel tank split, pouring fuel over him and his swinger (sidecar passenger). NSW rider Stan Bayliss, a giant of a man, muscled his Manx Norton outfit to the line. In eleven years, six different sidecar combos would claim Island victory. Bayliss rode outfits for 49 years and won three national titles.

In 1977, Neville Doyle turned up at the Island with three young guns: Murray Sayle, Rick Perry and flaxen-haired Queenslander Gregg Hansford. Two were motorcycle racers, and one—Hansford—was a sporting superstar, a natural talent of Brock-like proportions. He was the promotional product of a Sydney entrepreneur. Vince Tesoriero, a clever young advertising executive with the hots for bikes, had turned an essentially conservative sport, run by enthusiasts for enthusiasts, into a back-page sporting spectacle.

Vince invented the Castrol Six Hour for production bikes; turned dirt-track scrambles into the sex-on-two-wheels Mr. Motocross series, enhanced by airbrushed pop-art posters; coined the word 'superbikes'; persuaded the tobacco industry into sponsorship; and created two stars—Warren Willing and Gregg Hansford.

He discarded their black leathers in favour of multicoloured suits-of-light, and got willowy Willing to grow his hair long, exuding cross-gender appeal (it worked in the music industry, why not in motorcycling?). Hansford was presented as a Queensland surfer hunk. Both images were out of character, but in 1974 at Mount Panorama, Willing and Hansford, mounted for the first time on the newly arrived Yamaha TZ750 GP 'superbikes', staged an epic race that lifted motorcycling to page one. Willing won Bathurst's Chesterfield Grand Prix by the narrowest of margins.

By 1977, Willing had taken off to Europe and Hansford had defected to Kawasaki. Yamaha, keen to keep the brand battle alive, had given Willing's bike—all stars and stripes on its fairing—to Victorian Greg Johnson. Johnson hadn't had the Tesoriero treatment.

'Johnson was a maniac,' Mick Hone grinned. He was a bit unfinished around the edges, something of a loner. But they'd pitted him against Hansford in the Tom Phillis Memorial Trophy race and that was all the incentive he needed. Hone was in the box seat, off the second row on his Suzuki RG500, 'the best seat in the house'.

For the entire race Johnson clung to the polished Hansford, both of them under the lap record. On the last corner of the last lap, Johnson was poised for a kamikaze lunge—get in the tow and pull out to pass on the line. But when they arrived over Lukey Heights, there was a bunch of lapped bikes in front. Instant decision: Hansford in the lead forced his way under them. Johnson tried for the outside, the pair sandwiching the slower riders. The extra distance was just enough to break the invisible rubber band between them. Victory to Hansford, and a new lap record of 2 minutes 2 seconds (141.64 km/h). Hone, on a 500cc, came home a fighting fifth.

'Later there was an Unlimited scratch race, a chance for a repeat,' Hone said. But Phillip Island's rough surface decided the contest. Hansford's steering damper broke as a result of the pounding. Without it, he was powerless, unable to control the Kawasaki. Johnson cruised to an easy victory—a bit meaningless.

Hone won the 500cc Victorian Grand Prix. He was against Johnson, both of them on RG500 Suzukis. Johnson was the most formidable of competitors. But in practice his bike had seized.

It was the two-stroke engine's constant danger. Tune it too lean for maximum power and you ran the risk of it nipping up, instantly locking the entire drivetrain, turning the rear drive wheel into a sled. Riders raced with one finger on the clutch lever. If they felt the engine going, they pulled the lever in, disconnecting the clutch to keep the rear wheel spinning. If they were a fraction late, the bike would spit them down the road.

Dicing with Hone, Johnson seized again. Johnson had left no margin for error. Hone accepted the popular win.

In 1978, Neville Doyle took Gregg Hansford to Europe, chasing the 250cc and 350cc world championships. Hansford won ten grands prix, and was second in the 250cc title and third in the 350cc in '78 and '79: a world champion in the making until injury intervened.

Johnson raced at Phillip Island without Hansford to beat. In the Victorian Grand Prix in 1978 his nearest rival was Bob Rosenthal riding a Yamaha TZ750 for Milledge Brothers.

By then the circuit was breaking up badly. 'When it was hot, the plugs of concrete all around the track were lifting,' Mick

Hone recalled. 'At Repco Corner [Turn 4], the only way to get around was to lean in, then pick the bike up to miss the concrete, then lean in again.'

There was a morning warm-up race and Johnson made his ambition clear. He blasted past Rosenthal and set a new, almost unbelievable lap record in the process—1 minute 57 seconds (147.69 km/h), five seconds faster than Hansford's mark the previous year.

'That was the difference between the two of them,' Hone said. 'Harry'—Hansford's late father's name, by which Gregg was universally known—'would go just fast enough to win. He'd set a new lap record only if it secured him a win. Even if there was no one there to beat, Greg Johnson would have done that same lap. He knew only one speed.' The record on that version of Phillip Island stands for ever. Track degradation meant the grand prix would be the patched-up circuit's last.

Johnson bolted in the Unlimited Grand Prix. It was as if he'd set the metronome and couldn't change tempo. Daylight was second. But on lap nine, the Yamaha, stretched perhaps unnecessarily to its limit, seized. It cartwheeled over and over into Len Lukey's dam, by then without Johnson on board. Bob Rosenthal won. Johnson dusted himself off and rode to second place in the 500cc race later in the meeting.

Officials salvaged the Yamaha in several pieces.

A decade later, when the dam was drained as part of the next circuit iteration, its carburettors surfaced.

17

End of the Lukey Line

Sunday, 12 March 1978: the circle was complete. Phillip Island was over and out.

Its deteriorating surface paralleled the deteriorating relationship with landowner Len Lukey. With the circuit's operating budget in the red, even the most optimistic of PIARC members found it difficult to see a way forward. A contributing factor was the race crash at the 1978 Australia Day meeting.

A strong gust of wind, unusual from the east, had unsettled the tiny Scorpion race car of Peter Fermore and it had left the track, crossed the grass verge and crashed through a wire fence. Up to sixteen spectators (no one was sure) were injured, some flown by helicopter and others transported by ambulance to Wonthaggi, Dandenong and Frankston hospitals. Francis John

White, 58, a spectator, was dead. It was said he died of a heart attack, not from the impact, a moot point.

The crash had occurred in an area just beyond where spectators had been protected by a guardrail. Surely there was an urgent need for more expenditure on security. Where would the money come from?

There was some irony in the incident. The first race at Phillip Island had been marred by the track's only race fatality. Now this marvellous, free-flowing, high-speed circuit with an enviable record of safety appeared set to close after its second fatality. It was a tragic set of bookends.

Bob King, a leading Collins Street general practitioner, renowned as Australia's greatest authority on the Bugatti racing car, had a big idea. The very first race meeting on Phillip Island, on 31 March 1928, had been the initial Australian Grand Prix. Why not celebrate its Golden Jubilee with a re-creation?

'I didn't intend it as a swansong,' King, now 86, told me as we sat in the library of his gloriously preserved, Queen Anne–architecture home in Melbourne's increasingly trendy Brighton. He lives in a suburb of subterranean garages housing Ferraris and Bentleys.

Bob's ageing Alfa is parked at the kerb, and you can't help but wonder if his near neighbours know this is a bloke who has owned seven Bugattis, five of them the classic Straight Eight. 'Only one at a time,' he clarified. 'I could never afford two.'

Bob bought his first Bug when he was still a student. The Brescia was 'worth half a Holden'. But that's not why he bought it.

'I'd grown up on a diet of motoring books and magazines,' he declared, sweeping his arm around a library crammed with books by the great automotive writers and walls displaying original illustrations, mainly of Bugattis. His bible had been Ken W Purdy's *The Kings of the Road*, the 1952 landmark publication by the American writer describing 'those fabulous automobiles that have been conceived not as sources of commercial profit or mere means of transport but as instruments of pure sensuous pleasure'.

Bob King had not been at Phillip Island for the prewar golden years, but he could imagine them. The Golden Jubilee would be his chance. 'I was an ideas man,' he smiled. 'I sold it to others and left it to them to make it happen.' The idea germinated as early as 1974, long before the fate of Phillip Island was sealed. There was a heap of work to pull it together. By the time PIARC was staring down the barrel of closure, the Golden Jubilee was no longer being driven by the committee. It was driving them.

John Lanyon had built a village of people with complementary skills and a like-minded determination to succeed. In the Lukey–Lanyon era, PIARC had structure. It had become a highly effective hierarchy, so much so that, if need be, it could survive even the loss of the circuit.

In 1966 Peter Nelson, a fledgling pharmacist, and his girlfriend (and later wife) Marcia found a flyer under the windscreen wiper of his Austin-Healey Sprite. They were at Sandown and the pamphlet invited them to join PIARC—the opposition. It was an effective piece of ambush marketing. Nelson became the most organised person in motor racing at a time when laissez-faire management was all the rage. He'd go on to be appointed secretary of the meeting at the Australian F1 Grand Prix and MotoGP.

Geoff Bull was a banker. Naturally, he became the money man. Geoff joined PIARC in 1967, and found himself running the gate at eighteen years old, collecting and accounting the proceeds. He met his wife Dawn at a motorsport New Year's Eve party in 1968. In their brand-new Holden HQSS they became multiple PIARC club motorkhana champions.

Henk Duncan knew marketing. He worked for the big retailers—a high-pressure job for one so young—and used motorsport as his weekend release. He was a natural motivator of people. He helped create Phillip Island's race management team and became its clerk of the course. His family—officially the van den Dungens—populate the sport. His son Cameron is one of its leading commentators. 'It's always been a family affair,' Cam said over dinner at Phillip Island, beaming with obvious pride in his father's achievements.

Nelson, Bull and Duncan would become PIARC presidents, Peter Nelson for two long separate terms.

PIARC had influence. The circuit wasn't, then, one of the marquee venues. But there was something about the Island. It attracted the star-makers of the future. They set the corporate and cultural compass for the future of the sport.

John Roxburgh was too big for the Island. The winner of the first Armstrong 500 became PIARC's delegate to CAMS, then represented CAMS as its delegate to the FIA in Paris. And when the FIA's controversial president Jean-Marie Balestre fell ill, he became acting world president of FISA, the FIA's motorsport arm. Not bad for a knockabout bloke known to his mates as 'Rockerbox' (motorsport slang for a cylinder head), who got his rocks off roaring his 2.2-litre F2 Cooper, illegally, around the streets of inner Melbourne.

John Pryce, the second PIARC president after Winston Maguire, was the first to define motor racing as an industry. He bridged the divide between sport and business and firmly guided CAMS general secretary Donald Kingsley Thomson to embrace commercial reality. Thomson was a self-styled purist: 'So much money and publicity has forced its way into the door, that sporting concepts have had to fly out the window,' he wrote pretentiously. Try telling that to Peter Brock or Allan Moffat. A war could so easily have erupted. Pryce became the voice of conciliation.

'John was my friend,' Allan Moffat wrote in his autobiography. 'He was genuinely my mentor. When he succumbed to a virulent cancer in 1984 it was [my wife] Pauline who regularly drove his wife Marie to the hospital. One of the saddest memories I have is of John struggling for breath in his artificial lung.'

In 1976, John Lanyon was one of the initiators of the National Motor Racing Promoters Association, a grouping of circuit owners who demanded greater collective influence in the sport's commercialisation. It was akin to starting a new political party.

Lanyon had a finger in many pies. He crossed the streams.

He held the title of team manager of Ansett Team Elfin, according to John McCormack as a matter of expediency. 'He'd helped me enormously when I was trying to become a pro-driver.' Winning the support of Ansett had been a big deal. '[Lanyon] was writing a lot of letters on our behalf, representing us to commercial interests. We needed to give him a title. "PR manager" didn't seem big enough, neither did "sponsorship liaison". So we called him "team manager".'

According to McCormack, Lanyon adopted the persona. 'He had a giant-sized ego and he made sure he had access to every department in the Ansett building.' No problem there, surely? 'He could have told me more,' McCormack asserted. 'He was riding on my back.'

In 1972, John Harvey—speedway king, twice Australian sports car champion, winner of the Bathurst 1000 with Peter Brock—claimed the 100-mph lap record at Phillip Island. He used a sports car, the McLaren M6B, which had been constructed in the UK especially for Bob Jane by Bruce McLaren, to win the Endeavour Cup with a fastest lap of 1 minute 44.7 seconds (102.55 mph/165.04 km/h). Harvey dominated. He won five of the six rounds of the Australian Sports Car Championship that year.

The sight and sound of the McLaren sweeping across the Phillip Island skyline gave hope for a bold new future. Sports car racing could have been the next big thing. John Lanyon got behind it. Phillip Island hosted a round from 1970, when the championship began, right through to 1977 when the circuit became untenable.

In 1974, John McCormack had a big idea, one that could help cement the future of the sports car category, its principal local manufacturer Elfin and, through its commitment to the category, Phillip Island. 'I suggested we could do a lot more racing if Elfin built a sports car that could accept the drive train of an F5000 car,' McCormack said. 'It would essentially be a plug-in. You could just remove the F5000 tub and replace it with a sports car front end.' There was an economy of scale in using one rig to race in two series.

Garrie Cooper used the Elfin MS7 'hybrid' to win the Australian Sports Car Championship series in 1974. In 1975, Phillip Island hosted the title as a one-off race and Cooper won, lapping the largest field of sports cars ever assembled at the Island.

But it was too late for the concept to take hold. Lanyon's National Motor Racing Promoters Association had determined the championship would be held in future for series production sports cars. Porsche importer Alan Hamilton used a 934T to win the Phillip Island rounds in 1976 and 1977, conceding the national title to five-time Australian touring car champion Pete Geoghegan in 1976 and tying with John Latham in 1977, all in Porsches. It was a blow for Elfin, which was already suffering from the decline of F5000.

Garrie Cooper was in his workshop in 1982 when he was felled by a ruptured aortic aneurysm and died that night. He'd raced for several years with an artificial heart valve. He was just 46.

John McCormack and John Lanyon parted acrimoniously. A court case brought by McCormack over disbursement of funds did not, according to McCormack, result in a positive return.

The track was breaking up—not a little but a lot. Its degradation started almost from the first meeting—and it was ongoing.

'I used to tell him, "John, it will be fine,"' Henk Duncan smiled. 'I was working at Myer in the city and John Lanyon would call me and say, "We need to get a crew of twenty people together to fix the track for the coming weekend's race meeting." I'd get down there and he'd have twelve concrete trucks lined up.' Then John would go away and leave the fix to Henk.

The technique became second nature. Wednesday: clean out the holes of the broken track surface. Thursday: bring in a local contractor to fill them with a concrete blend. Friday: 'Watch the last topping of half an inch of concrete go on, with my fingers crossed,' Henk said.

Bert Stoppa was the local contractor. He was also caught up in the fervour. 'Many Saturday nights you'd see Bert sitting on the club's trailer, full of sand next to a concrete mixer, drinking the club's beer and yelling enthusiastic instructions to club members working under floodlights,' Mike Lanyon recalled. Running repairs were the norm.

'Where a weak spot was occurring after Saturday practice, we'd rapidly excavate a hole and in-fill it with a concrete plug for Sunday racing. The Stoppa family became expert at blending concrete patches so drivers [or riders] could not tell when they moved from one surface to another.' The Cowes tip, according to Lanyon, became a source of metal reinforcement for the increasingly gaping holes—'bedsteads, farm fences, any metal pieces we could scrounge', he recalled.

In the eleven years of Lukey–Lanyon custodianship, some 70 events occurred on the island, most at club level. The first race on the new track, 22 October 1967, had been for Formula Vees, the spindly, entry-level, almost affordable open-wheeler category. It was won by Melbourne dental technician and VW Australia works driver George Reynolds. The Island became the venue for the Vee Nationals, conga lines of massive fields drafting down the long straight, cutting in and out of their own high-speed tug of war like an orchestrated ballet. 'I throw the rule book away for the Vees,' latter-day driver standards officer Kevin Bartlett said. 'Even now their slipstreaming is wonderful to watch.'

Alfredo Costanzo, who would win the Gold Star four times, was the first to challenge Jack Brabham's lap record on the old circuit. Brabham did 2 minutes 2.6 seconds (140.95 km/h) in 1960. Eight years later, 24-year-old Costanzo achieved 2 minutes 1.07 seconds (142.73 km/h) in a borrowed 1600cc Elfin Monocoque. A year later, ex-motorcycle racer Maurie Quincey lowered it again to 1 minute 55.8 seconds (149.22 km/h) in an Elfin 600.

Quincey was the club-racing king of Phillip Island. He'd been injured on the Isle of Man in 1955. Doctors drilled a hole in his skull to relieve the pressure on his brain. Back in Australia, after a long recuperation and in deference to his wife Betty's concerns, he switched to car racing. In a succession of Clubman sports and then open-wheelers, he was consistently at the front of the field. He was never tempted to go pro.

But his son did. Young Ray, born in 1955 just before his dad's crash and named for works Norton rider Ray Amm, went motorbike racing. He won three Australian Road Racing Championships and two Australian Grands Prix, then took his prodigious talent to Europe. In 1978, he crashed on the Sint Joris street circuit in Belgium and used a wheelchair for the rest of his life. Ray was a regular visitor at Phillip Island's Australian

MotoGP as a guest of the international teams. They knew he could have been one of the greats.

Maurie Quincey died in 2019, aged 90. Ray passed away just three years later, aged 67, after suffering a major stroke.

The influence of Phillip Island on future generations was huge.

'My earliest memories are of a hot New Year's Day, swimming in the Phillip Island pool,' Peter Doyle, chief executive of Motorcycling Australia, recalled. 'That's where all the kids went while their parents were racing.' Peter's dad Neville ran Team Kawasaki pretty much globally. Before that, he had been a wrench for some pretty handy local riders. 'Ray Fisher, Ken Rumble and Ken Blake were my uncles,' Peter said. 'Gregg Hansford was my big brother.'

Len Lukey's Phillip Island, the Funland part, was a safe haven. But it was also a thorn in PIARC's side.

Lukey built a trout farm on the hill above Turn 1. He'd constructed it with a reticulation system that failed to account for the track beneath. 'He pumped water from the dam to irrigate the Japanese gardens, feed the trout farm, then return to the dam,' Mike Lanyon said. 'But its return path was through the spectator area and under Turn 1. On wet days it would cause considerable flooding of the track.'

Lukey's dam was a hazard. If a driver or rider missed the turn, they'd reach the water. 'We had to build a guardrail,' Mike Lanyon said. 'Many cars collected the guardrail, and one bounced over it and sank from sight.' Chief flag marshal Jimmy Gowans duck-dived to connect the tow rope.

Lukey loved plants. In 1970, he banned camping after he claimed bushes had been cut for firewood. PIARC conducted a forensic investigation and produced evidence that the bushes had been imported, not taken from the property. Lukey was unbending. Camping, one of the joys of a weekend at the Island, remained banned.

At least they agreed on the circuit's two infield airstrips. They gave the place character. Flight time from Moorabbin in Melbourne's southern suburbs was just twenty minutes. For big race meetings especially, many corporates chose to park and fly. There could be upwards of fifteen light aircraft on the airfield ramp between runway and racetrack. An air traffic controller was needed. 'The north–south [airstrip] was pretty manageable, but you had to be a really game pilot to use the east–west down near Southern Loop,' Henk Duncan said. Cattle fences inadvertently became catch fences.

Len would still use the PIARC volunteers as if they were farm labourers. The relationship had become strained.

In 1974, the ten-year contract between Lukey and PIARC expired. Lukey refused to renew it. He granted PIARC a rolling one-year extension. But that agreement was never committed to paper. His handshake was his bond. PIARC had no choice other than to accept it. They'd become, truly, vulnerable.

On 11 March 1978, the Golden Jubilee Grand Prix went ahead.

The Phillip Island Auto Racing Club and the Vintage Sports Car Club of Australia had pulled off a miracle. They'd convinced the Phillip Island Shire Council, the police and a multitude of authorities to support it. The Prime Minister of Australia, the Honourable Malcolm Fraser MP, a noted Lancia enthusiast, had willingly agreed to be patron. That may have helped.

Time retreated by half a century. Entrants would drive on the 10.4-kilometre road track on the Saturday, then race on the 'new' circuit on Sunday.

'We promised day one would be a low-speed demonstration,' Bob King smiled. 'But I was doing 150 kilometres an hour in my T35 Anzani Bugatti when the 1929 grand prix–winning T37 went past me at a much higher speed.' For two hours, from just after 1.45 p.m. on a red-hot early spring afternoon, almost 200 cars of the prewar period claimed the Phillip Island rectangle as their own. Crowds lined the course with no more protection than they'd had in 1928.

'The only difference was that the road was sealed,' King said. 'Back then, the dust was so thick they were steering by braille. You can only imagine . . .'

There were cars that had won grands prix: Les Miller, Sydney garagiste and former musician with Gary Shearston's folk group of the 1960s, had brought the Arthur Terdich Bugatti Type 37A, the 1929 grand prix victor. Miller loved the car. He'd rejected substantial offers from overseas suitors and instead, ultimately, sold it to Sydney's Powerhouse Museum for a fraction of its true value, so it would stay in Australia.

Noted New Zealand collector Lindsay Wogan brought the Riley Brooklands in which Bill Thompson had won the Australian Grand Prix in 1933. Melbourne vintage enthusiast Graeme Steinfort owned the engine and gearbox from the Austin 7 in which Arthur Waite had won the 1928 Australian Grand Prix, but not the body—it had been lost. Instead, Steinfort entered the 1935 MG P-type that won that year's grand prix.

From his home in Bluffton, South Carolina, Joel E Finn, IBM computer genius and later chair of several IT start-ups, brought the 1938 Australian Grand Prix–winning ERA R10B. The ERA may have won its grand prix at Mount Panorama, driven by 23-year-old Englishman Peter Whitehead, but it was still hugely significant—and worth Finn's journey.

There were, sadly, no grand prix winners in attendance. Arthur Terdich, 1929 grand prix victor and 'father' of Phillip Island, passed away in 1977, just short of the Golden Jubilee.

But Barney and Bess Dentry were there. The husband-and-wife team raced together in all but two Phillip Island Australian Grands Prix (Bess was pregnant both times). In their first grand prix together, 1929, they brought their French-built Senechal home second in class and sixth outright. Their best result came in 1931 in a Brooklands Riley—fourth outright. If it hadn't been for an unfavourable handicap, they said, they could have won.

Barney and Bess were the hit of the Golden Jubilee. 'As a combination we did pretty well, but without her I lost a certain amount of confidence,' the beaming Barney explained. Barney passed away in 1987, Bess in 2000. Their Brooklands Riley appeared at the 2023 Australian F1 Grand Prix, a backdrop to the induction of heroes in the Australian Motorsport Hall of Fame.

Joan Richmond, elegantly, attended the Golden Jubilee as an invited guest. The president of the Phillip Island Shire Council, WG (Bill) Papworth, unveiled a plaque.

'It was incredibly hot on Saturday, raining on Sunday.' Bob King's recollection was a commentary on the four-seasons-in-one-day reputation of Phillip Island. 'The "new" track was perhaps the more testing. It was in terminal stages of break-up.'

Bill Morris, the world's foremost authority on the British-built ERA racing car, had brought the marque's most revered example to the Golden Jubilee. It was Hanuman, the third of three ERAs once owned by the two racing princes of then-Siam, Prince Bira and his cousin Prince Chula. The princes acquired two ERAs for Bira's 21st birthday. They named them Remus and Romulus, a reference to the twin brothers of mythology who founded the great empire of Rome. The cousins could see a parallel. Their grandfather, after all, was the King of Siam.

Later, just for fun, they bought a third ERA, serial number R12B. They named it Hanuman after the Hindu god of celibacy. Given their lifestyle, the name was a source of some amusement.

On the wet and slippery Phillip Island surface, Hanuman lined up on the front row for the 50-mile (80-kilometre) Australian Grand Prix Jubilee scratch race. Alongside it was a cut-down A-model Ford, a hot rod rendition of the car that young Mick Smith had used to win the 1934 Victorian Centenary Grand Prix. The pair sped away.

South Australian Kevin Shearer dealt with handfuls of opposite lock from the 3.5-litre flathead Ford. Bill Morris was no less troubled with the spontaneous power delivered from the blown two-litre ERA.

Morris sat high in the saddle, his face encased in a bubble helmet, fighting for vision in the mist. Shearer spun twice and recovered. Morris bounced his way to victory; Shearer was a brave and applauded second. Prime Minister Fraser, wrapped in a waterproof Driza-Bone, presented the trophies.

If racing had to come to an end on Phillip Island, there could not have been a better way to close the circle.

Kevin Shearer, a tireless advocate for motorsport in Australia, died in 2010. There's a statue in his honour at Mallala Motorsport

Park north of Adelaide. Bill Morris passed away in 2018. By then Hanuman had been acquired by His Royal Highness King Bhumibol of Thailand.

On 27 October 1978, Len Lukey died. If there had been any chance of maintaining Phillip Island in working order, it died with him.

'My mother just was not interested,' Keith Lukey said. When his dad died, PIARC was locked out. Probate was made difficult by the lack of a contract. A lot of inherited wealth was at stake and whatever the Lukey family's individual opinions might have been, the lawyers and administrators had taken charge. Helen Lukey, Len's wife, was not in favour of continuation.

'PIARC was shocked,' Mike Lanyon and Peter Nelson asserted in a paper they later wrote. 'The administrator had formally written to PIARC advising them they would be considered trespassers, and that no racing activity of any sort was to occur on the property. PIARC had considerable infrastructure at the circuit over which they felt they had, if not proprietary rights, certainly a moral claim.'

Allegations of political intrigue emerged. Earlier that year, before Len Lukey's death, CAMS had moved the Australian Grand Prix, allocated to Phillip Island, to the LCCA-run Sandown. It was a sensible decision. The Island was in no state to host a grand prix. But its relocation to Sandown fuelled crossed wires. 'Members of the Light Car Club were vigorously trying to gain state government support to inject funds into [Phillip Island] and be the body that controlled racing at the rejuvenated circuit,' the Lanyon–Nelson paper claimed. The impasse would never be fully resolved.

The urgent requirement for major change had been brewing all year. In truth, Len Lukey's death had not been the catalyst but simply the full stop at the end of a long sentence.

'We had been about $10,000 in arrears and people were threatening to liquidate,' Geoff Bull, PIARC treasurer at the time, said. The successful Golden Jubilee meeting had done a lot to extinguish PIARC's debt. But there was no surplus to bring Phillip Island back on stream. Surface resealing was beyond the club's resources.

With that scenario in mind, PIARC's executive considered the future. The club was viable; it simply didn't have a venue. But it did have an organisational structure, arguably the best in the country.

Lanyon and Nelson acted swiftly. As a test of capability, PIARC ran a race meeting at the Winton club circuit, near Benalla in central Victoria. It was a round of the Victorian State Race Series, a championship constructed exclusively for amateur drivers. It proved a worthwhile experiment.

Lanyon and Nelson took their newfound confidence to Bob Jane, owner of Calder Park Raceway. PIARC held the rights to run the final round of the 1978 Australian Manufacturers' Championship for touring cars, a 500-kilometre race. Bob Jane had a venue. Why not combine efforts?

On 2 December, 35 days after Len Lukey's death, PIARC promoted the Manchamps race at Calder Park. Compared to Phillip Island, Calder was tiny, so PIARC split the field into two and ran two 250-kilometre races to accommodate the field. The innovation was unpopular with the main teams and with spectators. The Holden Dealer Team and Allan Moffat Racing stayed away, and just 1000 spectators turned up for Sunday's second race. Peter Janson (Torana A9X) won the outright class.

The event was a failure commercially but it was a big win for PIARC. The Jane camp was impressed with PIARC's ability, and Jane employed PIARC to run Calder's race meetings. 'Our style was to aggressively control a race meeting up to the level we wanted, while [Calder's] style was more to push the go button then cruise along, letting the race meeting just happen,' Peter Nelson said.

Two years later, the PIARC team was the organisational force behind the Australian Grand Prix at Calder Park that brought international F1 drivers back to Australia. Alan Jones, the country's own world champion crowned that year, won. PIARC hosted a dinner for him in the Great Hall of the National Gallery of Victoria.

In 1979, PIARC polled its members. It was no longer part of Phillip Island and yet its name remained the Phillip Island Auto Racing Club. Some people, tongue-in-cheek, were suggesting it could stand for 'People Interested in Automobile Racing Club'. But seriously, was it time for a change of name and identity? The referendum was decisive. 'Because the name had played a large and valued role in the history of Australian motorsport it should be retained,' Lanyon and Nelson reported.

In 1981, John Lanyon was made an Officer of the Order of the British Empire (OBE) for his services to motorsport. He died on Christmas Eve 1991, aged just 58. Russell Lanyon passed away in 2006, in the same week that Peter Brock and eco-adventurer Steve Irwin died.

Part Four

The Grand Prix Circuit 1989–2004

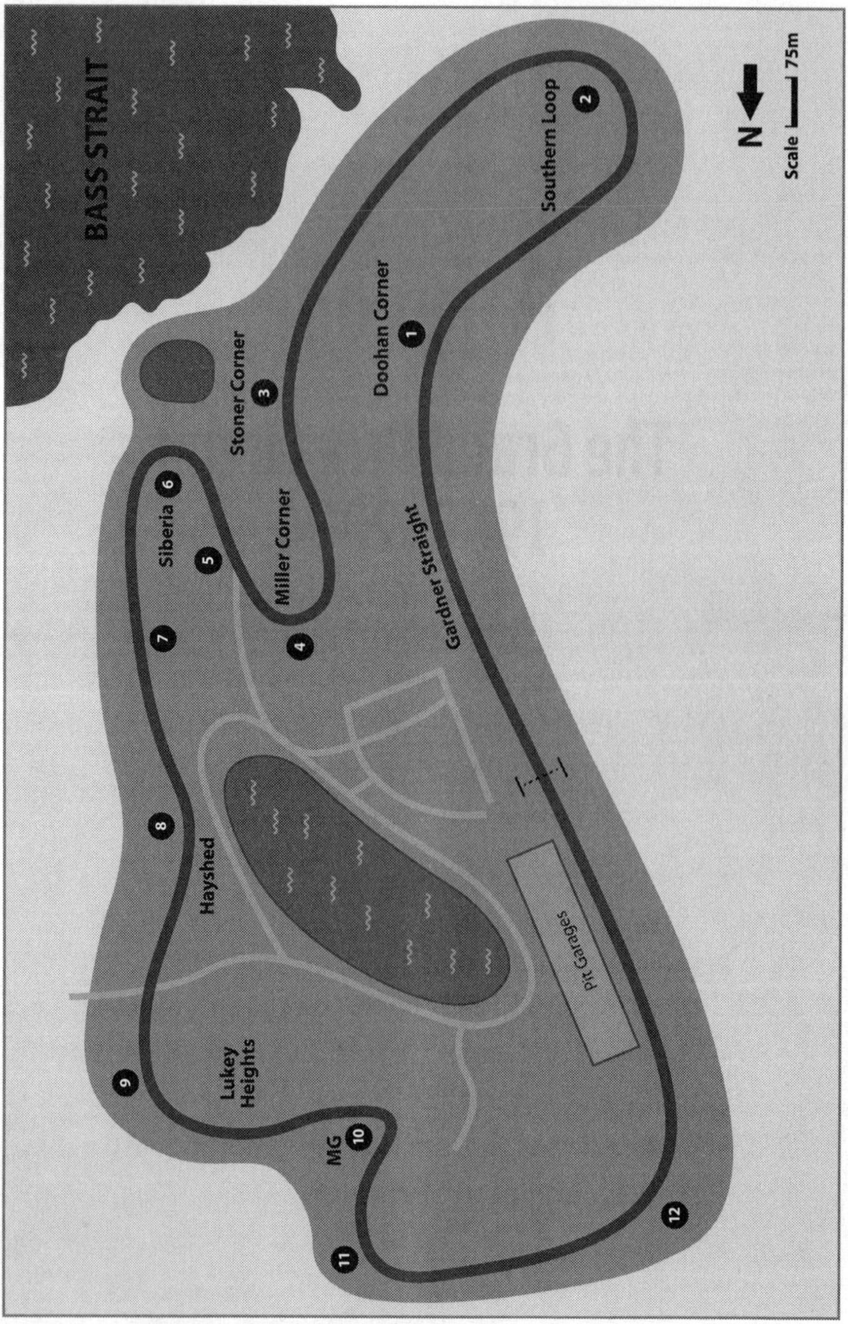

Phillip Island Grand Prix Circuit, 1988 to current
Distance: 4.445 kilometres (2.762 miles)

18

Saving the Circuit

On 15 June 1984, Placetac Pty Ltd, a shelf company, was registered with the Australian Securities and Investments Commission. It acquired from the estate of Len Lukey a parcel of prime grazing land formerly operated as one of Australia's best and most ambitious motor-racing tracks.

Placetac represented island landowners who knew a bargain when they saw one and who professed no greater interest than to turn Lukey's vision back into farmland.

Keith Lukey had tried to keep the dream alive. He'd ducked and weaved under the noses of the administrators and run two club meetings at the track in late 1979 and early 1980—not formal races as such, but lap dashes for one car at a time. Both were associated with high-performance driving instructor Jim Murcott, who provided training to participants in the name of road safety.

In 1980, Keith completed the core of his father's Funland project and Victorian premier Dick Hamer opened the Len Lukey Memorial Museum and Gardens on 27 July.

Keith also enabled Robert Shannon, a Melbourne devotee of historic race cars, to run two classic-car meetings at the end of October in 1981 and 1982. The meetings were well supported, progenitors of the historic-motoring movement. 'I was keen for Robert to buy the property,' Keith recalled. But Shannon was otherwise engaged. In 1981, he'd started Shannons Auctions, a haven for the trading of specialist vehicles, and backed it with an ambitious, highly successful insurance-underwriting business specifically for car enthusiasts. There was not enough gas in his tank to own a racetrack too, certainly not one in need of expensive restoration.

Shannon would conduct his speciality auctions as a feature of the Melbourne and Sydney International Motor Shows. He was curating the Melbourne auction in 2000 when he died at his home in Brighton.

The circuit and all within its perimeter had originally been valued at upwards of $1.2 million. After three years with no takers, an offer of around $800,000 would secure it.

Phillip Island is a tight-knit community. The rural sector understands the advantages of cooperative farming. 'I was part of a Lukey–Cameron company to run sheep,' Keith said. Along with near neighbour Fergus Cameron, a second-generation Phillip Islander, he'd joined the business for mutual benefit, a means of pooling resources to extract the best from their farmlands. Keith mentioned the property's reduced price to Cameron and 'he ran with it', Keith recalled.

Cameron worked fast. He was given just six weeks to raise the money, and he made it. He pulled together a like-minded group of farmers and property owners to complete the purchase, then leased back the land to graze sheep and cattle.

The Camerons were part of the island's aristocracy. 'Captain' Cameron, Fergus's war-veteran father, had developed farming and grazing property along Back Beach Road abutting the Lukeys' holding. It was glorious land, rolling down to Kitty Miller Bay where the SS *Speke*, a three-masted windjammer, went aground in 1906. The Camerons were great champions of the island. Fergus's older brother Donald was the first mayor of the expanded Bass Coast Council and a fifty-year stalwart of the island's Lions Club. In 2013 he was awarded the Medal of the Order of Australia in recognition of his contribution.

Fergus was a born promoter, active in the development of the nearby Phillip Island Nature Parks, instigator of a Devonshire-tea park in a historic home off Ventnor Road on the island's west side, a stock and station agent, and a farmer. He'd visited the motor races as a boy with his father. It was really just a short walk through the paddocks.

Peter Henderson, a prominent Melbourne ophthalmologist, was the son-in-law of Sir Charles 'Dave' McGrath, the boss of Repco who had bankrolled the circuit in the 1950s. Peter had met Helen McGrath at the Koala Cafe on the island. 'Charles McGrath had 100 acres [40 hectares] on the island, and we bought a property at Rhyll,' Henderson, now 84 and restoring a magnificent holding on the very tip of the Mornington Peninsula, told me over a sandwich lunch at Portsea Golf Club.

To describe Peter Henderson as part of the Melbourne establishment is an understatement—member of the Royal Melbourne, Kew and National golf clubs; Royal Melbourne Tennis Club; Mount Buller's Alkuna Ski Club; the Royal Yacht Club of Victoria; and Melbourne's Athenaeum Club. Professionally, he was a leader in the development of eye care, a president of the Royal Australian and New Zealand College of Ophthalmologists and awarded the College's highest honour, the Gold Medal, in 2004.

Peter Henderson had been educated at Melbourne's exclusive Scotch College. So had Fergus Cameron. It was natural that the now near neighbours (Henderson's holding was a holiday retreat, Cameron's a permanent residence) should become the core of Placetac Pty Ltd.

'There were nine entities [investors] in the original Placetac structure,' Henderson recalled. Little by little, Henderson bought them out. 'Ultimately, I had seventy-nine per cent of the company, the Camerons held fifteen per cent, and another investor had the remaining six per cent.'

Peter Henderson is relaxed about how it came about: 'We owned a racetrack so we thought we should run a race.' The official program for its first meeting in 1986 was unequivocal: 'Welcome to Phillip Island Motor Racing Circuit,' it read. 'Phillip Island, and particularly this racetrack, has had a long association with Motorcycle racing. It is our intention that the circuit once again become available to all forms of motorsport.' It was a clear statement of intent: open for business. Hartwell Motorcycle Club had the inside running.

'They invited us down for talks,' Mark Cadle and Paul Keam, committee members of Hartwell, recalled when we met in their club's rooms, an office-warehouse in Melbourne's industrial Bayswater, its high walls and trophy cabinets packed with the memorabilia of a club with nearly a century of sensational history.

'Dave Drechsler, our club president, went for a few laps on his sexy new RS BMW. Phillip Island was a big grassy paddock and there must have been 3000 sheep on it. Dave was doing 130 [km/h] down the straight when thirty of them decided to cross the track. We still don't know how he didn't end up with lamb cutlets in his fairing.'

As Cadle recalled, Cameron and Henderson, along with Keith Lukey's wife Lyn, outlined their plans to restore the circuit to host national, even international meetings. The key word was 'restore'. 'The track was badly broken up. Siberia Corner was exposed to the worst weather coming off Bass Strait, and the break-up of the surface was almost complete—just bare rock and stones. The run from Honda Corner [now called Miller Corner] down to Siberia was waterlogged. When we brought in resurfacing experts, their advice was to start again. But there was no money for that.'

'We formed a joint-venture company,' Keam said. 'It was called Hartron, a portmanteau of Hartwell and Cameron.' The company served several purposes. Largely, according to Cadle, it existed to give the directors of Placetac—the farmers who were still stakeholders in the land—some protection.

'They had to be shielded from the professional and personal liability that comes with running a race meeting.' Hartwell had some experience with that. The club had become a limited-liability company in 1977 when it was sued by the family of a competitor who lost a leg.

Hartron divided responsibilities. 'We provided six full-blooded weekends of working bees. They provided barrel on barrel of cold mix. The cost must have been in the tens of thousands of dollars,' Cadle said.

On 4–5 January 1986, Hartwell ran Thunder Down Under, a packed 33-race open meeting. 'We'd wanted to give it a big name, like the Victorian Grand Prix, but the Auto Cycle Union [of Victoria] wouldn't have it. They wanted us to prove ourselves first.'

There'd already been a false start.

Henderson and Cameron had fielded many proposals for the use of their newly purchased farming land, most centred on motorsport. The one that appealed was a suggestion from the local Gippsland chapter of the Victorian-based Motorcycle Riders Association (MRA), constituted in 1978 to represent the interests of the motorcycle community.

The Gippsland branch wanted to celebrate the centenary of motorcycling with a rally to Phillip Island, a weekend of camping at the circuit, a music concert over two nights and a historic race meeting on the Sunday. They called it the HAM Rally ('Hundredth Anniversary of Motorcycling'), and it would be held in November 1985. Bikers were getting a bad rap. The annual Easter motorcycle races at Bathurst—glorious contests on a fabulous circuit—had become media fodder. 'Bikie Riots at Bathurst' were headlines as predictable as the first shark sighting of summer, whether they happened or not.

Policing strategies were still developing. In 1979, the NSW

Police built a brick station with barred windows, a fortress, at the top of Mount Panorama; a year later they surrounded it with high wire fencing, turning it into a compound, and staffed it with members of the Tactical Response Group complete with shields and batons—an obvious target.

Damian Codognotto, the politically savvy spokesperson for the MRA, weighed in. 'They treat us like animals,' he said in defence of the motorcyclists. The MRA had embarked on a PR offensive. The HAM Rally, its Gippsland register believed, would be an opportunity to showcase motorcycling on their terms. Codognotto couldn't see it—'doomed to failure' were the words he used to motorcycle trade magazine *Revs*. But his branch went ahead with the rally, and when it got cold feet, three members took it up to run it privately. Hartwell was engaged to run the historic meeting on track.

'The locals were terrified,' Mark Cadle said. His words were perhaps an overstatement but also a reasonable summation of the mood of at least part of the island community. 'A Bridge Too Far for Violent Bikies', a local headline screamed, anticipating the worst.

Police went heavy. 'It was overpoliced,' Cadle asserted. Three hundred and fifty police were assigned, according to a report later prepared for presentation to the federal government's Criminology Research Advisory Council. 'They were stopping people at the bridge at San Remo and a lot didn't even get on the island.' As well, organisers had hired their own external security to patrol the on-circuit campground.

It was a lot of security for what turned out to be a small crowd. The numbers are rubbery. Promoters had anticipated 25,000, according to the report. Just 5000 turned up, thanks to 'a combination of poor marketing, media hysteria and over policing', the report claimed.

Organisers were facing a financial bath. By Sunday morning, an emergency meeting had called a halt to the festival. The Sunday-night concert featuring UK heavy metal band Uriah Heep, in the last stop on their Australian tour, and local band Kevin Borich Express, was cancelled to 'minimise financial loss'.

'On Sunday morning we were told their event had been cancelled, and they'd be going home,' Mark Cadle said. 'But our race meeting could go ahead. Placetac was really pleased with us. "[The cancellation] is not a reflection on you," they said.'

There was no riot. According to the report, police made nine arrests, seven of which were .05-related, one drug charge and one driving while disqualified. Six injuries occurred due to rowdiness, none of them serious. But all these years later, sitting in the Portsea Golf Club, Peter Henderson told me, 'They confiscated twenty-seven lethal weapons.' He was still aghast.

Revs dubbed HAM 'the monumental failure of 1985'.

Thunder Down Under didn't attract the superstars in 1986. 'The Team Kawasaki Australia transporter was in the pits, but only because Peter Doyle, team manager Neville's son, had used it to bring down his 250 and 900cc race bikes,' Mark Cadle said.

Peter was a promising B-grade rider. 'The track was melting,' he recalled. 'At the push start my feet were sticking to the surface. And it was still rough.'

Mark Cadle went one better: 'The concrete patches were so insecure you could stand on one side of the concrete and watch the other side rise.'

Hartron persevered throughout 1986 but it was a no-win situation. Hartwell committee member John Davis, a plumber—a useful skill in the circumstances—went to live on the island to coordinate constant reclamation and working bees. According to Cadle and Keam, 'We were fighting on several fronts. There were politics involved. The Bob-Jane-owned-Calder didn't want our circuit resurrected. Neither did Sandown.' In 1984, Sandown had vastly overspent on circuit improvements to host a round of the World Endurance Championship for sports cars, and in 1986 it was fighting for survival. Neither circuit, Cadle and Keam contended, wanted competition from struggling Phillip Island. 'While we were working on patching the track, Fergus was working hard to find sponsorship to run a race meeting, but without success,' Cadle said.

On 19 October 1986, Hartwell ran the Southern Classic on Phillip Island. 'We'd applied for an open licence but could only get a restricted club one,' Cadle said. 'The track condition was too poor.' Hartwell cheated a little: 'We didn't have enough classic bikes in our club to justify the meeting, so we invited a few others in.' Naturally it rained. 'It was so wet we had to ban bikes from using slicks.'

It would be the last race meeting held on that surface. Patching was not working and there was no point in continuing.

According to John Davis, 'Fergus and Peter told us they were going to go another way, take over the track themselves and find another means to continue.' There was no acrimony. Hartwell would stay in the loop. It had acquired the rights to run the 1987 Australian Grand Prix for motorcycles, winning it from Mount Panorama. All they needed was for Phillip Island to be in good shape to run it. They ended up running it at Winton.

19

Thinking Big

You only get one Bob Barnard in your life.

The towering, bearded, hard-talking English engineer built the 'new' Phillip Island. He delivered Australia a world-class motorcycle grand prix circuit, on time but nowhere near budget, and—incredibly—accepted the financial risk himself.

'Would Phillip Island have been rebuilt if I had not recognised its potential and had the guts to push through with the first Motorcycle GP against the odds? I somehow doubt it,' he challenged in his book *Seven Crazy Years*. Typical Barnard: big on self-belief. Many would argue the semantics, but he was right.

Barnard was Australian motorsport's Man of La Mancha, a Don Quixote character; the windmills he tilted at were huge. And ultimately they broke him (temporarily), bankrupted him and, unfairly, discredited him. Some accused him of leaving a trail of destruction. History suggests he left a legacy of successful construction.

Barnard was part of the team that built the Australian Formula One track around Adelaide's parkland. He'd emigrated from the UK in 1969, forged a career with the South Australian Roads Board and joined a private construction firm. When the car grand prix was proposed, he was the only person in the tender who'd had motor-racing experience.

'I raced a Morgan sports car, then an Elfin Formula Junior open-wheeler,' he told me down the video line from his home in the north of Spain: fit, suntanned and just back from his morning swim. Barnard knew road building, and Adelaide taught him about politics.

The team he belonged to—it's important not to characterise it as 'his' team—delivered a perfect inaugural Formula One event in 1985. Barnard was an integral part of the 3.78-kilometre circuit's design and, importantly, of its successful completion on time. 'Bernie Ecclestone [F1 supremo] told us we'd given him a real problem—we'd created a standard the Europeans couldn't match.'

In 1986 Barnard and another team member—the senior one, Mal Hemmerling—formed a company called Prixmotions to run the F1 grand prix externally. The government wouldn't have it and Hemmerling withdrew back into the public sector.

Prixmotions was dissolved. Barnard and three colleagues started Barnard Project Management (BPM). Jobs came amazingly quickly. BPM delivered the infrastructure for the new Brisbane Bears (later Lions) AFL club stadium; the Summernats (hot rod jamboree) in Canberra; lawn tennis in Adelaide; and the Ultimate Event, the grand opening of the Sanctuary Cove luxury community on the Gold Coast, complete with a concert by Frank Sinatra.

'We were also approached to run the International Six Day Trial'—one of world motorcycling's big events—'but as the promoter, not as the construction company,' he smiled, somewhat ruefully. 'Taking that role was a first.'

The offer introduced Barnard to a new world of politics. The possibility that a private promoter would seize the rights, and the presumed obvious profits, from running the Six Days Trial for the first time in Australia outraged factions within the sport. Motorcycle racing, then, was run by amateurs. 'When are you going to buy your Porsche?' a journalist demanded at an all-in media conference. The idea was stillborn, and the event was assigned to France, leaving residual ill-feeling. Barnard had caused offence but he had made his presence felt.

'David White tipped us to him,' Hartwell's Mark Cadle told me. White was the effervescent president of the Auto Cycle Union of Victoria, a prominent early influencer and navigator of the politics that brought the grand prix to Phillip Island. Cadle likens the protagonists in his account of the grand prix's genesis to politicians of the time. 'White was the Graham Richardson'—the fixer—while 'Barnard was the Paul Keating', the barnstormer.

Hartwell owned the rights to the domestic Australian Grand Prix. It was seeking someone who could resurface Phillip Island. Barnard saw greater potential. 'Around the second Adelaide Grand Prix, Mal Hemmerling had asked me to look at the rules for a motorcycle GP track to see if we could run one on the same street circuit,' Bob said. 'It could deliver us two races for the price of one set-up. I knew little about motorcycle GPs at the time, but it was obvious that a street circuit would not get approved. The idea planted a seed, though.'

Barnard's meeting with Hartwell ('They could never afford me') led to a serious discussion with circuit owners Fergus Cameron and Peter Henderson. Barnard had raced at Phillip Island in the Lukey era. 'It was a world-class circuit, in the rough.'

On 19 January 1988, they came to an agreement. Barfield, a shelf company, would be their umbrella to raise a loan, upgrade the track and stage a world championship grand prix. Barnard would build the new track and secure the race. Profit would be equally distributed. Share of risk, in Barnard's view anyway, was undetermined.

'There was no rights holder in those days,' David White, now retired, explained at the kitchen table of his bluestone cottage in the inner-Melbourne suburb of Fitzroy North. White is retained by Motorcycling Australia as its historian. As former CEO of Motorcycling Australia and a former vice president of the FIM (the Fédération Internationale de Motorcyclisme, the world motorcycling body), he's a good choice for the role. Few know more about motorcycling than White. But as the sport's ultimate fixer, according to Cadle, he's still guarded. Fixers do their best work behind the scenes.

'If you had a big idea, you brought it to the Auto Cycle Council of Australia,' David said, 'and if they supported it, they'd take it to the FIM. Once word got out Phillip Island wanted a world championship grand prix, everyone wanted one.' The internecine battle was intense.

'John Thompson, president of the Auto Cycle Council, was pushing for Sandown,' David said. 'He was a political animal. They called him Mac the Knife.'

Barnard, on the other hand, 'was difficult to deal with. He had a single purpose and couldn't understand anyone questioning his point of view.' Life wasn't easy for a fixer.

The FIM sent two delegates on separate visits: Mike Trimby, president of the International Road Racing Teams Association until his sudden death in 2023, and Joe Zegwaard, the official track technical inspector. 'Mike was fully in favour of Phillip Island,' David said. Zegwaard needed to be lobbied: 'I made it a point to get friendly with him,' Peter Henderson told me. Bob Barnard recalled: 'Bob Jane lent Zegwaard his helicopter but then pissed him off by doing flyovers of Phillip Island while he was there.'

Politics is a tough game. White watched while Barnard slugged it out with John Thompson. Not too much goodwill was left on the table, but deals were done. Ultimately the Auto Cycle Council president capitulated. 'It's up to the Auto Cycle Union of Victoria to decide,' he told White. 'I told him Phillip Island,' White responded. Thompson would later become a distinguished member of FIM committees.

White joined Barnard in Geneva to lay out their proposition to the FIM, and they got their date. 'It was the last time the FIM ever approved a track that had not been completed,' White said. 'It was built against all odds. I didn't know then how undercapitalised Bob was. He simply had vision.'

'Fergus Cameron was asking for proof of my financial ability to do the upgrades to the track and I'm sure that came from Peter Henderson,' Barnard said. 'Peter was paranoid about us tearing up the concrete and not being able to put it back. He was afraid he'd be left without a racetrack. He didn't realise he didn't have a track anyway, due to the condition it was in. At that stage I was just trying to assess the scope of the repairs.'

It was the first sign of difficulties in the Barfield partnership.

BPM had made $500,000 from Sanctuary Cove's Ultimate Event. Barnard bet it all on Phillip Island, then set out to raise the rest. He obtained an $800,000 loan from a local bank branch, then secured sponsorship from brewer Swan, owned by swashbuckling, later disgraced businessman Alan Bond. (Bond became a hero when his yacht won the America's Cup in 1983.) His grand prix sponsorship was paid upfront. Bond also owned broadcaster Channel Nine, and marketing arm PBL. 'There was good sense in keeping it in the "family",' Barnard said.

Barnard's situation remained precarious. Advance ticket sales provided cash flow, and he assigned them to capital works—never a wise strategy. 'We estimated total costs at $2 million. It ended up close to $5 million,' he admitted.

'I made his life a misery,' Keith Lukey told me. The Lukey family still owned its museum and a small parcel of land around it, including a Len Lukey–built dam. Barnard wanted free access for spectators to be able to walk the entire perimeter of the track, and he wanted the dam filled. 'It got pretty tense,' Lukey said. Lawyers got involved. A financial agreement was struck. 'He bought a dam, and I moved the fence,' Keith said.

'It was like trying to fight a war in a fog,' Barnard remembered. At every turn there were constraints and costs. The Victorian

Government endorsed Barnard's application to the FIM, even as its anti-tobacco lobby was in full flight. 'The race teams were in the main sponsored by big tobacco,' said Barnard, and it would soon become a major issue, one that brought opposing state premiers into play.

BPM co-promoted the Hartwell Club's 1987 domestic Australian Grand Prix at the tiny Winton circuit in central Victoria. 'It was a test run—to try out our officials and get our systems right.' It was a loss leader, not financially successful, and drew criticism from the not-invented-here crowd.

Separately: 'With only weeks to go, the Victorian Liquor Licensing Commission decided it needed written permission from the landowner before it would grant us a licence. I took that to Peter Henderson, who asked me for $150,000. He was very nice about it; he invited me to dinner at his home and we got it down to $100,000.'

Barnard felt he was being screwed. The Barfield relationship deteriorated.

'In the end, we had to buy them out,' he said. After the first race, Barnard, frustrated and staunchly autocratic, spent $600,000 to secure sole ownership of Barfield. 'They said to me: "We'll keep the land, and you can have it for one week for the grand prix."'

'It seemed a good deal,' Bob mused. 'I'd have control and we'd have years to pay it off.' He was gone from Phillip Island a year later.

Bob Barnard built a world-class track.

The 4.8-kilometre concrete quilt he used as his base became

a shorter 4.445-kilometre world grand prix benchmark. Honda Corner, the first hairpin, renamed Miller Corner in 2022 for Australian star Jack Miller, was dramatically shortened to move it away from the water table seeping from the nearby dam wall, as well as provide safety run-off for hard-braking bikes.

The run down to Siberia, the track's southernmost point, was realigned. The tight Turn 10, downhill into a steep uphill rise, was redesigned. 'I'd had trouble with it when I raced my Elfin there years before,' Bob said. 'So I raised the low point and eased the apex, especially to suit the GP bikes.'

Barnard sought expert advice: Wayne Gardner, superbike ace Rob Phillis, Australian international Gregg Hansford, and former racer-turned-team-owner/manager Warren Willing. Each contributed to promotional endorsements as well as track design.

For 30 years there'd been no infield access except across the track. 'There were some mighty close calls when people decided to cross as a bike came blasting out of Turn 12,' Paul Keam recalled.

Barnard built a tunnel, and a world-class pit area. The control tower was rebuilt. Much of his reclamation was invisible. For the first time the Island, so susceptible to weather, had near to proper drainage.

On Saturday, 19 November 1988, Hartwell held a club race day at Phillip Island—a soft launch.

'There was enormous interest,' Mark Cadle recalled. 'We had 220 entries. The big Sydney clubs, St George and Willoughby, turned up.' Hartwell and Barnard fell out over how it was run. Barnard remembers it as being 'run like a circus, uncontrolled and unsafe'. Hartwell remembers it as 'toilet-paper Saturday'. 'The toilets were overflowing, and we'd run out of toilet paper,' Mark Cadle said, placing blame for that at Barnard's feet.

Barnard moved to take more control.

Ross Martin, now a 30-year veteran of grand prix administration, was hired as clerk of the course. 'I've done many,' Martin told me. 'The biggest high was that first year.'

Peter Nelson from PIARC took over the role of race secretary. Peter invented the art of minute-to-minute organisation. 'I brought a race agenda back from the British Grand Prix,' David White said. 'Peter turned it into a world-leading document. Now every grand prix has one.'

'Bob brought in a lot of car officials to run the grand prix,' Mark Cadle remembered. 'They didn't understand bikes. When the two-stroke 125s got the chequered flag in practice, they'd do a plug chop,' immediately shutting down their engine so mechanics could assess the fuel/air mixture. 'Then they'd push back to the pits. It was hilarious to see the car guys believing the entire field had broken down simultaneously.'

On 4 December 1988, Phillip Island hosted the final round of the Swann International Road Race series (double-n Swann was an insurer, not a brewer). Like the Tasman Series for cars two decades before, the Swann gave Northern Hemisphere riders an opportunity for counter-seasonal racing. Local rider Mal Campbell won; emerging superstar Mick Doohan was a close second. Doohan's next ride would be as a member of the works Honda team.

The works teams tested at Phillip Island over the Australian summer and with great optimism pronounced it suitable. The 1989 Shell Australian Road Racing Championship, in March 1989, ended the learning curve. The grand prix was ready to run.

Principal sponsor Swan Brewery ramped up a national advertising campaign, 'They said you'd never make it'. Wayne Gardner was its star, but it could just as easily have been referencing Bob Barnard.

20

Wayne Gardner—Genesis and Genius

We're sitting in Wayne Gardner's time capsule, an industrial warehouse he built with some of his winnings from ten years of grand prix motorcycle racing. It's in a suburb of Wollongong, Australia's sole surviving steel city, 100 kilometres south of Sydney. He built this small enclave 34 years ago while he was still racing. Now, long retired, he's just finished another, much grander one further up the coast. He's a proud builder, managing his investments from afar. He lives in Monaco; when in Australia he stays with his dad Norm, sleeping in the second bedroom of the home unit he bought his folks overlooking Wollongong's North Beach.

The time capsule, in the industrial complex, holds the detritus of his incredibly successful vocation. It's dusty, decaying. So many trophies, their metal surfaces pitted with rust, wobbly on their bases. So many cardboard boxes, so limp at the edges they'll fall apart if you try to lift them. A crumpled tarp pulled back reveals upwards of 50 race suits, chronicles of his career. His mum, Shirley, used to care for them all. She died in 2016, aged 81. 'I know I should do something with it, maybe a museum,' he smiles, a bit apologetically. You bet he should.

Wayne Gardner, the Wollongong Whiz, invented motorcycle racing as a popularised sport in Australia.

There'd been world champions before, three of them, but none in the Senior class. And none who could put motorcycle racing on the front page of the national newspapers. Gardner was the man for his time.

Australia, caught up in the fervour of its bicentenary, was not short of heroes. In the year Gardner won his world title, Pat Cash won Wimbledon; Jeff Fenech was world super bantamweight champion, our first multi-weight title holder; and Greg Norman broke the nation's heart by choking at the US Augusta Masters. But when Australia's Sportsman of the Year was announced, Gardner was called forward, the first time for a motorcycle rider. The grand prix champions who came later—Mick Doohan and Casey Stoner—would be beneficiaries.

The Whiz has been well documented. In 2018 he even pioneered the art of the biopic—a 90-minute movie on his life (these days, it seems, every sportsperson has one). What was left to say?

'I've got an idea,' he says. Reaching forward to his phone on the desk, he punches in a speed-dial number and puts the call on speakerphone.

'It's your ex-husband,' Gardner announces, a huge grin on his face.

Donna is happy to talk.

They met on a blind date when Donna was not quite sixteen. 'We went to the Oxford Tavern, corner of Corrimal and Crown streets in Wollongong, a music venue. No need for fake ID. That wasn't an issue,' Donna smiled down the phone. She knew Wayne as an apprentice steelworker with an uncanny resemblance to pop star John Paul Young. Less than three years later they were in the UK. 'My dad was horrified, but my mum said, "Let her go." I would have gone anyway.'

The rough diamond had been partially polished. He'd turned up at Sydney's Oran Park with talent and attitude. Arthur and Jan Blizzard, who ran motorcycling in New South Wales, held him back in the junior grades. 'Otherwise he would have killed himself,' Arthur contended.

'Cracking the Sydney crowd was tough,' Donna said. 'We were from the 'Gong and the established riders didn't want us there.'

'Dickheads,' Gardner concurred.

Team Gardner was a bit fragile, a bit defensive. As a TV commentator at the time, I recall a blast from Donna over a perceived slight.

Tuner Peter Molloy got him next. Molloy was a driver whisperer. He was mainly an engine builder but practised sports psychology long before it became a science. Gardner was Molloy's first bike rider.

'Wayne was a scruffy little mutt, like a Jack Russell. Molloy cleaned him up,' Donna said.

Billy Hill, owner of Mentor Motorcycles, put him on a series of Molloy-prepared bikes. He won the Castrol Six Hour, then the Australian Superbike Championship.

Japanese tuner Mamoru Moriwaki took him global, to Japan

A new era for Phillip Island in 1956—on its own purpose-built 3-mile (4.8-kilometre) circuit. This PIARC program was the treasured possession of Hartwell Motorcycle Club pioneer Wes Brown. (Hartwell Motorcycle Club)

In March 1960, Jack Brabham was back in Australia as world F1 champion for the first time. Len Lukey built an entire race meeting around him, hiring the track from PIARC and becoming the promoter. (Ian Tate, VHRR)

Above: The F1 paddock for the 1960 Jack Brabham meeting was just that—a paddock. Brabham pulled a record crowd, naturally won, and set a new lap record. (Primotipo.com)

The man in pink. Len Lukey remains largely an unsung hero of Australian motorsport: promoter, circuit owner, benefactor and Gold Star winner. (Primotipo.com)

Peter Henderson, here on the viewing roof above the Phillip Island pits with Helen, his former wife, was chairman of Placetac, enablers of the continuation of racing at the island circuit. (Peter Henderson Collection)

March 1995—a tragic day. Australian motorsport's most successful all-rounder, Gregg Hansford, died in a Ford Mondeo in the opening round of the Australian Super Touring Championship. (Chevron)

Bob King, Bugatti aficionado, proposed the 1978 Phillip Island Golden Jubilee Grand Prix meeting and competed in it. (John Smailes)

1987 world champion Wayne Gardner created the impetus for Phillip Island to be rebuilt, and won the first and second world title grands prix held at the track. (Steve Reeves)

The magic moment. Donna Forbes (later Gardner) 'track invades' to greet her fiancé at the end of the 1989 Australian Motorcycle Grand Prix.

Wayne Gardner transitioned from two wheels to four, running his own team with Coca Cola sponsorship. He leads teammate, now senior Supercars commentator, Neil Crompton. (Chevron)

In 1990, Dick Johnson claimed the first 100-miles-per-hour lap for a touring car and won the championship race. He takes the start in Ford Sierra (17) alongside Tony Longhurst (25) and Shell teammate John Bowe (18). The pit area, built by Bob Barnard for the motorcycle race, was a vast improvement. (Chevron)

Open-wheeler driver John Smith escaped unharmed from the 1990 Gold Star crash that destroyed his Formula Holden, racing as a Lexcen, Toyota's badge-engineered version of the Holden Commodore. (John Smith Collection)

Future Supercars champions Marcos Ambrose (17) and Garth Tander (4) lead a packed field of Formula Fords. Phillip Island's long, sweeping layout has been a training ground for stars. (Chevron)

Three Australian world champions at their world-class circuit. Left to right: Mick Doohan (1994–98), Wayne Gardner (1987) and Casey Stoner (2007, 2011). (AAP)

Mick Doohan's greatest victory was at Phillip Island in 1998 when he won his home grand prix and the world title. A crash early the following season would force his retirement after five successive world titles. (AAP)

'A word in your ear, Guv': twice world champion Barry Sheene, like Valentino Rossi, had a personality far bigger than the sport. His influence was huge. Here (right) with Mick Doohan while commentating for Network Ten. (AAP)

Jeremy Burgess, one of the most successful crew chiefs in MotoGP, is a popular VIP attendee at the Australian Grand Prix; here on the fan stage with Wayne Gardner, who was the first of three world champions with whom Burgess worked. (John Smailes)

Burgess and Mick Doohan were regarded as the dream team—together through all five of Doohan's world titles. (Honda PR)

Jeremy Burgess was with Valentino Rossi for all seven of his senior world titles and through three different manufacturers—Honda, Yamaha and Ducati. (Old Bike Australasia)

Henk Duncan, a near-original member of PIARC, remains one of Australia's most senior race directors. His family has generational influence. (John Smailes)

The two Troys—Corser (left) and Bayliss (right)—dominated World Superbike racing at Phillip Island and between them claimed five world titles. (Russell Colvin)

Chris Vermeulen, one of several successful Barry Sheene protégés, raced with a stylised number seven, Sheene's race plate, in tribute to Sheene, who died of cancer in 2003. (Alamy)

Twice World Superbike champion Troy Corser rode for six manufacturers in a career spanning twenty years. He joined Suzuki in 2005 to win his second world title. (Old Bike Australasia)

Troy Bayliss won all three of his World Superbike championships, and a round of the World MotoGP title, exclusively on Ducati. Ducati named a model in his honour. (Old Bike Australasia)

Anthony Gobert—the Go-Show—was a winner at Phillip Island but ultimately unsuccessful in his pursuit of a World Superbike title. (Old Bike Australasia)

Ian Tate, president of the Victorian Historic Racing Register (VHRR), established in 1976 to preserve the sport's heritage. (John Smailes)

Twice Australian Gold Star winner Spencer Martin (left) with Peter Harburg, 'custodian' of the Ferrari 250 LM (no. 8) that featured in the VHRR's 2024 Phillip Island Classic. (John Smailes)

Peter Goddard, president of Motorcycling Australia, won a World Superbike round at Phillip Island and competed in seventeen world motorcycle grands prix. (John Smailes)

Jorge Viegas, president of the FIM, the world governing body of the sport, visited Phillip Island in 2023. He caught up with Australia's slide king Garry McCoy (left), winner of world championship grands prix in the 125cc and 500cc categories, and now coaching youngsters in the Oceania Junior Cup. (John Smailes)

Casey Stoner won six Australian grands prix at Phillip Island in succession—on Ducati and Honda. (Alamy)

In 2013, Carmelo Ezpeleta, chief executive of Dorna, the MotoGP rights holder, inducted Casey Stoner as a Legend in the Motorcycle Hall of Fame. (Alamy)

In 2022, Phillip Island declared Turn 4 'Miller Corner' in honour of Jack Miller, Australia's next MotoGP hero. Left to right: Carmelo Ezpeleta, Peter Miller (Jack's dad), Ruby (Jack's wife), Jack, Sonya (Jack's mum), Andrew Fox (Linfox), Andrew Westacott (long-serving CEO of the Australian Grand Prix Corporation). (Russell Colvin)

Jack Miller is a fan favourite, mobbed in the Phillip Island pits. Fans Colin Davis and his son Jack fashioned sports coats from Miller's racing no. 43. (John Smailes)

A question of balance. Jack Miller crests Lukey Heights, his right leg creating both an air brake and a fulcrum to better pivot the bike into the downhill run into Turn 10 (MG Corner). (AAP)

Phillip Island's whistleblower Tianda Watson—the friendly face of a modern circuit with old-world manners. (John Smailes)

Former Ferrari F1 driver Rubens Barrichello, twice runner-up in the world title to teammate Michael Schumacher, tested the new S5000 Australian Drivers' Championship car in 2019. (Chris Lambden)

Scott McLaughlin (left) and Fabian Coulthard (centre) won one Supercars championship SuperSprint race each at Phillip Island in 2019. Anton de Pasquale (Erebus Motorsport) (right) was third in the second heat. As of 2024 Supercars has not returned to Phillip Island, but many hope it will. (Ford PR)

Supercars star Will Davison knee-scraping on his Ducati V4R. Will took professional lessons at Phillip Island and at Motorcycle Australia's home track, Broadford. (Russell Colvin)

Next generation, part 1. Celebrating 30 years since Mick Doohan's first world title, Alpine F1 reserve driver Jack Doohan demonstrated the historic V10 2000 B200 Benetton F1 car at the 2024 Australian Grand Prix, with his five-times world motorcycle champion father, Mick, following on a Honda MotoGP RCV213. Jack hopes to be in F1 in 2025. (Alamy)

Next generation, part 2. Northern Territory rider Joel Kelso (right) took his first podium in the Moto3 world championship at Phillip Island in 2023. The rain-soaked race was won by Deniz Öncü, with Ayuna Sasaki second. (John Smailes)

Joel Kelso's mother Nayelle and sister Courtney celebrated beneath the podium—part rain, part champagne shower. (John Smailes)

Fergus Cameron, the face of Phillip Island for 40 years, with some of the sensational collection of historic racing motorcycles curated by the circuit's museum. (Old Bike Australasia)

for the Suzuka 8 Hours (pole), America for the Daytona 200 (fourth) and the UK for the British superbike championship (third—could have won but for a last-lap bike failure). Moriwaki rightly saw Australia as a pool full of rider talent.

In 1981 Wayne was in the UK, lonely in the spare room of teammate Roger Marshall's house in rural Lincolnshire, when he phoned home. 'If I had a seventeen-year-old daughter now, absolutely no way I'd let her go. But Mum and Dad paid my fare,' Donna said. She was on a mission. 'I had to protect him: from other girls, from the wheeler-dealers and sharks.' From other girls? 'He was a shocker, but we never discussed it. I'd never tarnish his reputation. I loved him, heart and soul.'

Gardner's first world championship race was almost his last. In the 1983 Dutch Grand Prix at Assen, he was an inadvertent participant in a race crash that almost killed world champion Franco Uncini.

'He went down,' Gardner remembered. 'Most others went right to miss him; I went left and hit him hard.' Uncini's helmet came off and he lay still.

'People attacked Wayne, told him he shouldn't have been racing [at that level],' Donna recalled.

'If Uncini had died I would have stopped,' Wayne agreed.

It would be 52 grands prix and almost five years before he'd crash in another world championship race. (A qualification: there were falls in non-title events, in testing and in practice.) By then he was world champion and he crashed trying to tame his evil-handling 1988 Honda NSR500 in a desperate and futile defence of his title.

'They'd sent me home because they thought I was a distraction,' Donna said of Wayne's opening season with Honda. Half a season later she was back, and Wayne's results improved.

In 1985, Rothmans had entered motorcycle racing to complement its successful sports car and rally program. Wayne was fourth for Rothmans Team Honda in 1985 and second to rival Eddie Lawson in 1986. In 1987 he was world champion. Donna was with him on the podium when he won it.

'The promoter pushed me up there,' she said. Wayne was alone on the winner's podium of the 1987 Brazilian Grand Prix, a white world-champion T-shirt pulled on hastily over his leathers, unsuccessfully fighting back tears, his Michelin cap clumsily on his head. 'He'd beaten Eddie, who refused to go up on the dais, so they sent me instead.' Donna clutched—hugged, actually—the trophy while Wayne sprayed the champagne. Donna's flared miniskirt did no harm to their image.

Gardner's world championship, and the notion of a boy from the 'Gong made good, set two-wheel sport alight.

On Saturday, 17 October 1987, it seemed all of Wollongong turned out to fete Gardner, and Donna, in the amphitheatre in Crown Street Mall. Wayne was presented with the key to the city. The 'key' was a new idea for Wollongong, so Gardner got the first. Because of Wayne, Wollongong led the national news.

Included in Australia's bicentennial celebrations, Wayne and Donna had breakfast with Prime Minister Bob Hawke at Kirribilli House on Australia Day, and met the Prince and Princess of Wales at the Royal Bicentennial Concert at the Sydney Opera House. The NSW Government held a state reception in his honour.

'I was at the Australian F1 Grand Prix in Adelaide, riding, doing a display thing, when Bob Barnard came up to me and said,

"I've got an idea,"' Gardner recalled. 'He wanted to run a world championship Australian Motorcycle Grand Prix.'

'"What circuit?" I asked. "Phillip Island," he replied. "Where the fuck is that?" I said. I'd never heard of it. We went down after Adelaide, just for a look. There was a little control tower, a lot of grass, sheep everywhere. "Is this it?" I asked.

'"Yep," he said. Then we went for a walk around. It was a very good track.'

Barnard needed Gardner's help.

'He asked me to lobby government and media and within the sport,' Gardner remembered. 'There was no money involved. I didn't get paid. I just wanted to see the race in Australia. I believed being a world champion had to stand for something.'

'Wayne worked his butt off,' Donna said. He arranged for Honda to lend Barnard bikes for display. He took time out of his season to make guest appearances. He hosted Barnard and his entourage at world championship rounds and introduced them to the right people.

He was battling to retain his title. The 1988 bike was 'a bucket of shit'. He rode its wheels off, crashed regularly and finished a frustrated second to Eddie Lawson. But he stayed loyal to Honda, and felt it should have been reciprocated.

'Honda asked me to get Mick Doohan for the team,' Wayne recalled. 'I rang him from South America and asked him. He said, "Wow, yeah." Then they gave Mick my crew chief Jeremy Burgess, and assigned Jerry's assistant Stuart Shenton to me.'

Then Honda hired Eddie Lawson, Gardner's number one rival, to join the team without telling Gardner. From Gardner's standpoint, it was a cold, hard slap in the face.

Gardner was embattled, the pressure huge. He and Donna had planned to marry at the end of the '88 season: 'We wrote a pre-nup on a table napkin in a little cafe,' Donna said. 'I needed to make it clear I didn't want his money.' The proposed wedding day came and went, postponed for a season.

Gardner spent the Australian summer doing media, promoting the Australian Motorcycle Grand Prix. Barnard had come through. The totally rebuilt Phillip Island track had been allocated second-round status in the 1989 world championship.

But first there was Japan, round one.

'I rode my balls off,' Gardner said, smiling at his intentional double entendre. He was the fastest Honda, but that still wasn't as quick as Yamaha and Suzuki. 'My goal was Eddie. I had to finish in front of him.' Leading Lawson, Gardner ran off the track in a huge tank slapper. He stayed on the bike but landed heavily on his groin. Lawson beat him to the podium, and the grand prix medico Dr Claudio Costa seriously considered removing his left testicle.

Gardner flew back to Australia with Channel Nine reporters Barry Sheene (twice world champion, living in Australia) and Darrell Eastlake. 'They were amused. I kept asking the steward for ice to put down the front of my pants. When Baz and Daz told him why, he was even more helpful.'

Australian Grand Prix week was a circus. Instead of giving Phillip Island his maximum attention, Gardner did media, all of it—talk shows, inane questions, well-meaning queues of well-wishers, corporates. Gardner, Mick Doohan and Yamaha rider Kevin Magee, the three prominent Australians, inaugurated the track for TV on Thursday. 'The only upside was that when I got pulled over by the cops driving back to Cowes, they let me off.'

In Saturday practice, he was taken out by slow-moving German rider Michael Rudroff, the 'Eddie the Eagle' of bike racing. 'He's actually a nice guy,' Wayne conceded. 'I was going to punch him, but realised I was probably on TV.' Gardner ran back to the pits, got his spare bike, and put it on the front row of the grid.

The first Australian Motorcycle Grand Prix is *the* classic. Wayne Gardner, on his Honda, won a race-long four-way duel by just 0.35 seconds from a brace of Yamahas. The lead had changed eighteen times. Lawson was fifth. Doohan, the lever Donna pulled to motivate her man in their pit caravan, was eighth, his hand stitched after a practice crash. Pole-sitter Kevin Schwantz crashed on the first corner. The Island's pernicious character was already evident.

'I never took a breath that last lap,' Donna said down the phone. 'I just wanted to see him come around the last turn. I was like Jello inside.' And then she was running, dressed for success in a black dress crafted by Australian Barry Taff's fashion label Covers ('I've still got it') and black snakeskin-pattern sneakers. Her feet seemed never to touch the ground as she ran out into no-man's land and up the main straight towards Gardner, seizing his helmeted head, screaming, 'You did it, you did it!' The team had boosted her over the fence. No decorum. The image of Donna and Wayne's moment is etched in motorcycle history.

The track invasion was huge: 'We want Wayne!' Bob Barnard in sports coat and tie was on the podium directly beneath Wayne. Wayne doused him with a bucketload of champagne from above.

It must have been some night, I suggested. There was a pause from Wayne and a silence from Donna on the phone. Then

Donna: 'He said, "Don, you go home." I waited all night, and he didn't come. About one a.m. I went to bed. He came home the next day. I wasn't included.'

There is no embarrassment, at least not outwardly. They are long since divorced. 'We are now the best of mates,' they agree.

Bob Barnard built the new Phillip Island Grand Prix Circuit, but Wayne Gardner enabled it. They did the same at Eastern Creek International Raceway (now Sydney Motorsport Park). Both world-class permanent tracks have hosted world championship events.

'I tell the story to the car crowd, and they shake their heads [in incredulity],' Jeremy Burgess—Australian motorcycle crew chief for Gardner, Doohan and Valentino Rossi, and surely our most capped and yet unsung motorsport hero—told me. 'But it's true. Without Wayne Gardner, we would not have either circuit.'

21

Winners and Losers

Wayne Gardner rode into the Grand Prix Ball on the Wednesday of the first event with a promotional model riding pillion—not on Phillip Island but 160 kilometres away in Melbourne. Who'd ever heard of a Grand Prix Ball? A new standard of promotion and professionalism had been declared.

Gardner won the first two Australian Grands Prix at Phillip Island.

Bob Barnard quit the track, built Eastern Creek International Raceway in Sydney, went broke and, with some dignity, left the country.

Hero or villain? It depends on who you talk to.

'Bob was shamefully treated,' his loyal clerk of course, Ross Martin, claimed. 'His vision was taken away from him.'

'I wanted to keep the grand prix at Phillip Island,' Peter

Henderson asserted. 'But Barnard had written the grand prix contract between himself and the Auto Cycle Council of Australia. There was no mention of Phillip Island.'

The first grand prix had confounded its critics. With hindsight, intermittent rain and parking areas that threatened to become quagmires had become fond memories. Barnard micromanaged each drama.

'Where's Bob?' someone asked Yamaha team manager Kel Carruthers.

'He's down there sorting it out,' Kel replied.

'By Friday I didn't want to get out of bed,' Barnard said, neatly mirroring Wayne Gardner's Sunday reluctance to race. But he did, and he was everywhere.

Alan Bond's Channel Nine promoted the event big time. Channel Seven angered racegoers by running old file footage of Bathurst bike-race riots.

At 9.35 p.m. on Sunday, a very real tragedy occurred. Senior Constable Richard Dufty was on point duty at the corner of Phillip Island Road and Churchill Road, trying to clear the never-ending traffic jam of racegoers. He stepped backwards into the path of a car and was killed. Police PR portrayed the incident as something 'not related to the grand prix'. Of course it was. Next year, a far more robust traffic management regime was introduced, including the introduction of the island's unique Blue Line, an extra lane used only on race weekends.

Ninety-two thousand people watched Sunday's race. It would prove to be an unbroken record, and it's assumed to be true.

Yet Bob Barnard knew he was a shot duck. Outgoings exceeded receipts. 'I can't work out why he didn't make money,' David White pondered. 'But he liked to do things on a grand scale. He was perhaps not as carefully budgeted as he should have been. In some ways, he overdelivered on a lot of things.'

'The Victorian premier John Cain called me a great entrepreneur but a bad businessman,' Barnard admitted. 'He could be correct.' But: 'No businessman would have taken the risk on the GP and they would have quit much earlier.'

Barnard was deeply in debt. He was trying to find funds in 1990 that could help pay off the debts of '89. It didn't help that the Australian economy was entering a recession, the one treasurer Paul Keating called 'the recession we had to have'. And it didn't help that the Victorian Government was tightening its anti-tobacco laws to a degree that the race teams found untenable.

As early as Christmas 1988, Barnard had chatted with Adelaide friend Bill O'Gorman. Sports car racer Bill was the enthusiast credited with planting the idea for the Australian F1 Grand Prix with the South Australian Government. He was the son-in-law of Sydney businessman Laurie O'Neill, a massive motor-racing fan who'd been the patron to drivers Frank Matich and Pete Geoghegan.

O'Neill owned a community recycling centre—a foul-smelling rubbish dump—in the foothills of Sydney's Blue Mountains. He thought it could become a motor-racing track. The idea started out as a separate project for BPM. It became its salvation.

Increasingly stymied by unfathomable Victorian pushback, Barnard began negotiations with the NSW Government. He had to deliver a motorcycle grand prix, but first he had to build a racetrack. It was déjà vu.

It's not possible to look at Phillip Island's predicament in isolation.

World motorcycle racing was in flux. In 1988, the Superbike World Championship (WSBK) had started in direct competition to the Motorcycle Grand Prix. 'Superbikes were derived from production machines,' explained Peter Doyle, chief executive of Motorcycling Australia and before that a leading team manager. 'People could relate to them. Grand prix bikes were like F1—just silhouettes.' There was, truly, a strong possibility that superbikes, supported by bike manufacturers seeking sales, could supplant GP.

Sydney's Oran Park successfully hosted a round of the first Superbike World Championship. With the enthusiastic agreement of his then partners in Barfield, Barnard stole it from the Sydney circuit for Phillip Island in 1990. 'I was always in favour of having more than one [world championship] race,' Peter Henderson agreed, adding that his friendship with Joe Zegwaard had precipitated the move.

A game of musical chairs had begun.

Phillip Island's first grand prix had been a huge success. The global grand prix organisers didn't want to lose that, especially if superbikes were going to take their place. Now, faced with the prospect of the grand prix going to New South Wales, the Victorian Government didn't want to lose it either.

Barnard, stuck in the middle, was no longer necessarily the main player, although he was a pivot. The NSW Government acted relatively swiftly to secure him. On 28 September 1989 it commissioned him to design and build the circuit to be known, unimaginatively, as Eastern Creek. The next day it gave him an advance on the $5.5 million loan it had agreed to guarantee to undertake construction. 'I immediately paid the pressing bills from the '89 event,' Bob admitted.

A week later, opening the Australian International Motor Show on the shores of Darling Harbour, NSW premier Nick Greiner announced that the grand prix would be moving to Sydney in 1990.

That was a tad premature. It would take more than six months to untangle the web. An Australian Grand Prix in 1990 was looking most unlikely.

Placetac's Peter Henderson changed the locks on the Phillip Island gates, denying Barnard access. Henderson is adamant he had the right. He was in control: 'Fergus Cameron was a very good circuit manager, but I was running the business.' A judge returned possession to Barnard.

Then, the Victorian Government reached a rapprochement with the International Road Racing Teams Association. If IRTA raced at Phillip Island in 1990, it could display its tobacco sponsors on its bikes and team apparel. But there could be no circuit signage. The Grand Prix was on, after all, and at its original venue.

Newly minted Eastern Creek, unfettered initially by government regulations on tobacco promotion, was guaranteed a round of the World Motorcycle Championship for 1991, time enough to get its act together.

Sponsorship was the next hurdle. Swan Brewery was facing liquidation, part of the systematic dismantling of Alan Bond's shaky empire. The Victorian Government stepped in. Through its Transport Accident Commission (TAC), it would become naming rights sponsor of the Phillip Island grand prix. It paid $75,000—according to Bob Barnard, 'about half Swan paid the previous year'. The TAC was running an anti-drink-driving campaign with the tagline 'If you drink, then drive, you're a bloody idiot'. Which is how the 1990 event became known as 'The Bloody Idiot Grand Prix'.

On 16 September 1990, Wayne Gardner won his second successive Australian Grand Prix at Phillip Island, promoted by Barfield.

On 11 November, Peter Goddard, now president of Motorcycling Australia, and Rob Phillis, Kawasaki superstar, each won a round of the Superbike World Championship on the windswept track. World Superbike, in future, would be promoted by Phillip Island's landowners.

'That was one of my greatest victories ever, the one that gave me the most personal satisfaction.' Wayne Gardner was pensive, poring over photographs of the 1990 Motorcycle Grand Prix on Phillip Island. 'World champion Wayne Rainey said, "How the fuck did you do that?"'

Gardner had been flung over the handlebars in a crash at Brno in the Czech Grand Prix and badly broken his wrist. 'I went to Phillip Island in a lot of pain. I had twenty-five micro-injections in the wrist, painkillers, and still my fingers were white.'

Mick Doohan, on the ascendancy, had won his first grand prix in Hungary just a fortnight before. At Phillip Island, he was on pole, having qualified 0.04 seconds faster than Gardner. Less than half a second covered the top four qualifiers. The race was over 30 laps (133.35 kilometres). Rainey, Texan Kevin Schwantz and the two Australians went physical, scraping fairings, elbows out. It was a race for the ages.

'I had a massive slide, came out of the saddle, and when I banged down, I broke my fairing on the left-hand side,' Gardner recalled. With aero compromised, 'the bike was hard to hold in a straight line'. And that was at 300 km/h.

'It was like I had an out-of-body experience,' Gardner said. Really? 'Yeah, you can do this—rise up and look down on yourself.' All the time, his wrist was on fire. 'I kept repeating to myself, "Deal with the pain after, deal with the pain after," over and over.'

Two laps to go and Doohan led from Gardner, Schwantz and Rainey. Gardner set up his move at the top of the straight, getting a faster exit from the final corner. The extra pace slingshotted him past Doohan into Turn 1. 'As Wayne came by, the wind almost blew me off the track,' Doohan recounted.

Doohan couldn't hold his line and suddenly Schwantz was through to second, hunting Gardner. One lap later, the Texan lunged into Turn 1. His front wheel washed out and he was high-sided at 240 km/h. 'That's the fastest I've ever crashed,' he told reporters. Schwantz landed on his back and slid forever into the grass. Reports at the time said that 'Schwantz had plenty of reason to thank Phillip Island for its inherent safety'.

Still, he broke a bone in his foot and another in his right hand, suffered extensive bruising and was coughing blood. Another day at the office.

Gardner won by a single second from Doohan—the first time, anywhere in the world, that Australians had finished first and second in a 500cc world championship race. 'When I saw Schwantz go down, it made me think that this was a bit more serious than us just enjoying ourselves,' Doohan said. 'All the same, it was the best race and the most fun I've had all year—better even than winning in Hungary.'

At the party that night, Gardner took a phone call from Belgian rider Didier de Radiguès, Gardner's old rival and good friend. 'Get your wrist checked out, quickly,' de Radiguès insisted.

'I went to Sydney's Royal North Shore Hospital,' Gardner said. 'Dr Tonkin told me it was really bad. I could lose use of the wrist.' The operation took bone from his hip and packed it around the scaphoid, securing it with a Herbert screw.

'We were just test pilots, doing stuff new to medical science,' Gardner quipped.

The 1990 Australian Grand Prix was Gardner's last win on two wheels in Australia. Over the next two years, he would win only one more grand prix—in Britain in 1992 (although he won two Suzuka 8 Hours: strong to the last). He retired at the end of that season.

The Australian Grand Prix became known as 'the Woodstock of grand prix racing'.

Phillip Island's wide-open spaces provided the perfect venue for a gathering of Woodstock proportions. Campers could be contained in a single area. That was a source of comfort to townsfolk, some of them nervous about an island influx.

The first year had been great. The atmosphere had been electric; no one much minded the paucity of ablution blocks and that a couple of big-name entertainment acts had failed to turn up.

In 1990, it just got better. Jimmy Barnes headlined acts that included Kevin Bloody Wilson, Noiseworks, The Black Sorrows and Paul Kelly and the Messengers. There was good food, hot showers, even a games arcade with state-of-the-art GP simulators. You couldn't ask for more.

Which is why it was so disappointing when an element 'piled into their cars', according to a report in enthusiast magazine *Australian Motorcycle News* (note the emphasis on cars) and 'wreaked havoc on the main town of Cowes. The rampage lasted until sun-up and left the town looking like a rubbish dump. The hooligans upended nearly every rubbish bin in the town, dispersing the contents and smashing a shop window.'

It could so easily have turned into a PR disaster. Even as the sun rose, GP rally organisers made an urgent appeal: 'Come with us into town to clean it up.' According to *Australian Motorcycle News*, 'around 600 to 1000 bikers rode into Cowes under police escort to assist with cleaning up. They were applauded by townsfolk on completion of the task as they rode back to the site.'

Peter Goddard, second-generation motorcycle racer and the world champion Australia should have had, raced in the 1990 Australian Grand Prix. His best lap on the Yamaha 500, built by former world champion Kenny Roberts, was 1 minute 37.6 seconds, which helped to secure a sensational eighth on his grand prix debut.

Two months later, he entered the first round of the Superbike World Championship at Phillip Island. He won the first of two superbike races, came second by 0.04 seconds in the next, and claimed the round. His best on the mighty Yamaha OW31 superbike, in high winds (gusts up to 90 km/h), was 1 minute 40.34 seconds.

No one was better credentialled to compare the two categories, back-to-back. 'The 500 was lighter, about 145 kilos, compared to the superbike at around 168 kilos, and it had more gearbox options, while the superbike had a fixed gearbox and you sorted out your ratios with final drive,' he explained in his Wollongong warehouse. He's now become a leading importer of electric trials and motocross bikes—no engine at all.

'But the superbike, being heavier, was more forgiving,' he continued—a good thing in Phillip Island's flukey conditions. Even now, his opinion on the racing he enjoyed the most is divided. But: 'There was a "holy shit" moment when I got on the 500. It was twenty kilometres an hour faster.'

In 1989, there'd been a superbike race supporting the grand prix and Goddard had won that too. The same crowd that cheered Wayne Gardner cheered him as well. 'It was unbelievable. I'd seen big crowds in Japan, but this was inspirational—so loud I couldn't hear myself.' Gardner enjoyed his track invasion, then they backed up for Goddard.

Goddard couldn't wait to get on a 500, just like Gardner. The opportunity came through his manager, Warren Willing.

'Warren was working with Kenny Roberts and he arranged for Yamaha to build a third Roberts bike for me, as a wildcard entry in the Australian Grand Prix,' Goddard said. 'It was built up out of spare parts. The first time I saw it was on the Tuesday before the race.'

Goddard already knew Roberts. Ted Goddard, Pete's father, was Australia's leading off-road endurance rider, a prototype Toby Price. He'd raced in the International Six Days Trial and even in the Baja 1000 in the USA. Pete followed in his dad's wheel tracks and won three Australian flat-track titles. Then he went to the States and met Kenny Roberts on the Californian flat tracks, Pete in the Junior category, Kenny in the Senior, both of them sparking flintstones with their steel-capped riding boots.

Flat tracks taught body control. They gave American Grand Prix champions—Roberts, Wayne Rainey, Eddie Lawson, Freddie Spencer—a dominant edge, the ability to minutely move their body mass on the bike in response to subtle inputs from their machine. A foot more heavily weighted on the peg, a shoulder dropped slightly . . .

'Kenny was keen to see how I'd go,' Goddard smiled. The first lap was a revelation. 'The bike had no over-rev. Some bikes let you roll on past the point where they're making maximum power. This one just stopped, like hitting the brakes. I was thrown forward into the fairing and smashed it with my helmet.'

Tyre selection at Phillip Island had always been critical. 'The tyre makers never gave you the good rubber until you'd proved yourself,' he recalled. On his fourth practice lap, Goddard's front tyre washed out in Turn 1 and put him down. 'I got back to the pits to find Kenny with a French tyre technician pinned by his throat to the wall: "You could have killed my rider!" he was shouting.'

Goddard finished eighth, progressively working his way through the field. It was a better than promising result. Goddard used it to secure a ride in the domestic All-Japan 500 championship. He won the title three times.

International riders in Phillip Island's first Superbike World Championship race in 1990 were nonplussed by the state of the circuit. 'It's bumpy in the dodgy places,' works Yamaha rider Rob McElnea reported. If anyone could tame the track, the powerfully built Englishman should. 'It's so important to get the right lines here because it's so fast,' he said. 'The difference is six inches between a good and bad line.'

The locals had the edge. 'The wind was brutal,' Peter Goddard said. 'You had to watch out for it. You'd look at the flags flying at track side, and you'd ride accordingly.' A big gust could blow you off line or put you down. 'You had to watch the birds too. I've had close calls at Phillip Island, screens smashed and air intakes broken. The worst are the Cape Barren geese. They weigh up to seven kilos.'

Goddard took pole and won the first of two races after fired-up local Rob Phillis fishtailed off into the grass on the right-hand Honda hairpin, then dropped the bike and broke his handlebar navigating back to the track. Phillis slipstreamed Goddard in the second race, then nipped out to win by the snap of a finger. Another local, Mal Campbell, used their draught to set a new lap record, 1 minute 39.08 seconds, and came in third.

The Superbike World Championship would become the constant feature of Phillip Island, and local dominance would be its hallmark, at least for the first decade. Why? Goddard saw it as a reward for good manners. 'Phillis and Campbell set the standard,' he opined. 'They left racing room. World championship people would ride dirty and try to run you off—no respect for other riders. When you're heading for a big crash, you don't want to get distracted by shit like that.'

While the superbike riders had good reason to believe they'd be returning in 1991, the grand prix riders knew they weren't. 'Why are we leaving Phillip Island? It's one of the best tracks in the world,' new champion and third in the 1990 Australian Grand Prix, Wayne Rainey, asked publicly from the podium, making himself a friend of the fans.

Michael Scott, doyen of race reporting, offered an optimistic response: 'If Eastern Creek manages to be half as good, it will still be one of the best tracks in the world.'

22

A Simple Case of Accounting

It was complicated.

By the early 1990s, motor racing—cars and bikes—had discovered its identity, and determined there was money in it. A Spanish company, Dorna Sports, had begun to introduce commercial reality to motorcycle grand prix racing. An Italian company, Flammini Group, was doing likewise with World Superbike.

For a short time, motor racing's supreme ringmaster Bernie Ecclestone owned a company called Two Wheel Promotions (start-up cost around $50,000), which held the rights to motorcycle grands prix. He sold it to Dorna for $52 million, all in the space of a year.

Bob Barnard and his Sydney saviours—Laurie O'Neill and partners Rod Hunwick, Craig Malouf and Sir Jack Brabham—

had secured a deal with the NSW Government to build a world-standard racetrack on Laurie's tip.

The state government had tried and failed to buy additional critical land, so Barnard modified his design. It was still good, though, in defiance of emerging trends. 'CAMS, representing the FIA, warned me that my sweeping Turn 1 was way too fast and F1 champion Alan Jones agreed,' Barnard recalled. 'He said I needed more right-angle corners.' Barnard countered by bringing in Warren Willing, who said it was just right for bikes.

Barnard ran his third World Motorcycle Championship grand prix at Eastern Creek International Raceway on 7 April 1991. Wayne Rainey won. Mick Doohan stormed up from ninth, and in front of a screaming partisan audience finished a flying second. He could have won but there weren't enough laps.

'The crowd was good, but not good enough. The sponsorship was okay but not enough, and corporate attendance wasn't sufficient,' Barnard said. 'We knew we were done.' The Barnard BPM partnership was labouring under debt and crumbling. The remaining shareholders tried unsuccessfully to sell Barfield, the company's operational arm, to media mogul Kerry Packer.

Packer had sold his media assets to Alan Bond in 1987 for $1.05 billion. He bought them back in 1990 for $250 million. He was in the middle of tidying up. Instead of buying Barfield, Packer's PBL marketing organisation applied for it to be wound up.

Barnard was bankrupted. To his credit, he worked through it, steadfastly paid back cents in the dollar from his salary in the construction industry to honourably discharge his obligations, and today designs and builds private country club motor-racing courses for high-net-worth individuals, operating behind securely locked gates. 'It's the only way to go; there's no money to be made in public racetracks,' he smiled from his Spanish home.

In place of Barnard the NSW Government asked the Auto Cycle Union of NSW to run the 1992 Australian Grand Prix. Three years later, the ACU, also, was bankrupt.

Ron Kivovich, an Australian 125cc short-circuit champion and twice NSW scrambles (motocross) title holder, was the whistleblower. 'I could see there was something wrong with their accounting,' the now 89-year-old Kivo (no one called him Ron), proudly wearing his Willoughby District Motor Cycle Club shirt, told me. Kivo had been president of the Willoughby club when it introduced the Castrol Six Hour production bike race, a game changer in motorcycle racing. He was an industry stalwart, Honda's then Yamaha's best salesman. 'I'd retired to go bike riding, but I could just see the grand prix wasn't right,' he said.

It was a simple case of accounting. 'They're bringing forward debt into the next accounting year,' he alleged publicly, incessantly, in meetings at the time. 'And it was compounding,' he told me. 'When it took on the grand prix in 1992, the Auto Cycle Union had funds of $1.2 million and was earning a cash surplus of $300,000 a year. When they went broke, they owed $800,000. They'd blown something like $2.2 to $3 million. Two of its board members, Arthur Blizzard and Sid Jackson, contributed $14,000 of their own money to keep it afloat on behalf of the members.' The trimmed-down Auto Cycle Union moved into an office 'behind an old bakery in Lidcombe'.

Kivo was kicked upstairs. He became the third president of Motorcycling Australia: 'We need an arsehole like you who won't take no for an answer,' he said they told him. He fulfilled the role for ten years.

In 1996, the NSW Government ran Eastern Creek's last motorcycle grand prix itself, employing international sports marketer IMG to help. The event's call to action was 'The Final Curtain'. Mick Doohan, just crowned triple world champion, led until the last lap, when his teammate and rival Alex Criville took them both out. Italian Loris Capirossi did a Bradbury and slipped by to claim his first GP victory.

A week later, Phillip Island hosted the grand final of the Superbike World Championship, the two events virtually back-to-back. Wollongong-born international Troy Corser won his first world title, grandstanding with massive high-speed wheelies to a crowd five deep on the fence. Then he confirmed his intention to join the 1997 grand prix field.

Email to the Hon Jeff Kennett AC, 9 November 2023:

> Dear Mr Kennett,
> I would appreciate a conversation with you to discuss
> how the MotoGP was regained for Phillip Island in 1997,
> and particularly the role played by you (as premier) and
> Ron Walker.
> Please let me know if you are able to assist.
> Regards,
> John Smailes

Just one day later, Victoria's highly visible and enthusiastic premier from 1992 to 1999 declined. He directed me instead to an early chief of the Victorian Major Events Company. The VMEC had been set up to separate the business of government from that of direct events promotion, a form of management requiring a different and perhaps more flexible skill set. Almost 30 years on, it seemed, the sensible division of responsibility was still in place.

By the mid- to late '90s, motorsport, at its elite level, had become big business for the state of Victoria. Along with the Australian Open tennis, and the perennials—the Spring Racing Carnival and the AFL Grand Final—the Australian F1 Grand Prix would soon become a source of major economic benefit for the state. By the time of Covid interruption, Victoria's Department of Premier and Cabinet pointed to a total events value of $1.8 billion. Post-pandemic, the theoretical equation returned to 84 per cent of pre-pandemic levels and was expected to grow.

Adelaide had inaugurated the Australian F1 Grand Prix in 1985. It had been a pacesetter—and a target. Ask any South Australian: Victoria stole it from them.

'I remember the day well,' former South Australian premier Dean Brown told the ABC. It was December 1993 and the Liberal leader had just won the state election. 'The day after I'd been sworn in, I received a telephone call from Ron Walker, who revealed a contract had been signed in extreme secrecy with Bernie Ecclestone a year before.' The grand prix would move to Melbourne in 1996.

Walker was a businessman, former lord mayor of Melbourne, and the Liberal Party's honorary federal treasurer for more than a decade. In the mid-'90s, he and Premier Kennett had ramped up the VMEC to attract world-leading sports to Victoria. The structure of Major Events separated its activities from the government, provided it with autonomy beyond that of a public-sector bureaucracy and, frankly, gave the government a shield should something go wrong. It took an amendment of state legislation to get it approved. Kennett's predecessor, Labor leader Joan Kirner, had appointed Walker its chair. Kennett invested in it. In this case, a good idea transcended party politics.

The Australian Grand Prix Corporation (AGPC) had been formed in 1994 to run the Australian F1 Grand Prix. Sensibly, it could handle motorcycle grands prix as well.

'There was opportunity to scale managerial responsibility across both events,' Judith Griggs, the first CEO of the Corporation, told me from her holiday location in Scotland. 'It was important though not to conflate them.' Each had to have its own identity.

Griggs is one of the great success stories of Australian motorsport. Trained as a commercial rights lawyer at the Adelaide Grand Prix (she wrote her own job description), she was plucked from her role with the grand prix to work with 'Mr Ecclestone' (even now she gives him the appellation) at Formula One Administration. Then it was back to Australia to run the first Melbourne grands prix, and to Europe as chief operating officer of Allsport Management, the Swiss money-making machine that defined product licensing and corporate hospitality in motor racing.

Griggs was one of two young prospects identified by Ron Walker for ascendancy. The other was John Harnden, a design engineer for an external company employed to help build the Albert Park F1 grand prix track. 'The plans were approved on

2 May 1994, the day after Ayrton Senna died,' Harnden recalled. 'Judith and Ron Walker invited me to leave my job and join them.' He became project manager at the AGPC, then deputy CEO, and succeeded Judith when she returned to the UK.

Griggs and Harnden were there to watch the deal go down that would bring the Australian Motorcycle Grand Prix back to Phillip Island in 1997. It was multi-levelled. 'Fergus Cameron kept pushing Ron to get it on the radar of the Victorian Government,' Harnden said.

In Europe: 'Mr Ecclestone and Carmelo Ezpeleta [the Ecclestone-like boss of Dorna] had a great amount of respect for each other,' Griggs said. 'They were great admirers of each other.' It's easy to see Ecclestone opening Ezpeleta's door for Ron Walker, already a Bernie confidante.

Even so, the motorcycle boss had a foot in another door with the NSW Government. Despite the problems at Eastern Creek, prising him loose could not have been easy. 'Victoria was very aggressive,' Harnden said. 'Both Ron and Jeff Kennett spoke to Carmelo. Ron did the deal. We knew it was coming before it was publicly announced in 1995.'

So, by the time the first Australian F1 Grand Prix occurred at Albert Park in 1996, the Australian Motorcycle Grand Prix was also locked up for the following year. It was a major coup for Ron Walker. 'People rarely acknowledged everything he did,' Griggs said. 'He worked without fees, just because he loved it.'

But if economies of scale were so important, why didn't the motorcycle grand prix go to Albert Park?

'Albert Park was very challenging. Its verge width didn't allow for motorcycle racing,' John Harnden said, providing the engineering answer. Unsaid, there was also the costly matter of closing a road circuit and installing temporary infrastructure. 'We went the other way. Because of our relationship with Phillip Island, we were able to use some of their overhead signs at Albert Park.'

Judith Griggs's caveat on confluence was paramount. 'Formula One is all about the racing. With MotoGP, you get a different sense: man versus machine versus track. It's a different experience.'

VMEC's charter, also, was to drive tourism to regional areas. Phillip Island met the brief. But there was, above all that, a far more compelling motivation. The Australian Motorcycle Grand Prix had been 'brought back to its spiritual home'.

Judith Griggs was named Telstra's Australian Business Woman of the Year in the public sector category in 1996. She is a co-director of Sports Right Management and Sports Rights Tech, companies with insight into the complex world of AI. John Harnden, a Member of the Order of Australia for his contribution to sports administration, was CEO of the 2006 Melbourne Commonwealth Games and a director of Cricket Australia, and is chief executive of the Melbourne and Olympic Parks Trust, overseeing all the state's major venues.

'My big moments in sports include Cathy Freeman winning the 400 metres at the Sydney Olympics; the final of the 2020 Women's T20 World Cup, which packed the MCG; and Mick Doohan winning at Phillip Island in 1998,' Harnden said.

'I'll never forget the first time I put my head over the pit wall at Phillip Island to see those incredible athletes—their ability to control a bike at that speed and hold it on trajectory,' Griggs recalled. 'It was difficult and dangerous. I was in awe.'

23

Four Wheels . . . Good

Ferociously talented open-wheeler driver John Smith was the first to feel the wrath of the resurfaced Phillip Island circuit. It was 25 March1990, and racing cars had been welcomed back to the Island in over-the-top style.

Four rounds of national championship series would be hosted on the one card: the Australian Touring Car Championship, Australian Drivers' Championship, Formula Ford and Australian Production Car Championship. It was a major statement of capability and intent, a 'we're back in business' shout-out. The promoter was Bob Barnard, still legally entitled—in fact obligated—to maximise his use of the track he built.

'I was on the front row of the grid for the Gold Star,' John Smith recalled. 'It was the first time any of us had been to the track and we were still learning. I lay in bed thinking how I could go faster. I was on the rev limiter in fourth over Lukey Heights. Could I do it in fifth?'

With six open-wheeler championships in his trophy cabinet, Smith was irrepressible. No one, domestically at least, held mid-corner speed like Smithy, dancing on the edge of disaster. People rushed to the fences to watch him—he was that exciting.

He'd secured a Ron Tauranac–designed Ralt RT21 for the Australian Drivers' Championship. It was a one-engine series: the cars were powered exclusively by a 3.8-litre Holden (Buick) V6. It was a big deal. Holden was right behind it.

Smithy, cheekily, had a big idea. General Motors-Holden was enduring a badge-sharing manufacturing partnership with Toyota. The federal government had forced the unwanted alliance on both domestic car makers as means of rationalising the local motor industry. It was a shotgun wedding.

United Australian Automobile Industries (UAAI)—Holden and Toyota combined—lasted just seven years. Holden's Commodore would be sold by Toyota as a Lexcen (named for the late Ben Lexcen, designer of the winged keel yacht that won the America's Cup). Toyota's Corolla and Camry would be sold as Holden's Nova and Apollo. It was a stupid plan and everyone hated it.

Smithy persuaded Toyota's general manager, marketing, Bob Miller, to sponsor his Holden-powered Ralt, badged up as a Lexcen. It was ambush marketing at its best. This was a golden chance to stick it up Holden—and to highlight the absurdity of the UAAI scheme. All Smithy had to do was win.

'It was early morning warm-up before the race and I did four laps, taking Lukey Heights progressively quicker in fourth, each time hitting the rev limit, and then I thought, "Now or never."' Smithy went for fifth with his right boot rammed to the pedal box.

'It went off the road at a great rate. It hit the bank backwards and tore off the engine and gearbox; it spun around and took off the front right-wheel assembly, which landed in my lap. It shed the left wheel too. By then it looked less like a race car and more like a canoe.' Leaking fuel started a grass fire.

'I walked back to the pits with the steering wheel in my hand and said to Dave Mawer [the car's owner and preparer]: "It's not good, Dave." He said, "I've got plenty of spares—let's get it rebuilt." I said, "No, mate, it's really not good. It's coming back on two trailers."'

Toyota kept its part of the bargain and paid enough of the sponsorship agreement to let the car be rebuilt. But Smithy never raced an open-wheeler again, at least not in the 'main game'. He moved to historic racing and ended up behind the wheel of the late John Dawson-Damer's collection of Lotus F1 cars.

Smithy became dealer principal of the family business, Sydney's Ferguson Toyota at Hurstville, the same workshop where Sir Jack Brabham had been an automotive apprentice 40 years before.

Five-time Australian touring car champion Dick Johnson was the first person to better 100 mph (160.934 km/h) in a touring car on the new Phillip Island circuit.

'I did it twice, actually,' Dick smiled down the line from his high-rise penthouse overlooking the Gold Coast's Broadwater. 'There was a test session a few days before the 1990 touring car championship race, and I surprised myself by breaking the ton then. Boy, that track was fast.' Dick was on the medium-compound Dunlop DS11 in the test.

'But Dunlop had also brought a new tyre, made especially for Phillip Island. It was the hardest compound they'd built at the time—the DS26—and they thought it would be the duck's guts at the Island.' The rock-hard DS26 was built to go race distance on the high corner speeds the Island served up, not act as qualifying rubber. But Dick got heat in the tyre over four laps then became the first to break the ton in official practice too, defying the laws of physics. Tony Longhurst and Glenn Seton, both on qualifying Yokohama rubber, ultimately went quicker, but nothing beats being first.

In the race, the hard compound Dunlops kept their grip, and Johnson and his wingman John Bowe stroked their Ford Sierra Cosworths to a one-two victory. 'Bowie pushed me all the way,' Johnson recalled. Team manager Neil Lowe had instructed them to slow down and not race each other. 'But you never knew what Bowie would do when he was desperate for a win, so I kept going,' said Johnson.

It's as well he did. His debut win at Phillip Island that day was also his last ever round victory in an Australian Touring Car Championship.

Johnson was immersed in the sport's politics. Phillip Island had relaunched at a critical time for the touring car series. 'Spectator attendance was down. TV ratings were dropping. Australian fans couldn't make sense of the cars they were watching,' Johnson said. 'Between them, CAMS and the promoters were deciding our future and they weren't doing a good job of it. We needed to have a voice. The teams started the

Touring Car Entrants Group of Australia to help stay alive. It all required funding and I kicked in $100,000, the lion's share of the contribution.'

The touring cars would not return to Phillip Island until 1993. When they did, they came back as rip-roaring V8s.

In 1993, Bob Barnard was gone. The circuit's owners had formed an operational company, Phillip Island Motor Sports Pty Ltd (PIMS), and along with PIARC they'd become joint-venture promoters. On 2 April 1993, they staged the third round of the Australian Touring Car Championship. It was the first year of the new V8 GP3A category. V8 Supercars had been born.

The new Phillip Island promoters named the main straight for touring car debutant Wayne Gardner. Never mind the four-wheel heroes: Gardner was Phillip Island's star. This was the return of the Island's prodigal.

Gardner had retired, hurt, from bikes in 1992. Back home and before he'd even begun to contemplate his next move, he'd been quickly snapped up by the V8 brigade. He'd run the rain-shortened Bathurst 1000 in '92, brought in by enthusiastic amateur Graham Moore. 'What was I going to do? Sit on a beach and drink beer?' Gardner shrugged. Then he went big time—to Tom Walkinshaw's Holden Racing Team, no less. This was no low-key entry into the world of touring car racing. Gardner was a big deal.

Phillip Island capitalised. Naming the straight for their two-time Australian Motorcycle Grand Prix winner was a masterstroke on several levels—good PR in Melbourne to draw a crowd, and a poke in the eye for Eastern Creek. The Sydney track might have stolen the motorcycle grand prix, but the Island had Gardner. (Much later, the new management at Sydney Motorsport Park, formerly Eastern Creek, named an entire track layout after him.) 'Fergus Cameron was dealing with Bernie Ecclestone, through Ron Walker, to get the grand prix back,' Peter Henderson confided.

In the third round of the 1993 Australian Touring Car Championship at Phillip Island, Gardner delivered. He made a sensational start in the preliminary 'Dash' race and again in the main event, so much so that officials, monitoring this newcomer carefully, fined him $500 for jumping the flag. Down into the hairpin Honda Corner for the first time, the other world champion in the field, 1980 F1 titleholder Alan Jones, hit him under brakes, turned him around and dropped him to last.

A clash between two world champions was great copy, and Jones and Gardner already had form. At the previous round at Symmons Plains in Tasmania, Gardner had speared past the field down the outside to win the Dash (his first win on four wheels). It was a manoeuvre way outside accepted technique and left a degree of mayhem in its wake. In the main race, Jones punted Gardner into a sand trap.

'I don't have a vendetta against Wayne,' Jones smiled after the Phillip Island incident. But clearly the car guys were keen to ensure the bike guy played by their rules. And it added to the show.

'The cars were not as big a challenge as people thought,' Wayne told me, all these years later, sitting in his time capsule in Wollongong. 'It was the same process, just with different parameters. For a start, you're sitting in a steel shell. With that degree of safety, you can push the limits more and know you can be a bit more cheeky.

'The bikes are far quicker at Phillip Island and there's a lot of run-off area. On a bike, if you make one little mistake, you're gone. In car racing, it's how good the car is; in bike racing it's about the rider. [For ultimate excitement] I'll take motorcycles every day. They give ten times more bang for the buck.' Thirty years on, his opinion might still rankle. But he's entitled to it. So, if a bike is a perfect ten at Phillip Island, what's a car? He thinks for a moment, gives a cheeky grin: 'A four.'

Gardner formed his own team the next year with major backing from Coca-Cola (Gardner had a close relationship with Coca-Cola's Australian chair, Dean Wills). Walkinshaw accused him of 'mutiny'. Gardner retained Coke right up to 1997, when the original energy-drink company splurged its budget on the 2000 Sydney Olympic Games. He raced successfully for Toyota in Japan, raced the 1998 Le Mans 24 Hour with his motorcycle buddy Didier de Radiguès, stormed to pole for the 2000 Bathurst 1000 and in 1995 claimed third place in Bathurst's Great Race, behind Alan Jones.

Gardner retired from racing in 2002.

'You've done motorsport a disservice.' Bob Jane, multi-millionaire owner of Calder Park Raceway and developer of its NASCAR-like Thunderdome had shirtfronted Kelvin O'Reilly, chief executive of the Australian Super Touring Championship.

Jane was furious that O'Reilly had not given the media access to the video of the death of Gregg Hansford. It was an unexpected and disturbing confrontation.

Hansford had been killed on 5 March 1995, on lap two of the

first round of the championship, ramming an earthen barrier at Phillip Island and recoiling back onto the track in front of an oncoming car. O'Reilly swears Jane wanted the vision released. 'We didn't have live TV,' O'Reilly said. 'We were recording and post-producing, so we had views of the crash from outside and from the in-car camera, but it had not gone to air.' It was not tape he would ever show anyone. 'I told Jane that,' O'Reilly said. 'He responded: "Well, if that's your attitude I don't want you to come and race at Calder." You can imagine what I replied.'

Most likely, Jane's demand wasn't motivated by a desire to showcase the titillating post-mortem vision, but rather a business decision to keep sweet with the networks. Motorsport needed television. By not releasing the vision, O'Reilly had not only defied Jane. He'd resisted the major TV networks, as Jane had feared, risking upsetting the delicate balance between broadcasters and race promoters.

'We weren't on *Sports Tonight* for a year because of it,' said O'Reilly, now CEO of Karting Australia, the breeding ground for future champions.

The Super Touring Championship for two-litre cars racing under international regulations pioneered the commercialisation of Australian motorsport. 'We were the first to be sold a category management agreement by CAMS,' O'Reilly proudly said. The deal preceded by two years a similar arrangement for V8s. Then, the two categories would fight out a war only one could win.

Phillip Island was in the thick of it, the first in; also the first out.

In 1993 they raced together, two-litres and five-litre V8s, in the same event. It was a shambles. Next year they separated.

Two high-flying local promoters, Terry Morris and Peter Adderton, joined forces with Aussie-expat boss of the British Touring Car Championship Alan Gow to seize control from CAMS and monetise motor racing. The plan was to import cars from the British Touring Car Championship, limited to two-litre engine capacity, and have them backed by local distributors. BMW was all for it. Audi joined them. Volvo came on board, Nissan and Toyota too.

In 1995, the series was relaunched as the Australian Super Touring Championship.

'They got me to run it for them,' O'Reilly said. He'd been the marketing manager of the Gold Coast IndyCar race. 'Fergus Cameron was on the Motorsport Promoters Association. He secured the rights to the first round of the new series.'

Gregg Hansford was the star. He was one of Australia's great international motorcycle racers, then had won the Bathurst 1000 (with Larry Perkins) and the Bathurst 12 Hour (with Neil Crompton).

'New regulations granting the cars greater aerodynamic freedoms were due on 1 April,' O'Reilly recalled. 'But Gregg was in last year's Ford Mondeo. It was to be the last race for that car before upgrading.'

Hansford aimed the car into Turn 1 and it could not hold its line. Its back came around and the car speared off to the right in a massive white-out of smoking rubber. When it rebounded from the tyre wall it was hit by the Peugeot of Mark Adderton, brother of the co-owner of the series.

The championship became big news, for totally the wrong reason.

Gregg Hansford's funeral was the largest Australian motor

racing had known (until Peter Brock's in 2006 which packed Melbourne's St Paul's Cathedral).

The Super Tourers upgraded their safety. New aerodynamics would better pin the cars to the racing surface. A regulation requiring two warm-up laps to get sufficient heat into the front-wheel drive and steer configuration would bring greater certainty on turn in.

In 1996, impresario Tony Cochrane, who had worked with Bob Barnard on the Ultimate Event opening of Sanctuary Cove, galvanised the V8 division into a cohesive marketing group he called Supercars and blew the Super Tourers out of the water.

It was an unfair contest. Cochrane was backed by local manufacturing powerhouses Ford and Holden. Super Tourers was reliant on low-volume importers. Toyota, the only one with mass-market clout, had withdrawn after the first season.

In 1999, Phillip Island declined to have Super Tourers on its calendar. 'It's just my speculation,' O'Reilly said, 'but we were charging circuits a sanction fee, somewhere between $10,000 and $20,000 a round. Phillip Island didn't want to pay that without a guarantee of return. The cost of operating a grand prix track was far in excess of opening the gates at Calder or Oran Park. We were squeezing the series really hard to make it commercially viable, so we were relegated to the smaller circuits.'

In the UK, rising costs nobbled Gow's British Touring Car Championship. Manufacturers withdrew with a flow-on effect to Australia. The series sank almost without trace. 'We pulled the pin on our series in September 2001,' O'Reilly said. 'I reckon by being proactive we dodged a bullet.'

V8 Supercars embraced Phillip Island. From 1993 to 2019, across 42 races and heats, fourteen drivers stood on the top step of the podium. In the best tribal tradition of Supercars, 21 victories went to Holden and 17 to Ford. The remaining four were claimed by a Volvo driven by promising youngster, now IndyCar hero, Scott McLaughlin. He tied with local hero Craig Lowndes for the most Supercar wins at the Island—seven each—and both would drive two brands: McLaughlin traded up from Volvo to Ford, while Lowndes controversially moved from Holden to Ford and back to Holden. His fans forgave him.

There was a time, when they were younger, that Supercar stars adopted superbikes as their midweek sport. It got pretty serious: road rides in street trim evolved into track days with superbike rubber and tyre warmers. Craig Lowndes became a Suzuki ambassador and willingly rode its GSX-R1000 to Phillip Island to watch the motorcycle GPs. Wide-eyed, he'd seek autographs from the riders. He revered Valentino Rossi and Casey Stoner, called them 'warrior-like, the last great daredevils of international motorsport, putting it on the line every time they go out'.

Will Davison, twice Island Supercar winner, went one better. He became a Ducati ambassador and took track-day lessons from Stoner and Wayne Maxwell, twice Australian superbike champion.

Davison is the only Supercar driver to have done serious two-wheel laps of the Island. He claims a 1 minute 40(ish) lap on a Ducati V4R 1000. (In 2023, the superbike lap record belonged to Jonathan Rae at 1 minute 30.07 seconds, so it's feasible.)

'The Island is much more a motorbike circuit than a car circuit,' Davison said. 'Places you take full throttle in a Supercar, you have to squeeze on with a bike. Where you'd start braking for Turn 1 at eighty metres in a Supercar, you have to start setting up 200 metres before on the bike, bleeding off the front brake, holding your weight down over the front, sliding the bike on throttle.' It took him a while to adjust. 'But then I was getting the rear wheel in the air during braking, and moving my body on the bike, corner to corner. It's a big adaption.'

Modern racing bikes have a lean angle of up to 65 degrees—40 degrees greater than the brain accepts as safe. Motorcycle racers wear sacrificial knee sliders to act as a buffer between knee and track. 'I was so proud when I came back with my sliders cracked,' Davison said.

'I was really reaching out to put my body—and my knees—in use. I thought I was Casey Stoner. But when I got back to the pits, the guys said, "Why?" Turns out the pros are so precise they don't wear them out, just lightly brush them to feel out the track surface.'

Davison, grandson of four-time Australian Grand Prix winner Lex, first saw Phillip Island as a fifteen-year-old 'at the grand prix where Mick Doohan crashed'. He was there the following year to see Doohan's greatest victory. He supported his older brother Alex with his fledgling Formula Ford career, then won his own first Formula Ford race at the Island.

Formula Ford played a big role in the development of Supercar drivers. In its twenty-year period (1993–2013) as an Australian championship and feeder series, fourteen Formula Ford winners graduated to Supercars and four became Supercar champions.

Jamie Whincup, seven-time Supercar champion, crashed his Van Diemen RF94—the Red Rabbit—at the Island in his debut year. The Rabbit had been a total surprise for the sixteen-year-old, the next phase in a career carefully curated by his father and uncle.

The Whincups epitomised the enthusiastic and ambitious families circling the flame of professional motorsport that had been lit by the burgeoning Supercar category. Jamie's mum and dad, Sandra and David, supported him absolutely from his first kart race, aged seven. In his early Supercar years, they set up a big yellow tent they called the 'Taj Mahal' at Turn 1, so family and friends could celebrate his success. When David died in 2012 of lymphoma, Jamie wrote: 'He wasn't just Dad to me—he was my best mate.'

Jamie won the Formula Ford title two years after his Red Rabbit debut.

Garth Tander, 2007 Supercar champion, and Marcos Ambrose, twice champion in 2003 and 2004, crashed their Formula Fords at Turn 1 in 1997. 'We were just being pig-headed and wouldn't give each other room,' Tander grinned. 'But when we got back to the pits, there were our fathers Dirk [Tander] and Ross [Ambrose], just shaking their heads and calling us dickheads.'

In 2000, Phillip Island hosted two heats of the Australian Formula Ford Championship. Will Power, twice IndyCar championship winner, barrel-rolled his Spectrum 07 out of Turn 12 in the second heat and ended up in hospital. Eighteen years later he won the Indianapolis 500. Will's dad Bob, a handy

F2 racer, had arranged for him to drive under tutelage of racing guru Mike Borland, who saw the crash as a pivotal moment: 'He didn't know whether to be aggressive or patient. When he returned he'd sorted his head out.'

At the same race meeting Power crashed, Leanne Ferrier became the first female to win a round of the Formula Ford championship. Her racer dad Mark was there to support her. She'd been going to his races since she was a kid; he'd been coming to hers since she started karting aged thirteen.

Leanne married Garth Tander (they're separated now) and they became the first husband and wife to simultaneously lead national championships. They formed TanderSport to provide an all-encompassing engineering and mentoring service to young hopefuls. It didn't work out: 'People want to pay nothing and get everything,' Ferrier ruefully observed.

Ferrier came so close to winning the Australian Drivers' Championship; she was beaten in 2007 by just two points and in 2008 by just four. In both series, she'd won a heat at Phillip Island. 'I loved the place—so daunting and so flowing. A true grand prix track,' she said.

She'd take Turn 1 'race-car-driver flat' (that's what Garth called it). 'You have a little lift and your brain doesn't even register you've done it.' It hurt when she missed out on the Gold Star—and the chance to be the only woman to win it. 'It's so historic, something I really wanted. To get so close was heartbreaking. I've replayed that season over in my mind so many times.'

Leanne Ferrier and Tander no longer race full-time. Garth is strategic director for Grove Racing, a multi-disciplinary team owned by businessman Stephen Grove, who entered Supercar in 2022. Tander and Ferrier's ten-year-old son Sebastian is a member of Grove's junior team, set up to foster next-generation talent. 'They told me they were signing him regardless of whether I came on board,' Garth smiled.

Glenn Seton won the first three championship rounds at Phillip Island in the V8 era, five races in all—a dominant performance. Second-generation racer Seton (his father Bo won the Bathurst 500 in 1965) used the Island as his test track. His rivals were quick to point out his advantage. But sometimes that benefit can be double-edged.

On 27 September 2000, testing for the upcoming Bathurst 1000, Seton's Tickford Racing Falcon stepped off the wet-racing line through the fast left-hand sweeper leading to Turn 12. 'There were no gravel traps, no tyre walls in those days,' Seton told reporter Aaron Noonan. The impact knocked him out. 'The guys got me out and I was lying on the ground. The pain was horrendous.' Wayne Gardner (who was driving with Seton's team at Bathurst) appeared. 'With his form, he's had a lot of injury. He was saying, "Stay there, mate, you'll be alright." I thought I'd broken my back,' Seton recalled.

Seton spent a week in Melbourne's Alfred Hospital, with massive concussion causing constant vomiting. 'It was a hard one to get over,' he said, and then he paused. 'I probably didn't get over it, to be honest, as a driver, because it really knocked me around.'

Seton had already won two Supercar championships and 40 races. He competed for another five seasons after that shunt and never won another Supercar event.

Supercars' last race at Phillip Island was in 2019; its two heats were won by Dick Johnson Racing teammates Scott McLaughlin and Fabian Coulthard. The circuit was not included in the Covid-shortened 2020 season, and Supercars did not return when full-time racing resumed. That's not to say they wouldn't in the future.

24

The Superbike World Championship—A Tale of Two Troys

Twice superbike world champion Troy Corser and I met for lunch on the day Anthony Gobert died. Gobert was the wild man of superbikes and perhaps the most talented rider of all. He was just 48, and his death was a consequence of unfortunate long-term substance abuse.

Corser and Gobert had been take-no-prisoners competitors with huge respect for each other, and it would have been understandable if Corser had passed on our appointment. But he would have none of it. Superbike racers are the hard men of motorcycle competition.

On the inside of Troy's forearm is the only tattoo he possesses: 'A zest for living must include a willingness to die.' He'd had it inked only relatively recently, at the end of his stellar career, not just as a reminder of the bullets he'd dodged but as a call to action for the young hopefuls he now trains. His star pupil is Jonathan Rea, six-time superbike world champion and seven-time victor at Phillip Island.

The Superbike World Championship and the Island were made for each other. In the first eighteen years of WSBK at Phillip Island, Australians won 23 of 36 rounds. And two Australians, Troy Corser and Troy Bayliss, between them won five world titles—three to Bayliss, two to Corser.

'The Italians, the Spanish, the French—they get too emotional. We don't let emotions get under our skin.' It's the only explanation Troy Corser can offer to explain Australian dominance in those early years. Determination is also a factor: 'Australians play for keeps,' twice world champion Barry Sheene, arguably the most recognisable racer of his era, once suggested to me. Barry had migrated to Australia to escape the brutal Northern Hemisphere cold that played merry hell with the metal inserts holding his battered body together. Sheene elected himself to the role of talent spotter.

'What you want to do is get out of Australia,' Sheene said to Corser. It was the second piece of advice the Wollongong racer had received from a world-title holder. Wayne Gardner was the first. They were both from Wollongong; the Gardner and the Corser families used to waterski together on Lake Conjola in the Shoalhaven, south of the steel city. Gardner was world champion when Corser was just fifteen. 'If you want to make a career, get off the dirt and onto the road,' the original Wollongong Whiz told the wannabe.

'At the time I was racing dirt track and the junior division of Mr. Motocross,' Corser explained. One of the guys he raced against was young Anthony Gobert from nearby Oakdale. The

Illawarra-Wollondilly region was a tight-knit motorcycle racing community, and a catchment for junior talent.

Corser put road tyres on his 125cc motocross bike, won a few races at Oran Park, borrowed money from his grandfather to buy a Suzuki RGV250 and won the 250cc production bike championship in 1990. Yamaha offered him a TZ250 grand prix bike for the following year. 'I took it as long as they'd pay me the same money I was making as an air-conditioning apprentice.' At nineteen, he quit his job and became a full-time professional. 'I crashed a lot; most of them were mechanical,' he said—the racer's way of saying 'not my fault'.

Like Supercars, superbikes had become Australia's premier domestic category. The concept of hot-rodding a showroom stock machine is particularly Australian. Australia led the superbike revolution in 1980 and even claims to have invented the name. Honda put Corser on a superbike and he won the national title in 1993 on its RC30. The RC was a purpose-designed homologation special, built to race while still complying with volume production rules. The bike was an international benchmark.

'Barry Sheene said, "We're going to America." He'd arranged a test for me with Ducati at Daytona,' Corser said. He would ride on the fearsome speedbowl. 'There were six guys testing for the Fast By Ferracci team.' Corser did six laps and set the fastest time: 'Barry was in pit lane, clapping.' Next season, Corser won the American Motorcyclist Association (AMA) Superbike Championship.

Sheene asked him what he wanted to do next. 'He arranged a wildcard entry for me in the Superbike World Championship,' said Corser. In 1996 Corser, riding for Ducati, won the first of his two world titles, the youngest ever superbike champion at the time.

Troy Bayliss was still spinning his wheels in Australia. Although two years Corser's senior, he was just graduating from proddies (production bikes) when Corser became world champ.

The first time Bayliss saw Phillip Island, 'I high-sided over Lukey Heights and broke my wrist.' Bayliss was an apprentice spray painter in hometown Taree; Kim, his childhood sweetheart and now his wife, was finishing school. 'We'd borrowed her dad's van to drive down and chase the production championship.'

Two years later, in 1997, he was back as a wildcard entry in the Phillip Island round of the 250cc World Motorcycle Championship, a ride arranged by speedway and motocross rider Gary Flood. 'I'd just busted my vertebrae in a superbike crash in Queensland, but I wasn't going to miss the chance,' Bayliss said.

'It was the first time I'd been on a grand prix bike. It braked, it cornered, it went where you pointed it.' Bayliss was at a disadvantage. 'I weighed sixty-eight kilos and the others, like world champion Max Biaggi, weighed under sixty kilos. A lot on a little bike.'

The other disadvantage may have been that he'd never raced at world championship level, but even now that subtlety eludes him. They raced elbow-to-elbow for 25 laps (111 kilometres) and Bayliss gave no quarter. He didn't win but he gave the world champion a mighty shake. When he came onto Gardner Straight on the last lap, he was third but finished sixth in the slipstreaming battle to the flag.

'Typhoon Troy', the headlines thundered. Even more influential: 'Barry Sheene gave me a great rap on TV.' It kickstarted his career. Darrell Healey, owner of GSE Construction—a big deal in the building industry in the UK—gave him a ride on his private team's Ducati in the British Superbike Championship, and a job as a forklift driver so he could eat. GSE would become the series' most successful entrant in the championship, and Bayliss won the 1999 title.

'In 2000 I was asked to substitute for Carl Fogarty, who was injured at Phillip Island.' Fogarty had already won four Superbike World Championships by then. 'I set myself a three-year plan: learn, win some races, then win the title. Or pack up and come home.' He won his first world championship in 2001.

Anthony Gobert was a natural self-promoter. He called himself 'The Go-Show'.

'Goey took over my local ride with Honda, the year I went to Europe,' Troy Corser offered. 'He won, too.' Gobert's death, the announcement made only that morning, was a topic I didn't want to raise. Just for a brief moment Corser looked out to sea. The Bombora restaurant in Wollongong's North Harbour is known for its views.

And then it came bubbling out. Gobert had won the national superbike title in the first half of 1994 and he was due to ride a works Honda RC45 in the Phillip Island round of the Superbike World Championship in late October. But at a test day at Phillip

Island on 19 October, his Honda was suddenly not available. The official line was that Honda had become aware of Gobert talking to other teams.

Corser swears otherwise. 'They fired him,' he asserted. They'd had enough of the unpredictable nineteen-year-old. And then, big grin on his face, Corser told me: 'He marched straight down the pits to Muzzy Kawasaki, helmet under his arm, and told team owner Rob Muzzy, "I'd like to ride your bike." And he let him. He was on the gas from the first lap. He was a massive natural talent.'

The story got better. Ten days later, in the Phillip Island world championship race, Gobert put the Muzzy Kawasaki on pole—against the best riders in the world—and brought it home third in the first 21-lap heat behind two world champions: Scott Russell, who was Gobert's teammate, and Carl Fogarty. In the second heat he smoked them, winning outright. 'If he hadn't yielded to Russell in the first heat he would have won the round on debut.' Corser, who'd had a high-side crash at Siberia in practice, was fifth and then third.

In 1996, it was at Phillip Island that Corser clinched his first World Superbike title, taking a safe third in heat one of the grand finale of the world championship—enough to make his points lead unassailable. Gobert charged to a win. In the second heat, Corser had planned to seal his title with a big grand slam victory, unfettered by points considerations. But an errant seagull smashed into his bike and broke his clutch lever. 'I did six or seven laps, but it was too dangerous. I pulled to the pits, fixed it, then came back and entertained the crowd with wheelies.' Two hundred klicks an hour on the back wheel—you'd think that would be a fitting finale.

But Gobert won again. On the podium, his hair dyed brilliant red, his earrings (a bit shocking for the time) glinting as he brandished two trophies, The Go-Show stripped off his leathers and flung them to the crowd. Down to his jocks. Chisel-jawed Corser, the new world champion in his celebratory, pristine white T-shirt, looked positively statuesque beside him. Goey's black T-shirt, donned later for modesty, said it all: 'I am what I am.' You couldn't help but love him. The pair were both heading for grand prix racing in 1997.

The two Troys—TB and TC—and Gobert aspired to grand prix careers. 'It's a different level,' Bayliss said. Bayliss rode his wildcard 250cc bike at Phillip Island in the same year Corser and Gobert entered the Senior category on the awesome two-stroke 500s. But neither got to experience the Island on a GP bike.

Corser stepped away from his ill-fated Power Horse Yamaha YZR 500 team mid-season in 1997. He wasn't getting results and he wasn't being paid. 'I didn't enjoy the GP paddock,' he said. 'No one talked to each other, like in WSBK. It wasn't that much fun.'

Gobert replaced Scott Russell in the Lucky Strike Suzuki team. He made it to round twelve at the fabulous 5.4-kilometre Brno Circuit in the Czech Republic, one of a very few to challenge Phillip Island in riders' estimation, then he failed a random drug test, the type they give all athletes. A zero-tolerance policy resulted in his instant dismissal.

It would be another six years before Troy Bayliss would convert his 1997 wildcard sixth place on a 250 into three full-time seasons of MotoGP racing. He came to the Senior grand prix category one season after it switched from two-stroke to four-stroke. He never got to race a 500. 'It didn't matter. It's about the rider, not the bike,' he said.

In 2006, Bayliss dominated the Superbike World Championship for Ducati; he won 50 per cent of the series' races and finished 95 points clear of his nearest rival. As a reward, Ducati put him on their grand prix bike for the last round of the World Motorcycle Championship at Circuit de Valencia and he won it outright by a scant 1.3 seconds from teammate Loris Capirossi. No one's achieved such a feat before or since.

In ten years, from 1999 to 2008, Troy Corser and Troy Bayliss won twelve of the nineteen World Superbike races at Phillip Island. Remarkably, they won six each. Anthony Gobert, struggling for consistency, won just one as his promising career went into freefall. Garry McCoy, another Barry Sheene protégé, won one more. The four Australians shared a win rate of better than 70 per cent. Phillip Island belonged to them.

In 2001 the Texas Tornado, Colin Edwards, had won the first superbike heat at the Island and bikes were starting to line up for the next. Troy Corser sensed disaster. There was rain coming—not just a shower but a deluge. He knew it, but officials didn't. They didn't have weather radar, but Troy had a sixth sense. He knew Phillip Island and its flukey weather. 'I rushed up to the control tower and said, "Don't start the race." They sent me away. I ran back down to the pit lane and started waving a red flag. Then I ran along the line of bikes and shut them down. The officials moved in. They thought I'd gone mad.'

But, suddenly, the rain came. 'Within thirty seconds you couldn't see a metre in front of you.' Disaster had been averted. Just the same, any rider who pulled that stunt would surely be censured. Instead, because of Troy's status at the Island, they thanked him.

The Bayliss and Corser families staked their claim on Phillip Island real estate.

The Corsers, with up to 50 or 60 friends, gathered at Turn 1. The Bayliss family grouped at the top of Gardner Straight, exiting Turn 12. The separation wasn't purposeful 'but we were rivals', Bayliss said. Corser agreed: 'When I first won in 1995 I went down to the family between races and there was my grandfather, Pop [Ron] proudly wearing a T-shirt emblazoned "The Gene Machine".' Taking credit. So much for Gobert's Go-Show. Troy had long since paid Pop back for his loan to buy his first production bike. 'I did it with the first sponsorship money I earned.'

The Island was good to them. Corser won both heats of its WSBK championship race in 1999 at the beginning of their decade of dominance, and then did it again in 2005, the year he claimed his second world title. Bayliss won both heats in 2002, then repeated the double in 2008. That was the year he won his third and last world title.

'I'd announced at the beginning of the year that this would be my last season,' Bayliss said. 'So I knew I was racing at Phillip Island for the last time.' There'd been a lot of pre-event media coverage and Bayliss was sent on a lap of honour in the course car on the morning of the race, lauded by 65,000 fans.

'I rode down pit lane after my second win, and there was Kim, and I just lost it,' Bayliss said. Shades of Wayne Gardner and Donna. 'I'd only gotten emotional twice before—when I won my first championship in 2001 and when I won the Valencia MotoGP in 2006.' The race was early in the year and he still had a world title to win, which he did, 122 points clear of Troy Corser.

After the Island win, he took a few days off to head for the Gold Coast to suss out schools for his kids. Bayliss, Corser and their families lived in Monaco, close to superbike central. Europe was where the bulk of the racing took place. Living in the principality wasn't a hardship, but both Troys are grounded; for world champions, they are as close as you'll get to humble. 'It's a twilight zone. I needed to get the kids out and get them back amongst ordinary people,' Bayliss said. 'I managed to get a couple of extra years out of Kim but it was time to come home.'

Troy Corser had promised himself he'd stop when he turned 40. He'd married Samantha Davies, introduced, naturally, through a Barry Sheene connection. When Corser pulled the pin, he moved near Sam's family in the UK.

'Stopping was the hardest thing,' Bayliss said. 'It was horrible. It took me years to get over it.'

Corser solved the problem by starting a performance riding school in partnership with BMW, the last of six factories for which he raced. They ran three events a year, each over three days, for 30 aspirants at a time. When we met in Wollongong, he'd recently returned to Australia to start a local Corser training academy.

In 2015, seven years after his retirement, Bayliss got Ducati to enter him in the Superbike World Championship at Phillip Island. 'I need to get beaten,' he told them. It was the only way to scratch the itch. He finished thirteenth in one heat, sixteenth in the other. But the itch was still there. In 2018, approaching his fiftieth birthday, he entered a Ducati Panigale (Ducati had named a model, the V2 Bayliss Replica, after him) in Australia's domestic superbike championship. He finished third, against riders half his age, and on 14 October he won the last race of the series—at Phillip Island. Then he retired.

Bayliss and Corser are entrenched in the top ten race winners of World Superbikes—Bayliss with 52 victories and fourth on the table, Corser with 33 and eighth.

Anthony Gobert retired at the end of 2007, not by choice. He'd fallen out of favour in Europe and America. In desperation he sold assets—his house, it's said—and purchased a Kawasaki to race locally. Unsuccessfully.

He died on 17 January 2024, his passing mourned by friends and fans who lamented what could have been. 'He had so much self-belief,' Troy Corser reminisced. 'Maybe too much.'

After Bayliss's twin-win in 2008, no Australian has won the Superbike World Championship, or won a World Superbike race at Phillip Island. It's incomprehensible how the tap could simply shut off. The Australian Superbike Championship, running in parallel, has bred champions, but none has been elevated to world-title status. Perhaps GP racing has put stars in their eyes. (Example: Brisbane's Chris Vermeulen, second to Corser in the

2005 world championship, transferred to GP without fulfilling his superbike objective.)

Australian enthusiasts claim Northern Irish racer Jonathan Rea OBE, the most capped superbike world champion ever, with six titles and seven wins at Phillip Island, as their own. He met Phillip Islander Tatiana Weston in a Cowes cafe, married, and they have a home on the island—not their full-time abode, but close. Rea, a third-generation racer, also holds the Keys to Phillip Island, the first ever presented. But he still races under the Union Jack.

The next champion may come from the next generation. Wayne Gardner's son Remy initially took the grand prix path. He joined his father as dual grand prix champions, one of only two father-and-son combinations to claim the accomplishment: Wayne in the Senior division, Remy in 2021 as Moto2 World Championship winner. Remy has transferred to World Superbikes.

Troy Bayliss's younger son, Oli, chose superbikes—first in the Junior division, then the Australian Superbike Championship, then graduating to the Supersport division of the Superbike World Championship. 'I watched him from Turn 12,' TB told me. 'I wished I hadn't. At that level, it's hard watching someone you love racing. They're mad as cut snakes. I called my mum and said, "Now I know what you went through."'

25

The Doohan Factor

Mick Doohan AM was the superstar. In 1997, the Australian Motorcycle Grand Prix was back at Phillip Island and there was huge expectation of a Doohan victory.

He had already confirmed his fourth consecutive World Motorcycle Championship win in that season—an extraordinary effort.

Now, *all* he had to do was win his home grand prix.

Mick was leading by seven seconds with only ten laps to go when it all went wrong.

'I was trying to conserve my tyres,' he said in a post-race debrief. 'I didn't want to blister them so I was taking it easy, holding nice constant throttle so the rear tyre wouldn't spin up too bad. I flicked it into Turn 1, hit some bumps and the front folded. I thought I could get it back so I dug my knee into the tarmac to take the weight off the front tyre. That usually does the trick, but it didn't this time. Instead the slide went on forever. You should see the hole in my leathers.'

Mighty Mick had used his knee to try to stay upright at something north of 280 km/h.

His only grand prix victory at Phillip Island would have to wait until 1998.

A year after that, in 1999, with his enforced retirement through injury imminent, the circuit's owners named Turn 1 for him. Gardner Straight led into Doohan Corner, one of the fastest combinations in world competition.

The Australian Grand Prix Corporation (AGPC) and Phillip Island Motor Sports (PIMS) had won back the Australian Motorcycle Grand Prix. But who could take the credit? Placetac and PIMS believed they had secured it. Ron Walker and the AGPC were certain they had.

'Fergus Cameron was talking directly to Bernie Ecclestone and we had a verbal agreement,' Placetac chair Peter Henderson asserted. 'Then we got a call from Ron Walker in London telling us effectively to "get off his grass".' Walker had inked a contract (better than a verbal agreement).

'All that was left for us was to come to an arrangement with the Victorian Government for the use of Phillip Island,' Henderson said. 'Fergus and I sat with the lawyers, and the AGPC's CEO Judith Griggs, for a marathon forty-hour session to write a heads of agreement,' he said, swearing that 40 hours was no exaggeration. 'Then Ron came back and said, "I don't agree with any of it." He screwed us.'

On 3 October 1997, in the first official practice, riders braved near-freezing temperatures, harsh winds coming off Bass Strait, seagulls and a paucity of gravel traps and run-off areas (a situation remedied progressively over the following 25 years).

Doohan was one of the first to crash, second-guessing the slower-moving Pete Goddard. It was the first of his two crashes in Turn 1. 'People think it's warm in Australia,' young 125cc rider Valentino Rossi said. 'Not here. They ought to call it the Grand Prix of Antarctica.'

Spaniard Alex Criville won the 500cc Australian Motorcycle Grand Prix in 1997. It was a unique double. In 1989, when the Bob Barnard–designed and built track first opened, Criville, then nineteen, won the 125cc grand prix—its inaugural race.

In 1998, the Doohan factor kicked in big time. 'Mighty Mick Makes It Five', one headline screamed. The Gold Coast tearaway, the hardest and most determined racer of his time, won his fifth consecutive 500cc World Motorcycle Championship at Phillip Island. He'd spent the practice sessions learning how to get heat into his cold tyres to combat the Island's track conditions and used that knowledge to open a gap that never closed.

He rode his victory lap carrying a huge Australian flag emblazoned with a gold '5'. Exceptional.

Only Giacomo Agostini, statistically the most successful racer of all time with fifteen titles across all divisions, had done better. Ago won seven 500cc titles in a row. Doohan was hunting him down. Strangely, Mick had detractors, people who claimed that the performance of his works Honda was the root cause of his success and that his consistent domination was boring. 'What do you want me to do?' he growled. 'Slow down?'

At the Island, 50,000 spectators cheered. Who was to know that they'd just witnessed Doohan's Phillip Island finale?

'If I wanted one guy riding for my life, it would be Mick,' said Jeremy Burgess, South Australia–born Honda crew chief throughout Doohan's grand prix career. It's a bold statement. Burgess had overseen fourteen world championship victories, been directly accountable for machines—and riders—that had won 157 motorcycle grands prix, and had amassed, by his count, close to 300 podiums. The three mega-star riders on his CV, in order, are Wayne Gardner, Mick Doohan and Valentino Rossi.

Burgess had to be forced to work with Wayne Gardner—nothing against the Whiz. 'When I went to the UK in 1980, I became a mechanic with the works Suzuki team and then with Honda. I was number two on world champion Freddie Spencer's bike when Wayne came on board. I said, "I'm perfectly happy where I am." Then Honda boss Agumi-san got on the phone and said, "If you don't take Wayne you are of no further use to Honda."' Okay. Wayne and Jerry (the name by which Burgess is known) won the 1987 world championship, then Mick Doohan joined the team. 'Honda wanted me to work with Mick.' Burgess had learned by then not to argue.

Burgess had been an A-grade racer in Australia—not a world beater but better than competent. He knew motorcycle racing as a rider and as a wrench. He preferred wrenching, 'although 1986 was the last time I got my hands dirty'. Crew chiefs are like chief operating officers in corporations. They take input from above, below and tangentially. They initiate, integrate, delegate, manage, motivate and, where necessary, manipulate. And while the buck should stop with the big boss, it usually comes to a screeching halt with the crew chief.

'You had to pump Wayne up,' Burgess confided. 'He was most insecure. When he found out Honda had hired rival Eddie Lawson to be his and Mick's third-man teammate, it set him off. Mick, on the other hand, was a man in a hurry. "I don't care who gets a Honda as long as I have one," he said.'

For more than a decade, the Mick and Jerry show dominated 500cc grand prix racing. They lived through Doohan's massive crashes, the worst in 1992 when he almost lost his leg and his life in an Assen hospital.

When he partially recovered, Mick's injured foot couldn't use the brake so they improvised, rigging up a thumb-operated rear-brake lever. 'To see him at São Paulo when he made his comeback, to see how much weight he'd lost, how his leg looked.' Jerry still empathises. 'You can share the disappointment but you can't feel the pain.'

They won five Senior world titles together. 'I was never really interested in the lower categories,' Doohan said. As far as Burgess was concerned, he was with Doohan for life. 'He's a man of steel—incredible,' Burgess told me, still in awe. But: 'It's a risk industry. You can fall down at any time.'

In March 1999, Doohan crashed for the last time. It was lap five of practice for the Spanish Grand Prix at Jerez among the sherry-producing vines of Andalusia. He broke his wrist and collarbone, and suffered severe muscle damage to his back. The main challenge was another break to the leg he almost lost in '92.

'I came home,' Burgess said. 'Honda told me I'd remain on Mick's team.' That was a bit odd: Burgess had built Doohan's team—a dedicated band of true take-no-prisoner professionals. Doohan worked hard all year to recover, but to no avail.

At the 1999 Australian Grand Prix, Phillip Island honoured him and named Turn 1 for him. Victorian premier Jeff Kennett applauded him as he limped, obviously painfully, to his Honda NSR. Organisers had arranged for him to do some parade laps for the crowd. Then he opened the throttles and put down a time that would have qualified mid-field for the GP. 'I've still got the feel for it,' he grinned when he returned to the pits. His mind was ready but his body was not. He made his retirement announcement at a Gold Coast media conference in mid-December.

A 'Vale'dictory

'I was sitting in the Honda pit at Phillip Island at seven p.m., just me alone,' Jeremy Burgess said.

'Valentino Rossi walked in, went right up and sat on Mick's bike—didn't ask for permission.' It was actually being raced by Sete Gibernau that weekend. 'He didn't say much, just got to know it.'

In 2000, Rossi, reigning 250cc world champion, was graduating to the 500cc division. The mercurial Italian, a talent with a persona that transcended the sport, was in demand. He agreed to join Honda on the proviso they would assign Burgess as crew chief. Had they not—had Doohan kept racing and claimed Burgess—it could have been a deal breaker. 'He was the guy making the big step, leaving the comfort of an Italian team

[Aprilia] with Italian mechanics to join a Japanese team with Australian mechanics,' Burgess smiled.

Rossi, known as Vale to his legions of fans, was already leading a resurgence of excitement in world motorcycle grand prix racing. He'd set the 250cc category alight.

In 2002, the Senior championship regrouped, discarding its screaming two-stroke engines and replacing them with howling four-strokes, reinventing themselves as MotoGP. Promoters saw Rossi as the standard-bearer for their revival.

With Burgess, Rossi won the last championship of the 500cc two-stroke era (2001) and the first of the new 990cc four-stroke age (2002). 'Someone had to do it,' Burgess quipped. 'It might as well be us.'

MotoGP elevated motorcycle racing to a level above anything it had ever attained before. Motorcycling Australia president Peter Goddard is in no doubt why: 'Dorna and Rossi.' Dorna invested in the change, while Rossi became its public face.

Valentino—the son of Graziano Rossi, a racer in five world 500cc championships (best place fifth)—was a huge talent and a natural showman. 'While Mick Doohan would race to win, and if that was twenty seconds ahead of the next rider so be it, Valentino would race to entertain,' Jerry Burgess told me. 'If he knew he had their measure, he'd keep the gap small and at the press conference afterwards he'd talk about how tight it was.' After enjoying Doohan's take-no-prisoners determination, Burgess had to learn to live with the new anxiety. 'People don't want to see long-gap victories,' Vale said.

Rossi, according to Burgess, had the ability to create magic. 'His fan connection was genuine,' Burgess said. 'When he celebrated by dressing up as Robin Hood in the UK or pretending to have a toilet stop in Spain, he was for real. Others tried to copy him, like Jorge Lorenzo planting his Lorenzo's Land flag after a win, but you could see their efforts were contrived.'

Rossi set out to be more than a racer. He became a brand. In his earlier, wilder years, he'd styled himself as 'Valentinik', a cartoon character intent on wreaking havoc. The brand came with a psycho-mouse logo. But as he matured, it was a tad unseemly. 'Il Dottore' was far more suitable—professional, clinical and unflappable. Even if his logo, the Doctor, was multi-coloured and splashed across the butt of his racing leathers.

'Jerry was like my dad in MotoGP,' Rossi said in a voice message to me.

It's a mark of the man's respect for Phillip Island and Burgess that he took the time to record his thoughts on his performance at a circuit he rates 'as one of my three favourites'. Three? 'Misano is my home track, just ten kilometres from my home in Tavullia and it's the track where I grew up with the bike and it is the track where I went for the first time.' English is Rossi's second language. He speaks it like Ernest Hemingway wrote it—lots of conjunctions building drama.

When Vale and Jerry got together in 2000, there was a bit of sorting out. Rossi wanted a place to sit in the pit garage. 'Mick never sat down,' Burgess said, affronted. '"If you want to sit down, sit on your bike," I told him.'

'He'd come into the pits in practice and he'd take off his helmet. "Don't do that," I told him. "I want you ready to go back out."' Rossi agreed to keep his helmet on, but he still wanted a chair. 'I sent one of the boys out to buy him one. He liked yellow, so we got it in that colour.'

Rossi's English, then, was limited. 'The language of this garage is English,' Burgess decreed. Even his Japanese bosses knew that. 'I was very grateful to Vale's parents,' Burgess said. 'They sent him to an English school in Pesaro.' Burgess is a fan of Graziano and Stefania: 'They gave him a grounded upbringing, made him respectful, a truly nice person,' he said.

Burgess's outlook on life is pragmatic. 'I never carried anyone's bags,' he said. It was a source of amusement to the Australian Grand Prix Corporation CEO at the time, Andrew Westacott, that on the drive to Phillip Island he once came across Rossi at the side of the road, changing a flat tyre on his team's rental car. Burgess claims no memory of the incident but 'if he did it, he should fix it'.

'I could see right from the start he was good,' Burgess said. 'The ability of his brain to process information was extraordinary. I liken him to Michael Schumacher.'

In our correspondence, Rossi nominated five races at Phillip Island he'd rate among his career's best. The first four: 'In 1999, when I won the 250 from Loris Capirossi; in 2001, when I won the race and the championship from Max Biaggi; in 2004, when I won the race and the championship, this time in the last lap from Sete Gibernau; in 2016, [when] I rode from fifteenth to second.'

Separately, Burgess and Rossi agree that his best-ever race of his entire career was at Phillip Island in 2003. 'He accidentally passed another rider under yellow flags'—a move that is forbidden—'when Troy Bayliss crashed and he was given a ten-second penalty,' Burgess said. 'He broke the lap record four times in four laps, made up the lost ground and won by ten seconds.

He told me it's the only time he'd concentrated 100 per cent for the entire race distance. I didn't breathe for the same time.' For Rossi it was special because 'I push really, really hard and win. I enjoy it very much.'

'Phillip Island is incredibly fast,' Rossi continued, 'a very high average speed which creates for the rider a lot of adrenaline. The end of the straight is the place you have the most scares of the season. It is one of the fastest corners [of all tracks]. It goes downhill and there are some bumps and the majority of the time there is a lot of wind. Always, I enjoyed it a lot.'

The Rossi–Burgess combination won five Senior world championships in succession (of their total seven) and claimed five grand prix victories at Phillip Island. 'Valentino had a real sense of the history of the sport,' Burgess said. It was more than simply knowledge. Motorcycling, and the heroes who'd gone before him, shaped his character.

In 2003, on the podium of the race they both rated as his greatest, Rossi unveiled a banner inked with the number 7—Barry Sheene's race plate. Sheene had succumbed to cancer six months before, aged only 52. Most riders wore black armbands. Rossi wanted to do more. 'We made a flag using a sheet from the hotel. Sorry, hotel,' he said on the podium. He did a full parade lap with Barry's flag. 'Barry Sheene was a magic person and changed a little bit the whole sport,' Vale said.

Mick Doohan rode Sheene's historic Manx Norton racer that day (Sheene had held the Phillip Island historic lap record on the bike) and did a lap of honour in the wet. The spectator areas were silent, the thump of the 500cc single the only sound.

Rossi won three world titles for Honda. Mick had won five and got to keep one of each of his winning bikes. 'Vale asked me where his were, and I told him Mick had written the bikes into his contract. Vale hadn't,' Jerry said. 'He loved the 500 on which he won the 2001 championship. He thought it was the sexiest bike he'd ever ridden.' But he still doesn't have it. According to Burgess, it's on display at Honda's museum in Motegi. 'There were at least six of them. It wouldn't surprise me at all if even now they paint one up and give it him.'

In 2003, Rossi's relationship with Honda was nearing the end of the line. 'Honda believed our bikes were so good anyone could win on them,' Burgess said. 'But just the same they gave me the brief to keep him.' When they met to discuss it, Vale told Jerry it wasn't about the bikes and it wasn't about the money. It was more than that. It was about respect. He was leaving.

'If it makes any difference, I'll come with you,' Burgess told his young champion. 'I knew I was burning my bridges.' When Burgess walked from Honda, his team came too: Alex Briggs ('I hired him on spec,' Jerry said. 'Just turn up with your tools. If you're no good we can always fire you') and Gary Coleman, Australian domestic racer-turned-mechanic and roustabout. On their first time out with Yamaha in 2004, the Rossi–Burgess team won the championship. Then they won another three.

Jeremy Burgess and Valentino Rossi dissolved their relationship at the end of the 2013 season. 'I was sixty and I didn't believe Vale could win another championship,' Burgess said, leaning back in his chair and looking out over the rolling landscape of

Aldgate in the Adelaide Hills. In 2011, Rossi and Burgess had moved again, this time to Ducati, and the pair had quit the team after a winless 2012 season. They'd shifted back to Yamaha, but the results hadn't come, at least not to their satisfaction. One win and a championship fourth was below their expectation.

'I'd signed a one-year contract for 2014, but [Rossi] said, "If we're going to change at the end of next year, we may as well change now."'

Burgess was half right. Rossi didn't win another title but he amassed another eight grand prix victories and won the Australian Grand Prix in 2014, his sixth victory.

The personality who put—and kept—MotoGP on the map had his last race in the Valencian Grand Prix in 2021. As a mark of the utmost respect, his trademark 46 plate was retired from competition in a ceremony at the Italian Grand Prix in 2022.

Whole treatises have been written about Rossi's influence on MotoGP. Should he have retired while on top? Why hang on? Jeremy Burgess has a theory. 'Barry Sheene had his last win in 1981 but didn't retire until 1984,' Burgess said. 'People had time to get used to the idea of him not winning. Valentino winding down progressively gave Dorna the opportunity to wean itself from dependence on him.'

Which doesn't explain why, now, his merchandise is still the top-selling brand at Phillip Island.

26

The Stoner Age

Casey Stoner is a once-in-a-generation talent.

For more than half a decade, his clashes with Valentino Rossi became legend. 'Your ambition outweighs your talent,' the determined young Australian told Rossi after they crashed at Jerez in 2011, Rossi putting his bike down mid-corner, leaving Stoner with nowhere to go but on top of him. The media hyped the conflict. It was great entertainment, good for the show.

Stoner's 'show' did not enjoy a long run. He first threw a leg over a MotoGP bike in 2006, and he retired at the end of the 2012 season. Rossi's run extended 21 years. Statistics are the devil's tool. They mask complexities: competition between rival tyre makers; a move to a control tyre to allegedly normalise competition; the adoption of the maligned 800cc MotoGP formula for the duration of Stoner's career; a crisscrossing path of manufacturer allegiances; even rider injuries and illnesses. They all influence the stats.

But raw data shows that in the period 2007 to 2012 (Ducati was happy to name it the 'Stoner Age'), Stoner claimed six successive victories on his home track Phillip Island, ending Rossi's chain of success. Casey and Valentino each secured two world championships in that six-year period—Stoner in 2007 and 2011, Rossi in 2008 and 2009. In the Stoner Age, Casey claimed 38 grands prix while Valentino won 21 (in fairness, his career total was 89, earning him the epithet of GOAT—Greatest Of All Time).

'Casey was the best,' Chris Vermeulen told me from his dad Pete's bakery in the historic tourist town of Maleny, overlooking Noosa and the Sunshine Coast. 'I rode against all of the riders of the era, with the exception of Marc Márquez, and I can tell you Casey's pure talent put all of them to shame.' Young hopefuls were lining up to take Mick Doohan's place. But grand prix racing is elite. Only a very few get the chance to test themselves at the pinnacle of sport.

When Doohan was racing, Daryl Beattie and Kevin Magee had given it their very best shot. Both had won world championship grands prix, and both had been taken out by injury.

Magee, three years older than Doohan, had claimed his only grand prix in Spain in 1988 for Yamaha, been injured in a shocking post-flag crash on a cool-down lap in 1989, retreated to World Superbikes, won twice at Phillip Island in 1991 and 1992, and then retired. Beattie, for Suzuki, was second in the world title to Doohan in 1995. He'd been Mick's Honda teammate in 1993 and claimed third in the championship ahead of a still-recovering Doohan. Beattie rode for three Japanese factories, won three grands prix, lost all five toes on one foot in a grisly crash at Le Mans, suffered severe head injuries in another crash and retired in 1997.

The risk-to-reward equation has never been favourable.

Barry Sheene was the enabler for a next generation of contenders. 'I was racing in an Australian superbike race in 1999 when Barry spotted me and got his co-commentator Leigh Diffey to introduce us. Barry took me to Phillip Island and walked me into the Suzuki pit,' Chris Vermeulen recalled. (Sheene had won both his world titles with Suzuki.) 'Nobu Aoki and Kenny Roberts Jnr were the riders. Barry said to team manager Garry Taylor, "Get rid of one of these blokes and put this guy (me) on the bike."' That didn't happen—not instantly. But: 'My parents were struggling to support my career. With one phone call, Barry got me a suite of Dainese leathers and full kit of AGV helmets.'

Sheene fostered Vermeulen's career, got him into British superbikes. 'Barry flew into the British Grand Prix in his helicopter. His motorhome was bigger than most of the riders', and the queue for his autograph was longer. I was just in awe.' Vermeulen won the Supersport World Championship in 2003, the year Sheene died, and joined MotoGP in 2006 with Suzuki, respectfully adopting number 7 as part of his race plate as a tribute to his mentor.

It was the same year Casey Stoner entered grand prix racing. They were on a similar trajectory, Vermeulen a little ahead. 'Honda wanted me to ride superbikes,' he said. 'But I rejected their offer of 1.5 million Euros and followed my grand prix dream.' Success comes down to choices.

In 2006, Vermeulen rode his works Suzuki to a brilliant second in the wet at Phillip Island in front of Rossi (third) and Stoner (sixth). He was the first Australian to stand on the podium since Doohan in 1998. In 2007, this time at Le Mans and again in the wet, he won his only grand prix.

But Suzuki was off the boil. 'The global financial crisis had hit them hard.' Vermeulen accepted a superbike ride from Kawasaki. At Phillip Island in 2010, a crushed right knee brought his career to an end. 'The bike locked up over Lukey Heights. I jumped off'—no easy feat—'but the bike landed on top of me. I could have continued but it's tough being an Aussie going to the other side of the world. If I was British or European I'd probably still be racing now. They get to go home every week.'

Garry McCoy won three 500cc grands prix. 'I was in only my second-ever road race when Barry Sheene noticed me in 1992,' Garry said. 'The next week he was in Suzuka, and there'd been a lot of crashes and riders were scarce, so he said to the Honda 125 team, "Give Garry a call." I got the phone call on 1 April and I thought it was an April Fools' Day joke. My fifth-ever road race was at the Australian Grand Prix, my first time on a 125 GP bike, my first time on slicks. Barry did it all.' McCoy's golden year was 2000; he scored all three 500 GP victories and fifth in the world title. Injury—a badly broken wrist in 2001—and retrospectively poor team choices concluded his career in 2010. He had, however, got eighteen years out of it.

Colin and Bronwyn Stoner did it their way. Their son was a precocious talent. He needed to be nurtured. I met them in 1999 at Channel Ten's Christmas party. The network, under sports boss David White, was having a big crack at becoming the Home of Motorsport. The Stoners had caught David's eye. They were a good story. Casey, just fourteen, had been denied a racing licence by the Australian Junior Road Racing Association, even though he was legally entitled. 'It was politics,' the Stoners claimed. 'Ambitious parents versus ambitious parents.'

Rather than hang around to fight, they were selling everything and heading off to the UK with just enough funds to buy a caravan and sign Casey up to a junior division. 'You're *what*? Be careful . . .' we expert commentators told them. 'It's a jungle.' Seven years later, Casey was world champion.

Cristian Gabarrini was a data engineer in Lucio Cecchinello's eponymous LCR (Lucio Cecchinello Racing) team when he first saw Stoner's telemetry. The seventeen-year-old was opening his throttle earlier, and holding it open longer, than Gabarrini had ever seen. Just as Valentino Rossi, an Italian, had formed a championship-winning alliance with Jeremy Burgess, Australia's Stoner and Italy's Gabarrini would provide the mirror image.

In 2005, as Rossi won his fifth successive Australian Grand Prix at Phillip Island, Stoner lost his chance to become 250cc world champion. He was leading on lap four when he high-sided LCR's Aprilia at MG Corner. Dani Pedrosa won the race and the title. 'I think Stoner will be the future of MotoGP,' Rossi told a Phillip Island media conference. 'He is Australian, he's young. I think for the future he is a good opportunity.' Be careful what you wish for.

In 2006 Cecchinello, Stoner's manager and ardent supporter, secured a Honda RC211V and formed a Honda satellite team—one bike, one rider. Casey claimed pole in his second race on it at Qatar, and was on the podium with a second place in Turkey. He was a frustrated sixth in Australia. Honda instructed LCR to change gearbox ratios at Phillip Island to conserve fuel so they got to full race distance. Stoner was sure it was a ploy to stop the satellite team beating their works bike. Marco Melandri won for Honda. No matter—Stoner was off to Ducati.

The Cecchinello plan had been to place Stoner on a Yamaha. Negotiations had been in play, but then the door slammed shut. One of Stoner's requests had been that he work out of the same garage as Rossi and Burgess to 'learn from them'. 'Someone didn't want me there,' Stoner said enigmatically. 'Valentino used his influence to veto Casey,' Jeremy Burgess told me for this book.

Ducati was no done deal. Livio Suppo, Ducati MotoGP boss, admitted years later Stoner had not been his first choice. Stoner got the ride only after negotiations with Marco Melandri, Sete Gibernau and Nicky Hayden fell through. Suppo got lucky.

2007 was a very good year. Twenty-one-year-old Casey Stoner married Adriana Tuchyna, eighteen, from Adelaide. They'd met in 2003 at Phillip Island when she'd asked for his autograph (on her torso—a request Stoner now says was 'way out of character' for the demure Adri). That same year Stoner also won his first world championship and delivered Ducati its first ever title. He dominated the Australian Grand Prix ahead of Loris Capirossi and Valentino Rossi.

Stoner had signed on with Ducati on a low salary supplemented with big, guaranteed-win bonuses. Ten wins in the season capped Casey's year.

The Ducati was made to suit Stoner. He and Gabarrini set it up so he could effectively steer the bike with the rear wheel, controlling the throttle to determine direction and drive. His style required great bravery. No one had backed a bike into corners before, certainly not at such extreme speeds. In 2012, in Stoner's last race at Phillip Island, organisers named Turn 3, the blazingly fast left-hand sweeper following Southern Loop, after him. It was Casey's favourite corner in the world. Gardner Straight now led into Doohan Corner, Southern Loop, then Stoner Corner.

'My will to win was greater than the fear. If I let fear control me, I never would have gone as fast,' Stoner told the *Gypsy Tales* podcast. 'Going through Turn 3 at Phillip Island . . . it's a lot to overcome . . . it's 265 [km/h] going into the corner, down through the dip. You're always getting a big push of wind from the inside going out to the ocean.' Casey's technique was the opposite of other riders'. 'I would slide before I even got to the corner . . . You have to get that rear to break before you get to the corner.'

Other riders, Casey said, slide after the corner: 'That's just sliding, that's not hard—these bikes have a lot of power,' he said, a bit dismissively. Their technique, he said, was inefficient. They were sideways all the way down to the next corner with the bike on the edge of its tyre. Stoner's way already had the bike standing up on the exit, powering to Turn 4 so he could brake into the hairpin from an upright position—far safer and far more effective. Casey was particularly proud that he maintained corner speed throughout the manoeuvre. 'The slowest point of the corner was 258 [km/h] . . . so we only lost seven k's an hour.'

Valentino Rossi was, frankly, in awe.

'He's able to enter it fast,' Rossi said of his rival. 'Especially, he's able to open the throttle twenty or thirty metres before the other guys. He puts the bike in oversteer and he gains ground all the way to the braking area for Turn 4.'

Phillip Island, Rossi said, 'is the last track on the world calendar where sliding helps the lap time'. Developments in tyre technology, on-board traction-control devices and circuits built by computer had meant that 'in the last two years you lose time. It's great to see Casey sideways in Turn 3 and I am able to do the same,' Rossi said.

In 2011, Stoner moved to Honda. For all his success, his time in MotoGP had not been easy. He'd been dogged by health problems, initially diagnosed as lactose intolerance and later confirmed as chronic fatigue syndrome. His demeanour—an inward withdrawal—led to a groundswell of unfounded derision and criticism. He was supposed to be having fun, and he wasn't. 'I wasn't the same person I was when I started racing.'

Honda was the panacea he needed. When he'd started racing as a kid, he'd been gifted a pair of Mick Doohan's boots and gloves. Rather than display them, he wore them. Doohan was his idol. Now, at the zenith of his own career, he was team leader for Repsol Honda, 'Doohan's team'.

On 16 October 2011, on his 26th birthday, he won his fifth successive grand prix at the Island and won his second world championship. Valentini Rossi crashed on the MG hairpin. He'd not been in major contention. Rossi had also swapped teams, taking Stoner's place at Ducati. His inability to perform on the bike had provided Stoner with some wry relief: 'Maybe I was better than people thought.'

At the French Grand Prix on 17 May 2012, Stoner announced his intention to retire at the end of the season. So early—he would be just 27. Trade press reported Honda had offered him US$15 million to stay: more than they paid world F1 champion Jenson Button. But he was adamant. A crash in qualifying at the US Grand Prix on the Indianapolis infield track solidified his decision. His electronic traction control had been caught out by the track surface: 'I was trying to get on the gas while it was shutting down.' It sent him sprawling. He was taken to the course hospital with leg injuries. He had his bootmaker modify a boot to be four times larger than its normal size, swallowed Aspalgin—a form of pain relief then readily available and now only by prescription—and bravely raced to fourth, which counted towards his third place in his world title defence.

On 28 October at Phillip Island, Mick Doohan suited up in his Honda leathers and took Stoner's bike for two typically Mick-swift parade laps, then Stoner reclaimed it, watched by Adri and their baby daughter Alessandra Maria, and won his last ever MotoGP, fittingly at the Island.

In 2008, Stoner had been named Young Australian of the Year. In 2013, he was made a Member of the Order of Australia (AM).

Part Five

A Class of Its Own
2004–Onwards

27

Selling the Farm

In 2002, Peter Henderson decided to sell the farm.

An advertisement in the Melbourne property press on 9 October offered 256 hectares on six titles, the 105.8-hectare grand prix circuit, and a permit for a 163-room seaside resort. The asking price was not quoted.

On 25 February 2004, almost eighteen months later, in an article titled, 'Fox Buys Island GP track for Resort,' *The Age* announced:

> Victorian property and trucking magnate Lindsay Fox will buy the Phillip Island motorcycle track and surrounding land with an eye to fulfilling a plan to add a holiday resort to the site.

> Placetac, the vendors . . . yesterday confirmed it had reached an agreement to sell the venue to Linfox Property Group, subject to a due diligence process.
>
> Placetac managing director Fergus Cameron would not disclose the price for the land, which includes the 106-hectare circuit and 4.4-kilometre track and a permit for a 163-room hotel, but industry sources put the figure at $10 million to $20 million.
>
> A report in *The Age* in 2002 quoted Placetac as estimating the site to be worth about $40 million but had been hoping to sell it for about half that amount.
>
> Mr Cameron said Placetac—a consortium of Phillip Island landowners—was selling the land because it did not have the resources to further develop it. The hotel resort permit gives approval for a two- to three-level development that must be completed by 2007.
>
> 'We felt that we were a small organisation and believed that we had taken the property as far as we could,' Mr Cameron said . . .
>
> Linfox director Andrew Fox would not comment yesterday . . .

Australian Grand Prix Corporation chairman Ron Walker was quoted: 'We are looking forward to working with Linfox.'

There had been partnership pressures. Placetac chair and majority shareholder Peter Henderson said he initiated the sale. 'We didn't get much out of the grand prix. We could have, but Ron Walker screwed us. Overall we weren't making big money, but enough to survive.' Fergus Cameron, he said, had 'been great at running the thing.' But 'Fergus and Christine [Fergus's wife] had become the Prince and Princess of Phillip Island and that pissed me off.' He reiterated their respective roles. 'I ran the business. Fergus was in charge of operating the circuit.' Henderson's time with the National Motor Racing Promoters Association had led him to believe 'motorsport needed people who could run a business. There were only two owners; the rest were managers.' Bob Jane from Calder Park was the other owner: 'I trusted Bob.'

It's not right to conclude Henderson is embittered. He doesn't come across as that; perhaps 'resigned' is a better description of the vibe he gives. 'When I stepped away, Fergus never spoke to me again, Fox never contacted me and I got no thanks from motorsport.'

In our meeting he was happy to provide me with paperwork in support of his position. He was, rightly, proud of the role he played in the development of Australia's pre-eminent grand prix circuit. 'My main achievement? We treated the sport very fairly. We didn't overcharge [for a premium venue].'

Henderson and Cameron had facilitated Bob Barnard's ambitious plans. Henderson bridled at any suggestion that they unduly benefited from Barnard's circuit improvements and subsequent bankruptcy. 'I've not a lot of time for Bob,' he mused. 'He had no idea of the support he got from government, or us. He didn't pay for the lease. We did the homologation. He should have made a lot of money out of it.'

Sitting in the sun on the Portsea Golf Club's veranda with golfers assiduously attacking the front nine below, and with water well under the bridge, Peter Henderson offered: 'At the start I wasn't interested in motorsport at all, but we owned a racetrack so we decided we should run a race.' Much later, with MotoGP restored: 'I enjoyed promoting motorsport, especially at another level, to have created one of the two or three best motorbike circuits in the world.'

'It was $12 million,' Andrew Fox said, reaching into his memory for the acquisition amount. On the surface Linfox had bought well, towards the lower end of *The Age*'s estimate. 'But it had [only] $700,000 of revenue and its contract with Supercars Australia was vulnerable,' Andrew said.

In Linfox's first year of ownership, Supercars passed on Phillip Island. 'They played hardball,' Fox told me. 'We wanted a ten-year contract and we would have invested in them. Instead they went to Symmons Plains in Tasmania and they were washed out.' The following year, Supercars was back at the Island, the first race, ironically, won by Tasmanian Marcos Ambrose.

Linfox House is a pristine five-storey building set back from Melbourne's St Kilda Road. It's a statement. Among the high-rises that distinguish the city's major boulevard as a powerhouse of commerce, the Fox building stands apart. Nothing showy, but a visitor can't help but be struck by the potential value of the airspace above.

Lindsay Fox AC, Andrew's dad, is a massive Australian success story. *The Australian Financial Review*'s 2023 Rich List rated him at number 23, with an estimated worth of $4.35 billion on the back of a dependable 3.6 per cent year-on-year increase. Fox started Linfox in 1956 with one truck.

He married Paula Peele in 1959, had six kids, and grew a transport and logistics business, right for its time, which transformed the way companies move and store goods. Linfox has been very good for Australia. Its business model has been based on partnership.

Andrew runs Linfox's Property Group. Brothers Peter and David are respectively executive chairman and managing director of Linfox Airports. It's a family business, with a heavyweight board and C-suite help. We met in Andrew's office on the second floor of Linfox House, facing St Kilda Road. It's crammed with sports memorabilia. This is a man who's been privileged to know and interact with elite sportspeople from all disciplines. He was laidback, dressed casually in an open-necked shirt. He's a father of five, granddad to two, but young in looks and demeanour. He was due in a board meeting shortly, flying to Europe that night.

We were supposed to be talking about Phillip Island but his focus was on his parents. His respect was palpable. His mum had recently survived melanoma. That led to the family galvanising, pulling together government and private support to build the Paula Fox Melanoma and Cancer Centre at Melbourne's Alfred Hospital, worth $152 million, seven storeys high and due to open in 2024. In 2022, the National Gallery of Victoria announced an 'extraordinary and unprecedented $100 million donation from Lindsay and Paula Fox and their family' to sit alongside the Victorian Government's $1.7 billion Melbourne Arts Precinct Transformation. The Fox: NGV Contemporary was soon to open.

Andrew Fox didn't have to tell me any of that, but he wasn't speaking boastfully—just providing context. Lindsay Fox's ownership of Phillip Island is a big deal. How did it come about?

'I got a phone call just before the MotoGP,' he recalled. 'Fergus Cameron invited me down for the race. I didn't go—a clashing date.' But he did visit the Island privately, 'jumped the fence' for a look around. 'Fergus was pushing me to acquire it. One of his motivations was to protect his employees.'

Linfox has an eye for a strategic purchase. In 1991 it bought and rebranded the Australian Automotive Research Centre (AARC) near Anglesea, a 1000-hectare, securely fenced test and development centre. Australia, then, had a domestic motor manufacturing industry. General Motors owned its own R&D centre at Lang Lang south-east of Melbourne; Ford had its centre in the You Yangs. The Anglesea site, sold by previous owner International Harvester, was rejuvenated by Fox to provide a discreet proving ground for the rest of the car industry and for the burgeoning defence sector.

Toyota, market leader for the first time in 1991, entered a partnership agreement. In return for a suitable lease, Linfox built Toyota its own purpose-designed matrix of test tracks behind locked gates within part of its complex. When local auto manufacturing ceased in 2017, the AARC paradoxically became even more relevant—a bastion of Australian-developed intellectual property.

In 1997, Linfox acquired the Avalon airstrip precinct midway between Geelong and Melbourne. It became a major transport hub, an alternative to Tullamarine for domestic carriers, and an Australian aircraft maintenance alternative to offshore services. A year later, in partnership with Fox's friend, developer Max Beck (a self-made magnate like Lindsay), Linfox secured a long-term lease for tired old Essendon Airport and transformed it into Essendon Fields, a model for a business and community precinct within an aeronautical environment. There's a synergy; wings and wheels are the common threads.

In 1997, the company inaugurated the Fox Classic Car Collection, with limited openings to the public, in the heritage

Queen's Warehouse building in Melbourne's Docklands district. Its purpose was to house 250 special vehicles the family, and especially the patriarch, had curated. The collection is currently valued at $68 million. Lindsay's original Ford F500 truck, restored from a barn find, takes pride of place.

Andrew's European trip the night we met would include a visit to Mercedes-Benz in Stuttgart to check the progress of Lindsay's new Project One, a limited-production, plug-in, dual-hybrid sports car, recommended retail price US$2.72 million. 'We have number 43 in the production series,' Andrew said. Lewis Hamilton, naturally, had 44, his racing number.

When Linfox bought Phillip Island, Fergus Cameron came with the deal. 'I asked him to stay on and run it,' Andrew said. 'He said he'd give us three months and he stayed for sixteen years.' The Island had created a very personal niche in the world of world championship motorcycle racing. As the business of motorsport became increasingly hidebound, Phillip Island kept it friendly.

'Fergus and Chris Cameron were the heart and soul of the place,' Motorcycling Australia president Peter Goddard told me. 'They were amazing hosts. They had a woolshed on their property just west of the track and they'd host fun family dinners. You'd get the chiefs of Dorna and the FIM attending, along with the major teams. It doesn't happen anywhere else.' It was something to look forward to at the end of a long journey across the world. Phillip Island came with a heap of goodwill.

And Fox added to it. 'We built Sunrise House on the cliff,' Andrew confided. The family's Island retreat is special and discreet. Carmelo Ezpeleta, the chief of Dorna, is a fan. 'Carmelo thinks it's just for him,' Andrew chuckled.

The hospitality is genuine, but there's also a business edge. 'My father says if you don't look after your customer, someone else will,' Andrew said. He likes quoting Lindsay.

The resort, so far, hasn't happened. 'We spent $1.5 million on concepts. We went to the UK and Baghdad. We consulted Greg Norman on the prospect of a championship golf course and looked at designs in the Napa Valley and at Huka Lodge in New Zealand.' A proposal Andrew put to the Bass Coast Shire Council coincided with the onslaught of the global financial crisis in 2007 (according to *The Age*, that was the year Phillip Island's development application expired). 'The council voted against our plan.' Because of the impact of the GFC, Fox regarded the refusal as a bullet dodged. 'I sent them a bottle of Dom Perignon to say thank you.'

'My father is a hard-nosed businessman,' Andrew said. Over his own twenty years of Linfox ownership of the racetrack, Andrew has firmed to a similar stance. 'My nature is not to be speculative. I'm not a developer, someone who invests to sell.' He's a keeper. The return on investment from building a resort doesn't compute, he said.

'If someone said they could do it, I'd consider it,' he said. 'I'd love to develop, but within the reality of the numbers.'

That doesn't imply the Phillip Island Grand Prix Circuit is in jeopardy. Just the opposite. 'It's not for sale,' Andrew firmly stated. Linfox had owned the track for two decades, equalling Placetac's record of longevity. 'It's an iconic property,' he said. 'One day we'll give it to the grandchildren to manage.'

Andrew is under no pressure. 'The only two shareholders I have to satisfy are my mother and father.'

28

Building on Heritage

In mid-February 2024, Peter Harburg, yachtsman and gentleman car racer, was on tenterhooks.

The ship carrying his latest acquisition, a Ferrari 250 LM with provenance so supreme that its drivers included world champions John Surtees and Jochen Rindt, had been diverted by the Israeli-Palestinian conflict. It was touch and go if it would land and clear customs in time to meet its late-summer Australian commitments.

The LM, one of only 32 ever constructed, would be a star attraction at the exclusive Sydney Harbour Concours D'Elegance held on Cockatoo Island, the Phillip Island Classic Festival of Motorsport and the Adelaide Motorsport Festival. After that it might travel to other great motorsport events throughout the world, at the determination of its new custodian.

'I'm excited,' offered Harburg, a particularly private person who derives great pleasure from his dual passions of ocean racing and car racing. The 250 LM would be the latest in a long line of highly desirable heritage racers he'd owned and raced on three continents. (He presents himself not as their owner but as their custodian.) They include a brace of RSR Porsches; a fearsome 1100-horsepower (820-kilowatt), twelve-cylinder Porsche 917/30 Le Mans, one of only six made; a ground-effects Lola T610 sports prototype; a shark-nose Ferrari SP 196 sports racer; and two cars with connection to Jack Brabham—the Cooper T51 sold by Brabham to David McKay, then on to Bib Stillwell, and the Brabham BT11 in which Jack came second in the 1965 Australian Grand Prix.

Harburg has an affinity with Brabham. His ocean racers have been named *Black Jack* in honour of his hero. 'I told him I wanted to name them after him. He'd ring me after a race and ask, "How'd you go?" and grunt a response. Typical Jack.' (Brief information gathering. No wasted words.) In 2021, Harburg's latest *Black Jack*, formerly *Alfa Romeo* when owned by fellow car-and-yacht racer Neville Chrichton, claimed line honours in the Sydney–Hobart yacht race.

'I'm an average helmsman and driver,' Harburg modestly assessed himself. 'That's why I have a professional on board the boat. In a car, though, it's just you and your helmet. It's a wonderful thing.' So—if he had to, which sport would he choose?

He took a while to cogitate. 'Cars are in my blood. I'd go without food for a month to enter a car race.'

In the stratospheric world of heritage car racing, Phillip Island aspires to be like Monaco, Spa, Le Mans and Goodwood: one of the blue riband events. In many respects, it's succeeded. 'It's ballsy, that's for sure,' Peter Harburg smiled. 'Every bone in your body is telling you not to turn into [Turn 1]. You're heading down the main straight with that magnificent ocean view in front of you and you know you shouldn't be looking at it.'

The Phillip Island Classic Festival of Motorsport is an annual event, run by the Victorian Historic Racing Register (VHRR), an organisation established in 1976 to promote and protect the legacy of old racing cars and, to a degree, their drivers. Ian Tate OAM, president of VHRR, is a lifelong devotee. 'I was twelve years old, sitting outside Harry Firth's garage, watching him work, when he sent Graham Hoinville to invite me in,' Tate told me in his home workshop, a half-restored historic aluminium sports car on the floor, memorabilia on the walls. Firth and Hoinville were legends. 'Pretty soon I was attending race meetings, pit-crewing for Harry at the early Phillip Island 500s,' he said. Tate became an integral part of Firth's Ford and then Holden touring car teams. When Tate went out on his own, 'Harry wouldn't talk to me. I was invisible.' While the mainstream of motorsport dedicated itself to V8 Supercars, Tate moved away from that too: 'You can get typecast.'

Historic racing became viable as the cars became valuable. The PIARC held its first dedicated race meeting in 1990. It attracted a remarkable 278 entries. The VHRR took control six years later. Entries expanded to well past 500, with an increasing smattering of international competitors. In 2023, Tate hosted six historic Formula One cars, their unbridled V10 and V12 engines providing a screaming, evocative soundtrack for a record spectator attendance.

The cost and complexity of travel makes it difficult for the VHRR to match the grand European and North American classics. Yet, reputationally, Phillip Island is up there with the best. Speak to anyone at the heritage events like Pau in France and they'll talk in awe of the Island.

The F1 cars and Peter Harburg's Ferrari are the cherries on top. Most of the Island's entries are dedicated to the eras of Australian racing—not necessarily locally made cars, but a snapshot of the categories of competition.

For internationals wanting to add the Island to their bucket list, there are always workarounds.

Melbourne enthusiast Chris Davison is the son of four-time Australian Grand Prix winner Lex, uncle of Will, and custodian of the family's race team, Ecurie Australie. He uses the Phillip Island Classic to provide a unique experience for paying European and American guests, not in Formula One cars but in spindly 1.6-litre Formula Fords. The nursery category bred champions. Mark Webber raced Formula Ford. He came third at Phillip Island in his debut year. The car he raced had carried Craig Lowndes to championship victory the season before.

Davison owns half a dozen of the entry-level race cars. They still achieve in excess of 220 km/h down Gardner Straight and the VHRR sometimes will start a field of fifty at a time. Their slipstreaming duels, darting and weaving, are legend. 'My overseas drivers are always satisfied,' Davison said.

It's hard for an amateur promoter like the VHRR when 'costs are in excess of $1.5 million and our best-ever surplus was $25,000'. It's a skinny margin, especially 'when a bad weather day could wipe us out,' according to Ian Tate. As he planned his next race meeting, he noted that 'costs are up better than six per cent. We'll need to pass half that on to our customers.'

Local historic racers, with some exceptions, aren't flush with funds. Tate is aware of his responsibility to them. But even those in the ultra-high-net-worth category aren't pushovers for ambitious promoters. 'You know, there are some concourses that want to charge an entry fee,' Peter Harburg told me, a little astonished. 'I tell them, "I'm providing you with a star attraction and you want me to pay for that privilege?"'

Old race cars are big business. At its very pinnacle, the global heritage race-car movement exists in a bubble of its own creation.

It's important to race and exhibit—not only for personal enjoyment but because values will continue to rise while ever-smart owners and promoters maintain an atmosphere of envy and desire. Increasingly, heritage racing cars are investments on wheels.

The major auction houses make a big deal of under-the-hammer results, but they're likely only the tip of the sales iceberg. Many more exchanges are off-market. 'I agreed with the American I bought the LM 250 from not to divulge details of the sale,' Peter Harburg answered when I asked about the sale. 'But you'll probably find out.' He's right. Once you know the build number of the vehicle—easy to acquire—it opens a cornucopia of pedigree details online: past owners, restorations, results and even crashes. In Peter's case, everything but price is available, and a gentleman never tells. (As a guide, the latest 250 LM to go to public auction was passed in at Monterey in California in 2023 at an estimate of US$18–20 million.)

'I tell them there are no sheep stations on the line,' Kevin Bartlett, driving standards officer for the VHRR, said. He's not too concerned about protecting the value of the metal but he's totally invested in saving lives. The hardest, toughest and yet fairest domestic open-wheeler competitor this side of Jack Brabham has in his later years become the gamekeeper, not the poacher. Bartlett knows every trick, and he's determined not to let the historic racers employ them—at least not at their own peril.

Driving standards is a recognised code of conduct in all motorsport categories, enforced rigorously in the professional divisions, sometimes determining the outcome of major events. Bartlett, typically, has interpreted the regulations to suit the requirements of a sector populated by enthusiastic amateurs. Competitors have to pass an observed High Performance Licence test. 'I've knocked a lot of people back,' Bartlett said. He goes out to Phillip Island's many corners to observe: 'Even MG, where there's a resident brown snake in the tyre barrier.'

His diligence doesn't imply universal distrust. 'Generally the guys who bring the F1 cars are competitors in the European Masters series, and they are very good. But there's a big difference in the speed differential in most of the classes and that requires special attention.' For the 2024 Classic, Bartlett was joined as a driving standards officer by Michael Stillwell, son of the late Bib (four-time Australian Drivers' Champion and early

Phillip Island stalwart). Michael, 73, had been a leading touring car competitor—second in the 1972 Australian championship—and had a lifetime's experience of racing at Phillip Island. 'In 1971 I speared off into the Hayshed in a Formula Ford. It was full of hay in those days,' he laughed. Hayshed corner now is just that, a corner. In Michael's day it was a hazard.

'Kevin [now 83] has been threatening retirement for several years,' Michael said. 'It's unlikely to happen.' Together they offered a source of knowledge for the historic racers. They'd take drivers for a few laps in the safety car tidying up their driving technique on the spot.

'I tell them to curb the aggression,' Bartlett said. 'Passing is a major concern.' Bartlett instituted his own standard, one unique to the Island: 'Unless the driver you're intending to pass can see your front wheel as you enter the braking area, you must pull out of it.'

Bartlett also sorted out the rolling starts of the ferociously powerful F5000 open-wheelers. 'It's a real concern getting them to enter Turn 1 on that first lap,' Stillwell said. 'It has to happen in an orderly manner. Kevin has disciplined them to take the start at 4200 rpm in third gear.'

Bartlett, a stylist, is a big fan of Phillip Island. 'The track flows more than any other in Australia. It allows drivers to express themselves, and their cars, a lot better.'

On 23 February 2002—two years before Kevin Bartlett was appointed driving standards officer—wealthy British enthusiast Spencer Flack was killed while racing his front-engine BRM

P25/258 Formula One car at Phillip Island. Flack was flung from the cockpit after striking an apparently unsighted car he was lapping and died on contact with the track. His BRM, at the time conservatively valued at £1.5 million, previously owned by the Hon Amschel Rothschild of the banking family, barrel-rolled and caught fire. Flack had been leading at the time of the collision.

Flack was a historic car and aircraft enthusiast. In 1979 he'd walked away from an aircraft crash in Germany when his Hawker Sea Fury FB11, a fighter that had seen service in the Korean War and the Cuban Bay of Pigs invasion, burst into flames on landing. Flack turned to cars.

His P25 had won the 1959 Dutch Grand Prix driven by Jo Bonnier. Stirling Moss regarded the P25 as the fastest front-engine race car of the 2.5-litre F1 era. Bonnier's win was the first of BRM's seventeen F1 victories, culminating in Graham Hill's landmark 1962 world championship in the team's rear-engine P57.

Flack's wife Carole had the wreckage shipped back to the UK and commissioned a full rebuild, using components her husband had fortuitously stored. She entered it in the 2003 Goodwood Revival meeting, the archetype for historic racing globally, driven by Rob Hall, a professional who specialises in providing services to historic racers. Then she onsold it through Bonhams in 2007. The auction house was able to report: 'Spencer Flack had raced the car with replica aluminium body panels attached, wisely preserving the original magnesium panels in storage. Of the body fitted today, only the tail cowl is new.'

Spencer Flack, 59 at the time of his death, is one of just seven drivers and riders to succumb in competition on the Phillip Island Grand Prix Circuit. 'Just' is an unusual way to describe fatalities. All lives are precious. Once, danger was accepted. Stirling Moss claimed that 'driving without danger is like cooking without salt'. It gave drivers more responsibility, he said.

Today, motorsport is a textbook study in risk mitigation. The requirement on sanctioning bodies to control the safety of machine, track and driver is growing exponentially. The Island's record is better than most. Comparison is unfair, but for perspective, Mount Panorama, surely an iconic equal, has endured 21 fatalities.

Of the Island's fatalities, two have been on bikes and the others in cars. Gregg Hansford, in 1995, remains the only professional competitor to have died. Phillip Rothfield's death in his Austin-Healey at the inaugural meeting in 1956 was followed by 39 fatality-free years for competitors until Hansford's crash. (In 1978, spectator Francis White died, apparently of heart failure, when hit by a Clubman racing car.)

Clinton Farr, a 21-year-old third-generation bike racer (Honda CVR600), died in a Supersport race near the Hayshed in 2001. Stewart McColl, a promising 23-year-old Newcastle driver—second to later IndyCar champion Will Power in the 2002 Australian Drivers' Championship title—died in 2003 when his VW Golf hit a wall at Honda Corner.

In 2012, seventeen-year-old Oscar McIntyre, riding his Yamaha YZF-R6 in the Superstock support race to the Superbike World Championship, failed to take Doohan Corner, skated through the run-off area and rejoined the track at the exit of Southern Loop. He had the misfortune to collide with two other riders and was fatally injured. A year later, 70-year-old Peter Hall (Datsun 260Z), a veteran of South Australian motor racing, failed to avoid a stalled Lamborghini Gallardo at the start of the Victorian State Circuit Racing Championship. The rear-end crash, estimated at 100 km/h, sent him into cardiac arrest. He died three days later without regaining consciousness.

Island Magic. It's the other face of the Island, the circuit getting back to its roots. 'We call it the pinnacle of non-national championships,' Geoff Bull, PIARC stalwart, proudly claimed. PIARC annually promotes Island Magic, a race meeting for drivers with names that will never be known outside the close circle of club sport.

'Michael Robinson is a real estate agent who races a Holden Monaro and is a multiple winner of our longstanding fifty-kilometre Sports Sedan Plate,' Bull said. 'Michael Miceli is a panelbeater who restores trams and trains for the Victorian Government and wins our Historic Touring Car division in his Boss Mustang. Darren Collins, a landscape gardener, swaps between a Camaro and a Mustang and is Michael's main rival.'

Grassroots motor racing is the backbone of Phillip Island's success. 'I came up with the Island Magic title thirty-five years ago, because Magic is what the island is,' Bull said. The Island community got behind it. The Ramada Resort on Phillip Island Road is its major sponsor. Isola di Capri, one of two go-to Italian restaurants on Thompson Avenue, is a prize-giver. PIARC gets more than 200 entries for its annual Magic meeting, enough with sponsorship and entry fees to make a profit to invest in the next one. 'At this level, you don't rely on a paying gate,' Bull said. 'We also run five annual sprint races—super sprints, they're now called—at the circuit. Each one attracts around 100 competitors.' At its height, PIARC was running 26 events a year at three circuits. The intensity has backed off a bit now since they've majored on Phillip Island.

PIARC has a symbiotic relationship with Phillip Island Operations (PIOPS), the management company that runs the circuit. PIARC owns the public address system that PIOPS uses for all its races, including the MotoGP. 'They still charge us a commercial hire rate, although they might go a bit easy on us,' Bull said. 'It's give and take.'

Phillip Island is an all-year-round affair. 'You're hard-pressed to get a booking,' Bull said. 'The MG Car Club, the Mini Club, the Sports Sedan Association, even Motorsport Australia all promote races at the track, and then there's the motorbike clubs.' The Australian Superbike Championship is an Island fixture. Multiple winners like Wayne Maxwell, Troy Herfoss and Glenn Allerton have all reinforced their reputations at the Island. In 2024, Josh Waters, cousin of Supercar driver Cam, clean-swept all three superbike races at the Island. 'There are drive and ride schools, test days and corporate bookings. Car companies use Phillip Island a lot for new vehicle launches.'

In 2019, Brazilian Formula One driver Rubens Barrichello, with 322 starts the fourth-most-capped premier-series driver ever, was hired by local entrepreneur Chris Lambden and his connections to test a new-concept open-wheeler—called an

S5000, based on a US-made Onroak-Ligier tub. 'It's not like the old F5000s at all,' Lambden defended, even though many people had high hopes it would be. The F5000s were monsters.

The S5000 deliberately presented a high power-to-grip ratio, making it skatey. Combined with the Island's high-speed sweepers, it was a challenge. 'What a track,' the 48-year-old Barrichello, once teammate to Michael Schumacher, enthused. 'I'm getting used to it gradually.'

'What do you think of the views?' his interviewer asked.

'Well, you don't have time to see them,' Barrichello said. 'It's quite fast.'

S5000 went on to become Australia's new Gold Star championship series. It delivered two national titles to young rising star Joey Mawson and another to 24-year-old Aaron Cameron before falling victim, hopefully temporarily, to the internecine battles for category supremacy that have become part of the business of Australian motorsport.

29

A Day at the Races—Australian MotoGP, 2023

Tianda Watson is Phillip Island's whistleblower. She spends each MotoGP at the mouth of the under-track tunnel Bob Barnard built in 1989. It's a narrow, one-way-at-a-time cylinder with rungs up its sides to dissuade enthusiastic wall-of-death stunts.

Tianda controls ingress and egress. It's a well-practised routine: stop cross-flowing foot traffic so vehicles can pass safely, allow one stream in, allow the other out, then release the impatient pedestrians. Repeat. Each sequence requires a minimum of five whistle blows, and there are approximately fifteen sequences an hour. The tunnel operates fourteen hours a day. That's a lot of blowing.

Tianda has been a security guard at Phillip Island for fifteen years. This is her fourth on the tunnel. She's the smiling face of the Island. Nothing phases her, and although people grumble that there should be two tunnels by now, it's just the way it is.

It's nice to be welcomed by a person, rather than a boom gate.

Phillip Island is, in its own style, pleasantly anachronistic. There are no infernally beeping F1-style electronic turnstiles to bar your way into the pits. If you're going to be refused, it will be done politely by a human being. There are no hectares of hot concrete parking pads. You park on freshly mown grass in a neatly fenced paddock. If you're riding, there's a secure tent where you can store your helmet.

The pedestrian footbridge over Gardner Straight has a sign imploring you to be kind to the resident possums, and when you emerge pit-side, the hedges are precisely trimmed and the manicured entrance archway has the arborist's touch. Bass Strait is in constant view. You might well be entering your upmarket golf club or the Birdcage at Flemington.

When Linfox purchased the Australian Automotive Research Centre two harbours away, it achieved a similar vibe. A tired industrial test facility was transformed into an attractive, prideful destination where engineers could confidently host their top brass. Professional presentation means a lot.

The 2023 Australian Motorcycle Grand Prix at Phillip Island was an amalgam of Linfox's infrastructure and the Australian Grand Prix Corporation's culture. In the pit building, there are no long concrete corridors pockmarked with anonymous doors, no obvious no-go zones, not like you find at the modern cookie-cutter circuits. You arrive at reception at the top of the stairs and you're greeted by Alison van den Dungen, wife of commentator Cameron and daughter-in-law of Henk Duncan, the circuit's long-term domestic race director. There's a sense of family.

'Andrew Fox gave me a choice of which corner I'd like,' Jack 'Thriller' Miller, Australia's latest MotoGP star, told me, widely grinning. 'I chose Turn 4 because that's where my family always gathers.' In 2022, Phillip Island bestowed its fourth permanent corner name. Gardner Straight led to Doohan Corner, then Stoner, and now Miller. There's something of a distinction. The first three were named for world champions. Jack had won just four Senior grands prix. Happily, there was still time for him to claim the title. Australia loves a homegrown hero. Jack is the latest, a prodigious talent with a Rossi-esque personality. Like Rossi, Miller had abandoned his earlier nickname 'Jackass' in favour of the wonderfully rhyming 'Thriller' (think Cassius Clay's 'Thrilla in Manila'). He was clearly part of the Phillip Island family.

'I first saw Phillip Island when I was fourteen,' he recalled. 'The only sealed-track riding I'd done was at Morgan Park'—a small club circuit near Warwick in Queensland. 'If I was going to chase a world title I had to know what a grand prix track was like.'

And?

'I was lost. It was so wide and the straight was so long. It just disappeared off into the abyss. Even on a 125 [Moto3], you're still doing 240 kilometres an hour into Turn 1.'

Sonya and Peter Miller and their other kids, Fergus and Maggie, always watch from Turn 4—once Honda Corner, now Miller Corner. They come down from Townsville, their hometown where Jack declared his ambition as a bike racer at age three on a PeeWee50. By the time he first saw the Island, he'd already broken fourteen bones in multiple motocross crashes, and Sonya and Peter had steered him to tar-track competition.

The Millers invested strongly in Jack's career. Peter hit up clients in the mining industry, where he's a freelance driller, and they took him to Europe. Sonya stayed with their teenager, while Peter returned to Australia to earn more. MotoGP's star-maker Mike Trimby recognised Jack's potential and the family's commitment, and rewarded both. Jack was on his way.

From Turn 4, the Miller family cheered Jack to victory in the 2014 Australian Moto3 Grand Prix, the year he finished a championship second on the works KTM by just two points to Alex Márquez. In 2017, the Millers were on their feet again. Against all odds, their boy was leading the Senior Australian Motorcycle Grand Prix.

He'd broken his leg in Japan just two weeks earlier, yet on a non-factory Honda he was off like a jackrabbit, leading Marc Márquez, Valentino Rossi, Jorge Lorenzo. 'To lead the first few laps of my home Grand Prix . . . it was fun, nerve-wracking as hell, but the most amazing feeling,' he told *Australian Motorcycle News*. Four laps later, the seasoned veterans stormed by. Jack tucked in behind and learned a lot about tyre management, the secret to success at the Island. He finished seventh.

In 2019, he put the experience to good use. He nursed his tyres ready for a last-lap surge. When Maverick Viñales crashed in front of him, he was on the podium, third in his home grand prix.

Now, in 2023, Jack was knocking on the door: fourth in the 2021 title, fifth in 2022.

The Australian Grand Prix came with personal milestones. The week before the 2022 race, he'd married Townsville sweetheart Ruby Mau. A month before the 2023 event, their daughter Pip was born. Jack had spent five years with Ducati. Now he was back with KTM. Qualifying wasn't great. He was only eighth on the grid, six behind his teammate Brad Binder. Phillip Island? 'It's all about speed,' he said.

At 5.30 p.m. on the evening of qualifying, Friday 20 October, Carlos Ezpeleta, chief sporting officer of Dorna, and son of its chief executive Carmelo, called a media conference. 'The weather forecast is quite bad for Sunday,' he said. It wasn't rain that worried Dorna; it was wind. In 2019 they'd had to red-flag practice when 70 km/h gusts blew several bikes off track. 'Those were the early days of aerodynamic aids on bikes,' Ezpeleta defended. 'We know much more now about how wind affects bikes.'

Dorna flipped the schedule. Sunday's 27-lap MotoGP would be held on Saturday. A short sprint race scheduled for Saturday would move to Sunday. It turned out to be a genius decision. Thirty-three-year-old Frenchman Johann Zarco—JoJo—won his first ever grand prix. Zarco had joined the Pramac Ducati team when Miller left it. 'If you can win here,' the first-time winner told the post-race press conference, 'you feel like you are one of the big guys.' Jack Miller was seventh.

On Sunday, Carlos's forecast came true. Step out of shelter at Miller Corner and an occasional strong gust could almost blow the unwary off their feet. The planned sprint race was abandoned.

'Everyone loves Phillip Island,' Motorcycling Australia chief Peter Doyle smiled. 'If we could just tow it 1000 kilometres north.'

Jorge Viegas, president of FIM for a second term, was at the Island for the first time in 22 years 'since the World Superbike race was cancelled because of rain', he joked, our conversation occurring before Ezpeleta's weather warning. Portuguese-born Viegas ('call me George') is a big fan of Australia and Australians. As we spoke in a pit garage, Troy Corser and Peter Goddard were standing outside. Viegas greeted them enthusiastically: 'I gave Troy his Diploma of Championship at Portimão in 2008.'

Why had Viegas chosen this year to return to the Island? He answered with a shrug. But it's inescapable that the Dorna contract with the AGPC expires in 2026, and it's important to address any issues that may exist. The FIA's consideration is the track itself. 'I compare it with Estoril in the 1990s,' Viegas told me. He had been president of the Portuguese seaside circuit, 30 kilometres west of Lisbon on Portugal's Riviera, during the transition from 500cc to MotoGP. 'It's very close to the sea; there's a big influence of wind—and we have seagulls there also.'

Estoril is no longer used for MotoGP or World superbikes. It's been supplanted by the Algarve International Circuit in Portimão, a three-hour drive south. Opened in 2008, Portimão is characterised as a modern complex, complete with karting track, off-road circuit, technology park, sports complex, apartments and a five-star hotel. Both Estoril and Phillip Island, Viegas said, 'are old style. I like that.'

Portimão, by comparison, was 'a velodrome, power-brake, power-brake'. He shook his head. Would there be any objection to retaining the classic circuit? 'As long as it's safe, perfectly safe,' he replied.

Carmelo Ezpeleta, the much-loved boss of Dorna, had taken up residence in the largest suite in PIOPS' permanent porta-cabin. Guarded by Carolina Mico, head of the CEO's office, but enabled by Ignacio Sagnier, communications director of Dorna, getting to Ezpeleta is a process. It's surprising, when access is granted, that Carmelo goes it alone. There's no minder to witness our conversation. In his youth, Carmelo was a five-time Spanish national champion in Jai Alai, a bat-and-ball sport requiring quick reflexes and finessed application of power. He's confident in his ability to handle a media encounter. Carmelo is old school.

Like Jorge Viegas, he has history with Australia. In the 1990s, he was manager of fellow Spaniard Carlos Sainz Snr, twice world rally champion and recently four-time Dakar winner, when Sainz barrel-rolled out of contention in the Perth round of Rally Australia.

'I first came to Phillip Island in 1990 with ROPA,' Carmelo said. ROPA is the consortium of circuit owners; Ezpeleta had been a director of Spain's Jarama and Barcelona-Catalunya tracks. 'I was surprised by the lack of facilities. I'd been accustomed to a lot of grandstands.'

Dorna took control of the sport in 1992–93 when it bought commercial rights from Bernie Ecclestone. Ezpeleta has been at its pinnacle ever since, the very definition of a benevolent dictator. When Ecclestone was a frontline F1 operator he was feared and revered in equal parts. Carmelo is universally admired.

'Phillip Island is a different situation than when we are in Europe,' he told me. 'I understand it is difficult to upgrade here.' The Australian MotoGP already provided 'disproportionate attendance compared to its population. We must be careful not to compare.'

Ezpeleta acknowledged discussions with Australia's newest grand-prix-sized circuit, Tailem Bend, just across the border in South Australia and built by Adelaide's super-enthusiastic Shahin family. 'We talked some time ago.' But then, definitively, he said, 'Phillip Island *is* Australia. It is the only possibility. The layout is the best in the world.'

Had contract renewal discussions begun? 'We are talking to the Victorian Government through the Australian Grand Prix Corporation,' he said, noting that Martin Pakula, former Victorian sports minister, had become 'president' of the AGPC. Pakula, the AGPC's chair, had played a role in Melbourne, locking in hosting rights for the Australian F1 Grand Prix until 2037. It's the longest F1 contract ever negotiated.

Phillip Island hosts MotoGP and World Superbike each under different management structures, requiring different agreements. In 2013, Dorna added the Superbike World Championship to its portfolio. 'They run as two separate companies,' Ezpeleta explained. 'The requirements also are separate—a little less difficult for superbikes.' Carmelo reiterated his charter: 'We need to be in good connection with our teams. It is important to achieve the best possible solution. We need to think into the future. We are happy to be in Australia.'

Carmelo's son Carlos had just made his rain warning, prompting the senior Ezpeleta to hit the phones, alerting broadcasters around the world to changed schedules, a massive undertaking. At 78, he exhibited obvious pride in Carlos, a member of Dorna's management team since 2007: 'He's doing a good job.'

Was Carlos part of his succession plan? 'I am not the biggest shareholder,' he smiled, deflecting the question with all the skill of a Jai Alai 'chula' shot.

Within a month of our meeting, Carmelo Ezpeleta had gone public in response to emerging reports that Dorna was on the market for upwards of €2 billion. In answer to media probing, he revealed Dorna's senior management owned approximately 20 per cent of the corporation's shares, 'of which I am the largest holder'. The other 80 per cent was held almost equally by British investor Bridgepoint Capital and CPP, the Canadian Pension Plan. 'I am surprised that information intended only for stock-holders' consumption would leak,' he said.

Six months later, the deal was done. On 1 April 2024, Liberty Media Corporation, proprietors of Formula One since 2017, announced they had entered into an agreement to acquire Dorna Sports from Bridgepoint and CPP Investments. It was April Fool's Day, but this was no joke.

'Liberty Media will acquire 86% of MotoGP with MotoGP management retaining approximately 14% of their equity in the business,' the ambitious and diversified conglomerate announced. 'The transaction reflects an enterprise value for MotoGP of €4.2 billion and an equity value of €3.5 billion.'

Liberty Media is the precocious child of 83-year-old US Telco billionaire John C Malone. Its portfolio encompasses sporting associations stretching from motorsport through to the Kentucky Derby. Liberty's team, headquartered not in Europe but in Englewood, Colorado, seemed to be doing everything right. One month before making its Dorna announcement, Liberty's Formula One Group proudly reported a 25 per cent rise in F1's revenue during the 2023 financial year, up to US$3.2 billion.

Liberty had acquired Dorna, it said, because of its 'attractive financial profile with diversified and contracted revenue streams, high EBITDA margins and low capital intensity resulting in significant free cash flow'. The acquisition was expected to be completed by 'year-end 2024', subject to 'the receipt of clearances and approvals by competition and foreign investment law authorities in various jurisdictions'.

Importantly 'Carmelo Ezpeleta, CEO of Dorna since 1994, will continue to run the business headquartered in Madrid'.

Almost 2000 enthusiasts are camped comfortably on a total of 973 sites within the grand prix precinct. The numbers disprove the long-held myth of a seething mass of fan-zone debauchery. Maybe, sometime in the past, it might have been on. But that was in a less regulated environment. Now the volume of campers is strictly limited by the availability of amenities.

There's no such thing as sleeping rough. The Australian Grand Prix Corporation offered five grades of campsite, right up to pre-erected glamping opportunities. Clearly the majority of spectators were sleeping elsewhere. The grand prix contributes mightily to the Island's economy.

When it bought the circuit, Linfox built a karting track, a near-exact 750-metre, twelve-corner miniature of the main circuit. A Lilliputian Phillip Island is a clever idea. It operates year-round as a tourist attraction, except on MotoGP weekend when it is blanketed by tents. A good lap time in one of its French-built Sodi RT8 Evo2 hire karts powered by a Honda GX270 engine is around 48 seconds, an average speed approaching 60 km/h.

The Phillip Island History of Motorsport Museum had better than 30 bikes on show. Among them were nine world championship winners that between them had won 51 grands prix and placed their riders on 106 podiums. Andrew Fox secured fifteen Aprilias and another nine Cagivas from two European collectors, including the 125 that launched Valentino Rossi's career when he won the 1997 Ultra Lightweight Championship.

In town, the Phillip Island waterfront was transformed into the 'Cowes Entertainment Precinct'. A super-screen and stage on the corner of Thompson Avenue and The Esplanade hosted live bands and racing replays. Crowd estimation is always difficult, but in the enclosed area a little looked a lot, maybe a thousand at a time. It was enough for the mayor of Bass Coast Shire Council, Michael Whelan, to sell up the MotoGP as a 'major driver of off-season tourism'.

The only disappointment was the cancellation of the annual Barry Sheene Tribute Ride from Bairnsdale to the Island. The ride had been run to commemorate the late Baz, and at its height it attracted more than 1000 riders. This year marked twenty years since Sheene's death, surely something to be noted, but participation had gradually decreased and organisers pulled the pin.

Across the island, the locals and their annual MotoGP guests, once wary of each other, had settled into a state of convivial acceptance. Most of the on-circuit campers, it seemed, were content to stay on site, grooving to two cover bands, Rewinder and Redline. It was almost like a family gathering on a grand scale.

Garry McCoy, 'The Slide King', winner of three Senior 500cc world championship grands prix and 2004 World Superbike winner at Phillip Island, was having an identity crisis.

He'd been hired by Motorcycling Australia to mentor young riders in the Oceania Junior Cup (OJC), designed for children aged between eleven and sixteen, and not only did many of them not know him but few were curious to find out. 'It's hard to get their noses out of their phones and tablets,' he mock-complained. Even the oldest of the aspirants hadn't been born when Garry stopped racing.

Motorcycling Australia inaugurated OJC in 2019 to provide a structured path to local and international competition. It's consistent with development programs in all sports, except these youngsters are achieving 150 km/h down Gardner Straight. They're all riding identical single-cylinder 155cc Yamaha YZF-R15s. The highly subsidised program costs their parents $5100 for bike, tutoring, consumables and clothing. It's a bargain. But at Phillip Island? 'It's quite okay,' Trevor Manley, a former 125cc Australian champion and McCoy's co-coach, explained. 'They'll learn a lot about drafting on the long straight, and they're not going any faster here than they would at any other track.'

Two thirteen-year-olds—Archie Schmidt from South Australia and John Pelgrave from Queensland—emerged from the slipstream to win a race each; the third race was cancelled because of the rain-shortened schedule. Archie went on to secure a place in the Asia Talent Cup for 2024.

Nayelle Kelso, a single mum from Darwin, was all over the podium ceremony, homemade team flag draped over her shoulders. Her son Joel, for whose career she'd worked two jobs, seven days a week, seemingly forever, had just claimed third in the wet Australian Moto3 Grand Prix.

The twenty-year-old had started from the front row, been as high as second and conceded that place only when the need to bag a secure podium overcame his will to win. A little disappointing. You expect young firebrands to press on regardless. Kelso had that morning locked in a full-time Moto3 ride for the next season with Spain's BOE Motorsports, and he didn't want to throw it away by doing something rash. 'It wasn't the place on the podium I was looking for, but it feels good,' he explained.

Kelso might well be the last young Australian to make it in MotoGP outside the Motorcycling Australia OJC pathway. With the help of aspiring Victorian team owner Jake Skate, he won his first national title, the 70cc championship, aged ten, and bagged three championships by fourteen.

Nayelle had spent every dollar, and more, on getting him there. She'd even tried crowdfunding.

Now he was on his way. In the future—Kelso Corner? She could only dream.

30

Future Shock

On Valentine's Day 2024, Motorsport Australia presented the Victorian Government with a business case which, if it got up, could change the face of the sport. The white paper was entitled 'The Home of Motorsport' and it proposed the construction of a motor-racing campus encompassing all facets of competition up to and including an FIA Grade 1 circuit able to hold an F1 grand prix or a MotoGP.

The government knew the paper was coming. It had funded it—$1.7 million allocated in its 2022 budget to seek advice and proposals from global experts. Tim Bamford, former CEO of the Australian Grand Prix Corporation, had been contracted by Motorsport Australia to project-manage the investigation. He sought business advice from Ernst & Young and, crucially, commissioned preliminary designs from German firm Tilke

Engineers & Architects. Tilke are world leaders in circuit design.

Motor racing in Australia is controlled by five federations represented under a peak umbrella organisation called the Australian Motorsport Council. Cars, motorcycles, drags, speedway and karts had all been consulted as key stakeholders.

The campus would be sited adjacent to Avalon Airport on the multi-lane Princes Freeway, 58 kilometres from the Melbourne GPO and 28 kilometres from Geelong. Speedway already had a high-quality facility, hosting World Series Sprintcars, across the road from the proposed complex. The land was owned by the federal Department of Defence and leased to Linfox. 'We are happy to look at negotiating anything,' Andrew Fox told me. 'Tim Bamford,' he said, 'had to explore it.'

It's an exciting prospect. Australia's three marquee events—the Australian F1 Grand Prix, the Australian Motorcycle Grand Prix and the Superbike World Championship all reside in Victoria, and there is real determination to retain them. A purpose-built facility would provide certainty, although as Fox pointed out it would be a tough ask to miss the economic benefit of showcasing the Melbourne CBD with the Australian F1 Grand Prix at its Albert Park location. Ditto, it would seem, for Phillip Island, which holds a unique place in world motorsport.

Motorsport Australia's vision was broad. For years there had been uncertainty about the future of Melbourne's suburban Sandown track. In 2022, the Melbourne (horse) Racing Club, which controls the venue, gained approval to move to community consultation on a rezoning proposal that could transform the venue into a suburb with 7500 homes. Calder Park, to the north, had recently attempted a resurgence, achieving a Motorsport

Australia licence to run events up to state-championship level. But with suburbia encroaching, the sport's administrators—across all disciplines—could see sense, in fact an imperative, in exploring a new Home of Motorsport.

'The proposal has gone to the [Victorian] Department of Sport and Recreation for consideration by the Minister,' a spokesperson told me. 'If it passes that phase, it will go to Cabinet for determination in the State budget.'

Travis Auld, CEO of the Australian Grand Prix Corporation, is one of a new breed of administrators at the top end of Australian motor racing. He'd been CFO and GM of Broadcasting and Clubs for the all-powerful AFL, an exalted role, and moved to the AGPC when seventeen-year veteran Andrew Westacott pulled the pin. Westy joined the board of his beloved Western Bulldogs football club, in a neat juxtaposition.

Auld's appointment created wry amusement within the tight coterie of motorsport CEOs. 'The AFL is so powerful that they dictate terms,' one told me. 'At the AGPC, he has to answer to the FIM and FIA and they say, "Don't question us, just do it."' Auld, casually dressed, inquisitive, with face stubble to make Mark Webber envious, is unphased. As soon as he came on board in mid-2023, he travelled to Catalunya for the MotoGP and to the new Las Vegas F1 GP. 'They appreciated I went to meet them,' he said. Travis is all about 'creating an experience befitting the history of the Phillip Island circuit'. His 'number one goal', he said, 'is to retain the event for Victoria'.

Auld had commissioned an Ernst & Young report on the economic benefit of the MotoGP. If you can't measure it, you can't manage it. He was already in no doubt that the race at Phillip Island represented Victoria's 'biggest regional event', a proposition supported by then Bass Coast mayor Michael Whelan, who estimated annual island revenue from the grand prix at $42 million. 'That's the hole it left in our economy when it was cancelled by Covid,' Whelan, mayor when we spoke in late 2023, told me.

'There's a uniqueness about Phillip Island,' Auld went on. 'The MotoGP is best experienced there.' Covid had caused some difficulty. 'People who had holiday homes on the island had retreated to them and remained permanently,' he said, 'creating a strain on accommodation.' As a solution for the next MotoGP, he and his team were getting creative, looking outside the box, perhaps a cruise ship moored off the Cowes pier.

Travis's operational contact at Phillip Island is Dave Bennett, general manager of the Grand Prix circuit. Bennett took over from Fergus Cameron when the man regarded as the 'father' of Phillip Island retired after almost 40 years. Bennett and Auld had both worked at the Gold Coast Suns football club, Bennett as stadium manager and Auld as CEO. They'd been there when the Suns' stadium was totally rebuilt at a cost of $144 million. 'Sometimes it's easier to knock it over, rather than try to tack something on the back,' Auld said. In regard to the Avalon greenfield proposal, he was remaining 'open-minded. It's important to put our best foot forward as a state.'

A consideration was the upcoming contract renewal with Dorna. 'Tenure allows you to do a lot of things. Our F1 contract [to 2037] allows us to lift our eyes to larger horizons in order to justify our investments. It's difficult to do that with a three-year horizon,' Auld noted. MotoGP requires renewal at the end of 2026. 'It would be good to have a result by 2024,' he said.

Quite rightly, the new CEO is an agent of change. 'People love Phillip Island,' he said. His anticipation is for positive, progressive improvement. 'If it looks like it does now in ten years, it won't have a GP.' Not harsh—just realistic.

Bass Coast mayor Michael Whelan was certain of the economic benefit of Phillip Island's grand prix track. He'd already identified the value of the MotoGP alone at $42 million. The historic race meeting brought in another $8 million. He couldn't provide figures on the overall impact on the island's economy but it would be substantial. 'Penguins are our number one crowd draw. They're all year round,' he told me over breakfast coffee in Cafe Lugano on Thompson Avenue.

Whelan was a relatively recent island resident. He came to retire but stood for council to make a point. His proud achievement as we spoke was the soon-to-open $28 million Berninneit cultural centre a few doors away. 'They'd been trying to get it up for twenty years. We did it in two.'

Whelan was a big supporter of Destination Phillip Island, the local tourism authority of which Fergus Cameron had been an influential member. But as the island's demographic changed, with more permanent residents, Whelan was taking a longer view: 'I'm trying not to rely on any one thing. We've been very reliant on penguins and bikes for our island economy.'

In the future, the mayor saw the island as being more vegetated, with its towns more densely populated, yet with the same rural flavour. Light industry would be accommodated sympathetically.

That night, Whelan's council voted on a development plan for a new $85 million waterfront hotel on the site of the former Isle of Wight Hotel, destroyed by fire in 2010. The Isle of Wight had been the epicentre of motor-racing life on the island almost a century before. The plan got up, delivering a further 163 rooms and four restaurants to the grand prix circuit's need for additional accommodation. It was a back-to-the-future moment.

Michael Whelan served two single-year terms as mayor. He stepped down in November 2023.

Competitors in the first round of the 2024 Superbike World Championship arrived at Phillip Island to find it totally resurfaced. It wasn't a surprise. Andrew Fox had flagged it at our meeting before Christmas. It was the fourth resurfacing since Bob Barnard's major makeover in 1989 and the second in the Linfox era. Dorna's own circuit consultants, an Italian specialist firm, had been at the track during the 2023 MotoGP, consulting teams and making millimetre-precise measurements. Linfox had funded the resurface, the AGPC confirmed.

The superbikes and the Supersport support category each carved around a second off their lap records. The new surface still needed to be rubbered in, and a few bumps had appeared during the resurfacing that hadn't been there before. They would need to be shaved in time for the MotoGP at year's end. But 24-year-old Nicolò Bulega, on debut for the works Ducati team, won his first superbike race and set a new pole time of 1 minute 27.916 seconds (182.01 km/h). It was the first time a superbike had dipped below 1 minute 28 seconds and the first time one had averaged above 180 km/h. Local riders in the domestic superbike series achieved similar gains, about two seconds a lap slower.

There was great hope the new surface would establish Phillip Island without doubt as the fastest MotoGP circuit in the world. That accolade had always been under challenge. Austria's Red Bull Ring was for a time considered faster, but a chicane—for bikes, not cars—installed for safety on its Turn 2 in 2022 took it out of contention.

So which track is quickest? It's between Phillip Island and the Chang International Circuit in Thailand.

The most reliable guide is to compare contemporary pole-position average speeds achieved by MotoGP machinery of the same era. In 2023, Spain's Jorge Martín (Ducati) provided a truly scientific benchmark, statistically close to perfect. Grands Prix at both circuits occurred a week apart in October. The same rider was on the same bike. At Phillip Island, Martín claimed pole with a lap average of 183.536 km/h. A week later he claimed pole again in Thailand at an average of 183.614 km/h. Thailand was faster by 0.078 km/h. Phillip Island's new surface was likely to redress that deficit the next time the MotoGP bikes hit out.

Issues still existed in regard to the pit area, the size of each pit and, specifically, the width of the lane. Former Supercar team owner Roland Dane had been outspoken in his comments, calling the pits substandard and the pit lane 'so tight it's dangerous'. A Motorsport Australia spokesperson said, 'It's wrong to say there's a major concern. If it was built like that now it wouldn't comply, but we inspected it last year and issued it with a Grade 3 FIA licence that allows racing to occur.' Supercars Australia, which had not returned to the circuit since 2019, declined discussion.

Veteran John Bowe was one of the first to drive on the new surface. 'I thought it had more bumps in it,' he confirmed. But he thought it could have been the car. The $284,000 BMW M4 GT4 he was testing 'felt like a go-kart with a roof, very aggressive with the way it takes the throttle'.

Bowe had been hired to be the 'Pro' in a Pro-Am combination contesting the inaugural Australian SRO GT4 series over six rounds in 2024. The first race would be at Phillip Island, two days before Bowe's 70th birthday.

'It was like a gift from God,' Bowe exhaled. 'I love the act of driving a racing car.' By his own calculation—as twice winner of the Gold Star, twice Australian touring car champion, once Australian sports car champion—Bowe has driven more makes of racing car in more series at Phillip Island than anyone else: sixteen that he can readily count. He'd crashed an open wheeler just the once.

'I'd never driven a F5000 at the Island and in 2008 New Zealand owner David Abbott offered me the ex-Alf Costanzo Lola.' Four-time Gold Star winner Costanzo had been Bowe's bête noire. The opportunity to discover Costanzo's secrets was enticing. 'I came onto the main straight, around 280 kilometres an hour, and the rear wing fell off. I must have spun fifty times [exaggeration] before I backed into the pit wall. We repaired the car and every lap onto the straight I looked in the mirror to make sure the wing was still there.'

Bowe had first raced at the Island as teammate to Dick Johnson in the 1990 Australian Touring Car Championship. His two-litre turbocharged Ford Sierra featured massive turbo lag, and tyres that he struggled not to blister on the harsh surface. He'd dutifully finished second to Dick. Now, 34 years later, channelling the perfect lap-by-lap recall with which top drivers are blessed, he compared the Sierra to the BMW, 'a racing car you buy straight from the factory with little to be done to it'.

The Stephane Ratel Organisation (SRO) has homogenised motor racing. Its global GT racing series has caused performance-car makers to produce racing cars on their production lines. Audi, BMW, Mercedes and Porsche have all come on board. They even provide a pool of professional racers to co-drive with wealthy amateur owners. Ratel prides himself on providing unique experience. He delights in presenting the classics—Spa, the Nürburgring, Mount Panorama and, for his domestic GT4 series, Phillip Island.

Bowe had been hired by 30-year-old newcomer Jacob Lawrence to coach and co-drive. 'At least it's not a sixteen-year-old who knows everything,' Bowe joked. His first test at the Island highlighted the developments over three decades since he drove the Sierra. 'It's got more grip and better brakes. It's twenty kilometres an hour slower down the straight, but it's so much faster in the corners. It can take Hayshed flat. If I tried that in the Sierra, I would have been in the lake. I did more than 100 laps and the control tyres did their job. There are ten knobs on the steering wheel and there's telemetry and data for every purpose.'

But: 'The Sierra had grunt. There was nothing like it when it kicked you in the back.'

By no means is Bowe advocating a return to times past. He's grateful for the opportunity to 'fuel my addiction' and extend his career. 'I love Phillip Island. It gives me a sense of satisfaction better than most. It's a real, serious racetrack.'

Epilogue

It's October 2019, 30 years since Wayne Gardner won his hallmark race at Phillip Island. We're packed into the Greenway Chapel, near Gosford on the Central Coast north of Sydney, for the funeral of Peter Molloy, the driver-and-rider whisperer. Molloy—always 'Molloy', never 'Peter'—had died, aged 84, of brain cancer. Warwick Brown, winner of the Australian and New Zealand Grands Prix, and Wayne Gardner were both to deliver eulogies. Brown and Gardner were the Golden Ones, the shining achievements in Molloy's career.

Wayne came from behind, heading for the pulpit, and I looked back to see who he was with. It was Donna. Wasn't expecting that—not after all these years, with other marriages for them both and children with other partners. Donna looks just as she did those decades before. The original and the best.

They'd broken up two years after Wayne stopped racing bikes, only five years into their marriage but sixteen into their intense relationship. 'When he stopped racing, we just lost purpose,' Donna said. They'd tried unsuccessfully for children; IVF hadn't helped.

Wayne met Toni Atkinson; they married and had two sons: Remy, who was 2021 Moto2 GP champion, and Luca. That marriage had ended and Wayne lived in Monaco with 'a much younger girl, who keeps me young', he grinned, that cheeky, apologetic 'understand me, I'll always be this way' grin.

Donna married Sydney agribusiness specialist Johnny Kahlbetzer and they had sons Colt and Cruz. Donna and Johnny have done very well. (*The Australian*'s annual Richest 250 list in 2024 had Johnny and his brother Markus at numbers 110 and 111, with an estimated combined wealth of $1.3 billion.)

'So you came here separately?' I asked cautiously at the wake.

'No, together,' Donna smiled. 'We drove up in my FF Ferrari. I think that's why Wayne came with me.' It's a simple deflection to a much deeper question. Throughout all these years, they'd stayed respectfully close. They'd been soulmates and neither can nor wants to deny that time in their lives. They are, simply, mates.

'The world championship was great,' Donna said. 'But the Australian Grand Prix, and Phillip Island—that will always be the one. You just can't replace that high with anything else.'

Acknowledgements

Like koalas and penguins, Fergus Cameron is protected on Phillip Island. 'We love Fergus like a member of the family,' Andrew Fox told me in an emotional early-evening phone call. 'He's frail. I kissed him [when I saw him] on Saturday.' Fergus, for 40 years the face of the Phillip Island Grand Prix circuit, is not well and his friends have moved to shelter him. That's why there are no direct quotes from him in this book. 'Ferg built the most amazing, loyal team and we were so very lucky to have him at the helm,' Ingrid Roepers, his friend and communications guru for most of that time, told me in an email. 'He is respected across the globe in the world of motorsport and on the island in his work with Destination Phillip Island (he was chair for quite a long time). He somehow managed to juggle all the stakeholders on the island with all their varying interests and opinions, and in the main carried the people of Phillip Island on the ride.'

It would have been good to speak with Fergus, understandable that I could not—equally, the late Ron Walker AC. Both contributed mightily to the development of elite motorsport in Australia.

The emotional connection to Phillip Island is incredibly strong. More than 70 people—competitors, administrators, volunteers and promoters, all deeply invested in their Island paradise—willingly gave up their time and knowledge to this project. Happily and, in many cases, surprisingly, each contributed fresh intel. Most are listed in this addendum. My sincere appreciation to them all, and to others with whom I conversed.

The keepers of the Phillip Island faith are an eclectic group—two groups, actually. On four wheels, it's PIARC; on two wheels, it's Hartwell Motorcycle Club. So many assisted in research. To Geoff Bull and Henk Duncan from PIARC, Paul Keam and Mark Cadle from Hartwell, my special thanks.

It was particularly pleasing also to discover Peter Henderson, the founding chairman of Placetac, long moved on from his Phillip Island experience and able to impart first-person insight.

The historians were a huge help. Mark Bisset, proprietor of Primotipo.com, arguably the country's pre-eminent motorsport heritage site, was generous in sharing recollections and pictures, and introducing me to Bugatti authority Bob King. Jim Scaysbrook OAM, whose own book on the Island published two decades ago provided a reliable guide to early bike races, unlocked pictures never before published. Ian Tate OAM, president of the Victorian Historic Racing Register, bridged the gap between heritage and contemporary as promoter of the annual Island Classic.

For Mark Bisset this book will be a frustration. Mark is a proponent of the proposition that the first Australian Grand Prix was held in Goulburn, New South Wales, in 1927. I discount that. The Goulburn event, although grandly called the Australian Grand Prix, was a lap dash over six laps of a 1-mile (1.6-kilometre) track and that does not count as a GP. Yet I'm not certain that Phillip Island in 1928 qualifies either. It was 'only' over 100 miles (161 kilometres), not a proper Grand Prix length. The 1929 race got the distance right, and perhaps therefore deserves the mantle of our first GP. Conjecture remains ongoing.

Three good friends made their precious magazine and book collections available: Colin Bond (*Racing Car News*), Ray Berghouse (*Australian Motor Racing Year*) and Dean Mellor (*Australian Motorcycle News*). There's nothing more accurate than reading eyewitness reports of motor races, recorded directly after they occurred and before they're skewed by recollection. Thanks also to their colleagues Kel Buckley and Chris Currie.

Visiting the Island is always a pleasure—no matter the weather. Thanks to my Grossard Point housemates, Tim and Frances Jardine, Greg Rust and Steve Wood, the senior production team at Zspace who make GPTV informative and entertaining on the Island's big screens (they produce GPTV for the Australian F1 Grand Prix at Albert Park, too).

This is my sixth motorsport book for Allen & Unwin. It's been a pleasure to renew our association post-Covid and to work with Tom Bailey-Smith, senior editor and commissioning editor, who suggested this book, as well as with the 'regular' team, senior editor Samantha Kent and freelance copy editor Emma Driver, cover designer Luke Causby, typesetter Lynne Jones and proofreader Hilary Reynolds. Sam asks the smartest left-field questions in the business. Emma does her darnedest to keep me politically and socially correct.

Phillip Island came at a time of happy turmoil for the Smailes family. To Jenny, Andrew, Karen, Cameron, Matilda, Kate and Dan, thanks for your support and understanding. And to twins Amelia and Lucinda, born to Kate and Dan mid-manuscript, welcome to our world. See you at the races.

Bibliography

Books

Barker, S., *Valentino Rossi: The definitive biography*, London: John Blake Publishing, 2021

Barker, S., *Barry Sheene: 1950–2003: The biography*, London: HarperCollins, 2003

Barnard, B., *Seven Crazy Years (And That Was Just the Start)*, Spain: B. Barnard, 2020

Bartlett, K., and Shepherd, J., *Big Rev Kev*, Sydney: Lansdowne, 1983

Bell, R., and Loxley, T., *F5000 Thunder: The Titans of Road Racing 1970–1982*, Glenbrook, NSW: Full Throttle Publishing, 2012

Beretta, M., and Cadigan, N., *The Riders: Australia's Motorbike Champs*, Sydney: HarperCollins, 2010

Blanden, J.B., *A History of Australian Grand Prix 1928–1939*, Adelaide: Museum Publishing Co., 1981

Brabham, J., and Nye, D., *The Jack Brabham Story*, Windsor, NSW: Minidi, 2004

Buchanan, G., *Penguin Land*, Melbourne: Mitchell House Publishing, 2015

Clark, M., *The Puzzles of Childhood*, Melbourne: Viking Penguin, 1989

Cox, D., and Hagon, W., *Australian Motorcycle Heroes 1949–1980*, Sydney: Angus & Robertson, 1989

Cuttriss, L., and Bird, E., *500 Million Years on Phillip Island*, 2nd ed., Cowes, Vic.: KMBay Press, 2021

Dale, W., and Noonan, A., *Dick Johnson Racing/DJR Team Penske: 40 years of cars 1980–2019*, Melbourne: Authentic Collectables and AN1 Media, 2020

Davis, P., *Australians on the Road*, Sydney: Rigby, 1979

Davis, P., *Wheels Across Australia*, Sydney: Marque Publishing, 1987

Dowsey, D., *Elfin: The Spirit of Speed*, Melbourne: Elfin Heritage Centre, 2020

Floyd, T.B., *The Official 50-Race History of the Australian Grand Prix*, Sydney: R&T Publishing, 1986

Gliddon, J., *Phillip Island in Picture and Story*, Melbourne: J. Gliddon, 1977

Green, B., *Glory Days: Albert Park 1953–1958*, Brisbane: B. Green, 2002

Greenhalgh, D., Floyd, T.B., and Tuckey, B., *Australia's Greatest Motor Race 1960–1999: The first 40 years*, Sydney: Chevron Publishing, 2000

Harrison, R., *Austin Racing History*, London: Cable Publishing Company, 1968

Hartgerink, N., *Gardner: A dream come true*, Sydney: Century Hutchinson, 1989

Howard, G., *Lex Davison: Larger than life*, Sydney: Turton & Armstrong, 2004

Irving, P., *Phil Irving: An autobiography*, Sydney: Turton & Armstrong, 1992

Jones, A., and Botsford, K., *Alan Jones: Driving ambition*, London: Hutchinson Publishing Group, 1981

Jones, A., and Clarke, A., *AJ: How Alan Jones climbed to the top of Formula One*, Sydney: Penguin Random House, 2017

King, B., and McGann, P., *Bugattis in Australia and New Zealand 1920 to 2012*, Black Rock, Vic.: Viglione Press, 2012

Lanyon, M., and Nelson, P., 'The history of PIARC', Melbourne: Phillip Island Auto Racing Club, unpublished manuscript

Lowndes, C., and Fogarty, M., *Craig Lowndes: The inside line*, Sydney: HarperCollins, 2010

McKay, D., *David McKay's Scuderia Veloce: The autobiography*, Sydney: Turton & Armstrong, 2001

Malsher, D., *The Sheer Force of Will Power*, Sydney: HarperCollins, 2015

Normoyle, S., *The Great Race*, vols 16–24, Sydney: Chevron Publishing, 1996–2004

Oswin, A., McKay, E., and Hudson S., *Once Upon an Island: The early days of Phillip Island*, Cowes, Vic.: Chicory Publishing, 2023

Oxley, M., *Mick Doohan: Thunder from Down Under*, Windsor, NSW: Minidi, 2000

Parrish, S., and Harris, N., *Barry: The story of motorcycle legend Barry Sheene MBE*, London: Sphere, 2007

Patrick, K., *Bill Thompson: Australian motor racing champion*, Adelaide: K. Patrick, 2011

Pearson, B., *Birthplaces of Australian Motor Racing: The history of 150 defunct car racing venues*, London: Austin Macauley, 2022

Scaysbrook, J., *Phillip Island: A history of motorsport since 1928*, Sydney: Bookworks, 2005

Scaysbrook, J., *Motorcycle Grand Prix World: History, heroes and hopefuls*, Melbourne: William Heinemann Australia, 1989

Smailes, J., *Formula One: The Australian and New Zealand story*, Sydney: Allen & Unwin, 2021

Smith, B., *Whispering Smith*, Melbourne: B. Smith, 2014

Stoner, C., and Roberts, M., *Casey Stoner: My story, my way*, Sydney: Hachette Australia, 2013

Tuckey, B., *Australia's Greatest Motor Race: The complete history*, Sydney: Landsdowne Press, 1981

Tuckey, B., *On Solid Ground: 90 years of VACC*, Melbourne: Victorian Automobile Chamber of Commerce, 2010

Tuckey, W.P., *The Book of Australian Motor Racing*, Sydney: KG Murray Publishing, 1965

Watson, B., *Phillip Island to Fangio: The history of the Light Car Club of Australia*, Melbourne: B. Watson, 2010

Whincup J., and Gover, P., *My Championship Year: Behind the wheel with the V8 champion and his Vodafone team*, Sydney: Allen & Unwin, 2010

Whincup, J., and Gullan, S., *Jamie Whincup: Drive of a lifetime: The autobiography*, Melbourne: Penguin Random House, 2021

Wilson, S., and Floyd, T.B., *Australian Motor Racing Year*, vols 18–25, Sydney: Chevron Publishing, 1988–1995

Woods, B., *Legends of Speed: The story of Australia's great race drivers*, Sydney: HarperCollins, 2004

Periodicals

Australian Motor Racing Annual 1974, Sydney, 1974

Australian Motorcycle News, vols 38–69, 1989–2020. Loaned by Dean Mellor.

Racing Car News, vols 6–20, 1966–1980. Loaned by Colin Bond OAM.

Online

Australian Motorcycle Grand Prix, www.motogp.com.au

Australian Motorcycle News, www.amcn.com.au

AutoAction, www.autoaction.com.au

Crash, www.crash.net

Primotipo, www.primotipo.com

Speedcafe, www.speedcafe.com.au

Trove, www.trove.nla.gov.au

V8 Sleuth, www.V8sleuth.com.au

Interviews

Auld, Travis: Melbourne, January 2024

Bamford, Tim: Melbourne, September 2023, February 2024

Barnard, Bob: Spain, September 2023

Bartlett, Kevin: Maleny, Qld, December 2023

BIBLIOGRAPHY

Bayliss, Troy: Gold Coast, Qld, January 2024
Beechey, Norm and Margaret: Melbourne, October 2023
Bond, Colin OAM and Robyn: Sydney, December 2023
Bowe, John AM: Melbourne, February 2024
Bull, Geoff and Dawn: Melbourne, October 2023, February 2024
Burgess, Jeremy and Claudine: Adelaide, September 2023, February 2024
Cadle, Mark: Melbourne, October 2023, various dates in 2024
Carruthers, Kelvin: Murrieta, California, November 2024
Corrigan, David: Melbourne, January 2024
Corser, Troy: Wollongong, NSW, January 2024
Davison, Chris: Freshwater Creek, Vic., November 2023
Davison, Will: Gold Coast, Qld, February 2024
Doohan, Mick AM: Gold Coast, Qld, October 2023
Dove, Geoff: Melbourne, September 2023
Doyle, Peter: Melbourne, December 2023
Duncan, Henk: Melbourne, October 2023
Ezpeleta, Carmelo: Phillip Island, October 2023
Ferrier, Leanne: Melbourne, February 2024
Foley, Brian Patrick: Southern Highlands, NSW, November 2023
Fox, Andrew: Melbourne, September 2023
Gardner, Wayne AM: Wollongong, NSW, October 2023
Goddard, Peter: Wollongong, NSW, January 2024
Griggs, Judith: Scotland, September 2023
Harburg, Peter: Brisbane, February 2024
Harnden, John AM: Melbourne, October 2023
Henderson, Peter: Portsea, Vic., October 2023, January 2024
Hone, Mick: Phillip Island, December 2023
Jardine, Tim: Sydney, September 2023
Johnson, Dick AM: Gold Coast, Qld, January 2024
Jones, Alan MBE: Gold Coast, Qld, November 2023
Kahlbetzer, Donna: Wollongong, October 2023; Sydney, January 2024
Keam, Paul: Melbourne, October 2023, various dates in 2024
Keeffe, John OAM: Melbourne, January 2024
Kelso, Nayelle: Phillip Island, October 2023
King, Bob: Melbourne, December 2023
Kivovich, Ron: Sydney, January 2024
Lambden, Chris: Melbourne, January 2024
Lanyon, Michael: Ocean Grove, Vic., October 2023, various dates in 2023–24
Little, Shannon: Phillip Island, September 2023
Lukey, Keith and Lyn: Tarwin Lower, Vic., September 2023

Manley, Trevor: Phillip Island, October 2023
Martin, Ross: Melbourne, September 2023
McCormack, John: Tasmania, December 2023
McCoy, Garry: Phillip Island, October 2023
McLachlan, Wayne: Phillip Island, September 2023
Miller, Jack: Phillip Island, October 2023; Buriram, Thailand, November 2023
Moffat, Allan OBE: Melbourne, September 2017
O'Reilly, Kelvin: Gold Coast, Qld, January 2024
Oldfield, Chris: Phillip Island, October 2023
Prendergast, Kevin: Perth, January 2024
Richards, Steven: Melbourne, February 2024
Ritchie, Gordon: Phillip Island, February 2024
Roepers, Ingrid: Sydney, September 2023
Rossi, Valentino (courtesy of Alberto Tebaldi): Tavullia, Italy, January 2024
Smith, John: Sydney, January 2024
Smith, Michael: Melbourne, February 2024
Stillwell, Michael: Melbourne, February 2024
Tander, Garth: Melbourne, February 2024
Taramasso, Piero: Phillip Island, October 2023
Tate, Ian OAM: Melbourne, January 2024
van Venrooy, Kally: Phillip Island, September 2023
Vermeulen, Chris: Maleny, Qld, February 2024
Viegas, Jorge: Phillip Island, October 2023
Watson, Tianda: Phillip Island, October 2023
Westacott, Andrew: Melbourne, September 2023
Whelan, Michael: Phillip Island, September 2023
White, David: Melbourne, December 2023
Yates, David: Melbourne, December 2023
Zarco, Johann: Phillip Island, October 2023
Zeitz, Lynette: Adelaide, September 2023

Index

INDEX

INDEX

INDEX

INDEX

INDEX

INDEX